Essays in Trespassing
Economics to Politics and Beyond

Essays in Trespassing
Economics to Politics and Beyond

ALBERT O. HIRSCHMAN

CAMBRIDGE UNIVERSITY PRESS

Cambridge
London   New York   New Rochelle
Melbourne   Sydney

Published by the Press Syndicate of the University of Cambridge
The Pitt Building, Trumpington Street, Cambridge CB2 1RP
32 East 57th Street, New York, NY 10022, USA
296 Beaconsfield Parade, Middle Park, Melbourne 3206, Australia

First published 1981

Printed in the United States of America
Typeset by Huron Valley Graphics, Inc., Ann Arbor, Michigan
Printed and bound by Halliday Lithograph Corp., West Hanover, Massachusetts

Library of Congress Cataloging in Publication Data
Hirschman, Albert O
Essays in trespassing.
Includes bibliographical references and index.
1. Economics – Addresses, essays, lectures.
2. Economic development – Addresses, essays, lectures.
3. Latin America – Economic policy – Addresses,
essays, lectures. 4. Political science – Addresses,
essays, lectures. 5. Social science – Addresses,
essays, lectures. I. Title.
HB171.H638   330   80–29654
ISBN 0 521 23826 9   hard covers   AACR1
ISBN 0 521 28243 8   paperback

Preface

"... the discipline [of economics] became progressively more narrow at precisely the moment when the problems demanded broader, more political, and social insights ..."

Thus speaks a foundation which is a leading supporter of social science research.[1] It is an increasingly common lament. Under the circumstances, it may be useful to document the existence of exceptions and countertrends. While I dare not vouch for those "broader insights," I can at least claim that the essays assembled here ignore any narrow disciplinary boundaries. Their unifying characteristic is the propensity to trespass from one social science domain to another and beyond.

Written over the past decade, the essays deal with themes that have engaged me over a much longer time. Once I put the volume together, I was indeed rather pleased to find that it also serves to tie together my own work: Virtually each of my previous book-length studies has a strong intellectual bond with one or several of the essays. This observation yielded a plausible, if egocentric, thematic subdivision (see Contents), which in turn facilitated the drafting of introductory notes to the resulting groups of essays, where appropriate. The notes provide background on the circumstances and intellectual climate in which the essays were written and orient the reader to some of the numerous interrelationships.

The arrangement makes plain that my interests have moved away from the exclusive concern with development issues that characterized my previous volume of collected papers, *A Bias for Hope: Essays on Development and Latin America* (1971). First place has been given to the essay "The Rise and Decline of Development Economics," in part because it helps explain this shift. It is

---

[1] Russell Sage Foundation, *Annual Report, 1979*, New York, 1980, p. 12.

v

not so much that the "decline" made me move on to greener pastures; rather, I came to feel that progress with some of the major puzzles in economic-political development requires considerable detours and forays into other areas. Some success can already be claimed for this circuitous approach: My work in intellectual history, published as *The Passions and the Interests* in 1977, has allowed me to reinterpret some particularly vexing development problems (see pages 23–4 and 99–105). Naturally, in addition to such utility, I found much that was worth pursuing for its own sake in those new areas.

Presenting the essays as being related to my previous books does not mean, I hasten to add, that they are mere postscripts. Afterthoughts some of them may be, but then an afterthought that comes to the author just as he publishes his book often expresses the essence of what he was really after and did not quite manage to catch while still laboring on the manuscript. Some of the essays do indeed testify to this curious occurrence, but most stand on their own feet as posterior works that are simply indebted to earlier ones.

Within each group, the essays are presented in chronological order. Their text is almost wholly unchanged, except for the correction of errors and the updating of references. When the same topic is discussed in two or more essays, cross-references have been provided. In a few instances, passages have been added at the time of preparing this volume for publication, for purposes of clarification or because intervening events invited further comment; those passages have been placed within brackets.

A number of acknowledgments are in order. I spent three of the last ten years at Harvard and the remainder at the Institute for Advanced Study, which I joined in 1974 after having been a visitor in 1972–73. Chapters 3 and 6 were written at Harvard, the others at the Institute. I am grateful to both institutions. The volume was prepared for publication in the summer of 1980 at the University of California at Berkeley where the Institute of International Studies kindly offered me its hospitality. Finally, I have been most fortunate to have Johanna M. Cornelissen as secretary for the past four years; her intelligent, skillful, and dedicated help has been invaluable.

Princeton, New Jersey   **ALBERT O. HIRSCHMAN**
September 1980

Contents

1 The Rise and Decline of Development Economics   *page* 1

Around *National Power and the Structure of*
Foreign Trade   25

2 Beyond Asymmetry: Critical Notes on Myself as a
   Young Man and on Some Other Old Friends   27

Around *The Strategy of Economic Development*   35

Introductory Note   37
3 The Changing Tolerance for Income Inequality in the
   Course of Economic Development   39
4 A Generalized Linkage Approach to Development,
   with Special Reference to Staples   59
5 The Turn to Authoritarianism in Latin America and
   the Search for Its Economic Determinants   98

Around *Journeys Toward Progress*   137

Introductory Note   139
6 Policymaking and Policy Analysis in Latin America –
   A Return Journey   142
7 On Hegel, Imperialism, and Structural Stagnation   167
8 The Social and Political Matrix of Inflation:
   Elaborations on the Latin American Experience   177

Contents

Around *Exit, Voice, and Loyalty*   209

Introductory Note   211

9   Exit, Voice, and Loyalty: Further Reflections and a Survey of Recent Contributions   213

10   Exit and Voice: Some Further Distinctions   236

11   Exit, Voice, and the State   246

12   Three Uses of Political Economy in Analyzing European Integration   266

Around *The Passions and the Interests*   285

Introductory Note   287

13   An Alternative Explanation of Contemporary Harriedness   290

14   Morality and the Social Sciences: A Durable Tension   294

Index of Authors Cited   307

1

The rise and decline
of development economics

Development economics is a comparatively young area of inquiry. It was born just about a generation ago, as a subdiscipline of economics, with a number of other social sciences looking on both skeptically and jealously from a distance. The forties and especially the fifties saw a remarkable outpouring of fundamental ideas and models which were to dominate the new field and to generate controversies that contributed much to its liveliness. In that eminently "exciting" era, development economics did much better than the object of its study, the economic development of the poorer regions of the world, located primarily in Asia, Latin America, and Africa. Lately it seems that at least this particular gap has been narrowing, not so much unfortunately because of a sudden spurt in economic development, but rather because the forward movement of our subdiscipline has notably slowed down. This is of course a subjective judgment. Articles and books are still being produced. But as an observer and long-time participant I cannot help feeling that the old liveliness is no longer there, that new ideas are ever harder to come by and that the field is not adequately reproducing itself.

This retrospective essay, which is also to appear in the forthcoming collection in honor of Sir Arthur Lewis (London: George Allen and Unwin), is of course a highly selective review. In particular, it does not treat the development of our factual knowledge about the development process which has often included the testing of theories; here the main debt is owed to such figures as Simon Kuznets and Hollis Chenery. A number of other surveys of the sort here attempted have appeared recently. See, in particular, Paul Streeten, "Development ideas in historical perspective," in *Toward a New Strategy for Development*, Rothko Chapel Colloquium (New York: Pergamon Press, 1979), pp. 21–52, and Fernando Henrique Cardoso, "The originality of a copy: CEPAL and the idea of development," *CEPAL Review* (second half of 1977), UN Commission for Latin America, UN Publication E.77.II.G.5, pp. 7–40. See also the introductory section of Chapter 4 for a brief review of "theorizing on economic development in historical perspective" with a rather different focus.

When scientific activity is specifically directed at solving a pressing problem, one can immediately think of two reasons why, after a while, interest in this activity should flag. One is that the problem is in fact disappearing–either because of the scientific discoveries of the preceding phase or for other reasons. For example, the near demise of interest in business-cycle theory since the end of World War II was no doubt due to the remarkably shock-free growth experienced during that period by the advanced industrial countries, at least up to the mid-seventies. But this reason cannot possibly be invoked in the present case: The problems of poverty in the Third World are still very much with us.

The other obvious reason for the decline of scientific interest in a problem is the opposite experience, that is, the disappointing realization that a "solution" is by no means at hand and that little if any progress is being made. Again, this explanation does not sound right in our case, for in the last thirty years considerable advances have taken place in many erstwhile "underdeveloped" countries–even a balance sheet for the Third World as a whole is by no means discouraging.[1]

In sum, the conditions for healthy growth of development economics would seem to be remarkably favorable: the problem of world poverty is far from solved, but encouraging inroads on the problem have been and are being made. It is therefore something of a puzzle why development economics flourished so briefly.

In looking for an explanation, I find it helpful to take a look at the conditions under which our subdiscipline came into being. It can be shown, I believe, that this happened as a result of an a priori unlikely conjunction of distinct ideological currents. The conjunction proved to be extraordinarily productive, but also created problems for the future. First of all, because of its heterogeneous ideological makeup, the new science was shot through with tensions that would prove disruptive at the first opportunity. Secondly, because of the circumstances under which it arose, development economics became overloaded with unreasonable hopes and ambitions that soon had to be clipped back. Put very briefly and schematically, this is the tale I shall tell– plus a few stories and reflections on the side.

[1] See, for example, David Morawetz, *Twenty-Five Years of Economic Development: 1950 to 1975* (Washington, D.C.: World Bank, 1977).

I. A simple classification of development theories

The develpment ideas that were put forward in the forties and fifties shared two basic ingredients in the area of economics. They also were based on one unspoken political assumption with which I will deal in the last section of this paper.

The two basic economic ingredients were what I shall call the rejection of the *monoeconomics claim* and the assertion of the *mutual-benefit claim*. By rejection of the monoeconomics claim I mean the view that underdeveloped countries as a group are set apart, through a number of specific economic characteristics common to them, from the advanced industrial countries and that traditional economic analysis, which has concentrated on the industrial countries, must therefore be recast in significant respects when dealing with underdeveloped countries. The mutual-benefit claim is the assertion that economic relations between these two groups of countries could be shaped in such a way as to yield gains for both. The two claims can be either asserted or rejected, and, as a result, four basic positions exist, as shown in the following table.

Types of development theories

	Monoeconomics claim:	
	asserted	*rejected*
Mutual-benefit claim: *asserted*	Orthodox economics	Development economics
rejected	Marx?	Neo-Marxist theories

Even though there are of course positions that do not fit neatly just one of its cells, this simple table yields a surprisingly comprehensive typology for the major theories on development of the periphery. In the process, it makes us realize that there are two unified systems of thought, orthodox economics and neo-Marxism, and two other less consistent positions that are therefore likely to be unstable: Marx's scattered thoughts on de-velopment of "backward" and colonial areas, on the one hand, and modern development economics, on the other. I shall take up these four positions in turn, but shall give major attention to development economics and to its evolving relations with – and harassment by – the two adjoining positions.

The orthodox position holds to the following two proposi- tions: (a) economics consists of a number of simple, yet "power- ful" theorems of universal validity: there is only one economics ("just as there is only one physics"); (b) one of these theorems is that, in a market economy, benefits flow to all participants, be they individuals or countries, from all voluntary acts of eco- nomic intercourse ("or else they would not engage in those acts"). In this manner, both the monoeconomics and the mutual- benefit claims are asserted.

The opposite position is that of the major neo-Marxist theories of development which hold: (a) exploitation or "unequal ex- change" is the essential, permanent feature of the relations be- tween the underdeveloped "periphery" and the capitalist "center"; (b) as a result of this long process of exploitation, the political-economic structure of the peripheral countries is very different from anything ever experienced by the center, and their development cannot possibly follow the same path – for example, it has been argued that they cannot have a successful industrial- ization experience under capitalist auspices. Here, both the mu- tual-benefit claim and the monoeconomics claim are rejected.

A cozy internal consistency, bent on simplifying (and oversim- plifying) reality and therefore favorable to ideology formation, is immediately apparent in both the orthodox and the neo-Marxist positions. This is in contrast with the remaining two positions. It should be clear why I have placed Marx into the southwesterly cell (mutual-benefit claim rejected, monoeconomics claim as- serted). Writing in *Capital* on primitive accumulation on the one hand, Marx describes the process of spoliation to which the pe- riphery has been subject in the course of the early development of capitalism in the center. Thus he denies any claim of mutual benefit from trade between capitalist and "backward" countries. On the other hand, his well-known statement, "The industrially most developed country does nothing but hold up to those who follow it on the industrial ladder, the image of its own future," coupled with the way in which he viewed England's role in India as "objectively" progressive in opening the way to indus- trialization by railroad construction, suggests that he did not perceive the "laws of motion" of countries such as India as being substantially different from those of the industrially advanced ones. Marx's opinions on this latter topic are notoriously complex and subject to a range of interpretations, as is indicated by the question mark in the table. But to root *neo*-Marxist thought firmly in the southeasterly cell took considerable labors (which involved, among other things, *uprooting* an important component of the thought of Marx). The story of these labors and revisions has been told elsewhere,[2] and my task here is to deal with the origin and dynamics of the other "hybrid" position: development economics.

It is easy to see that the conjunction of the two propositions – (a) certain special features of the economic structure of the underdeveloped countries make an important portion of orthodox analysis inapplicable and misleading, and (b) there is a possibility for relations between the developed and underdeveloped countries to be mutually beneficial and for the former to contribute to the development of the latter – was essential for our subdiscipline to arise where and when it did: namely, in the advanced industrial countries of the West, primarily in England and the United States, at the end of World War II. The first proposition is required for the creation of a separate theoretical structure, and the second was needed if Western economists were to take a strong interest in the matter – if the likelihood or at least the hope could be held out that their own countries could play a positive role in the development process, perhaps after certain achievable reforms in international economic relations. In the absence of this perception it would simply not have been possible to mobilize a large group of activist "problem solvers."

II. The inapplicability of orthodox monoeconomics to underdeveloped areas

Once a genuinely new current of ideas is firmly established and is being busily developed by a large group of scholars and re-

---

[2] B. Sutcliffe, "Imperialism and Industrialization in the Third World," in R. Owen and B. Sutcliffe, eds., *Studies in the Theory of Imperialism* (London: Longman, 1972), pp. 180–86, and P. Singer, "Multinacionais: internacionalização e crise," Caderno CEBRAP No. 28 (São Paulo: Editora Brasiliense, 1977), pp. 50–56. On the complexity of Marx's views, even in the preface of *Capital* where the cited phrase appears, see Chapter 4, this volume, pp. 89–90.

searchers, it becomes almost impossible to appreciate how difficult it was for the new to be born and to assert itself. Such
difficulties are particularly formidable in economics with its
dominant paradigm and analytical tradition – a well-known
source of both strength and weakness for that social science.
Accordingly, there is need for an explanation of the rise and at
least temporary success of the heretical, though today familiar,
claim that large portions of the conventional body of economic
thought and policy advice are not applicable to the poorer countries – the more so as much of this intellectual movement arose
in the very "Anglo-Saxon" environment which had long served
as home for the orthodox tradition.

Elements of such an explanation are actually not far to seek.
Development economics took advantage of the unprecedented
discredit orthodox economics had fallen into as a result of the
depression of the thirties and of the equally unprecedented success of an attack on orthodoxy from within the economics "establishment." I am talking of course about the Keynesian Revolution
of the thirties, which became the "new economics" and almost a
new orthodoxy in the forties and fifties. Keynes had firmly established the view that there were *two* kinds of economics: one – the
orthodox or classical tradition – which applied, as he was wont to
put it, to the "special case" in which the economy was fully employed; and a very different system of analytical propositions and
of policy prescriptions (newly worked out by Keynes) that took
over when there was substantial unemployment of human and
material resources.[3] The Keynesian step from one to two economics was crucial: the ice of monoeconomics had been broken and
the idea that there might be yet another economics had instant
credibility – particularly among the then highly influential group
of Keynesian economists, of course.

Among the various observations that were central to the new
development economics and implicitly or explicitly made the
case for treating the underdeveloped countries as a sui generis

[3] Dudley Seers leaned on this established terminological usage with his article "The
Limitations of the Special Case," *Bulletin of the Oxford University Institute of Economics
and Statistics*, 25 (May 1963): 77–98, in which he pleaded for recasting the teaching of
economics so as to make it more useful in dealing with the problems of the less-
developed countries. The "special case" that had falsely claimed generality was, for
Keynes, the fully employed economy; for Seers, it was the economy of the advanced
capitalist countries, in contrast to conditions of underdevelopment.

group of economies, two major ones stand out, that relating to rural underemployment and that stressing the late-coming syndrome in relation to industrialization.

1. *Rural underemployment.* The early writers on our subject may have looked for an even closer and more specific connection with the Keynesian system than was provided by the general proposition that different kinds of economies require different kinds of economics. Such a connection was achieved by the unanimous stress of the pioneering contributions – by Kurt Mandelbaum, Paul Rosenstein-Rodan and Ragnar Nurkse – on *underemployment* as a crucial characteristic of underdevelopment. The focus on rural *under*employment was sufficiently similar to the Keynesian concern with *un*employment to give the pioneers a highly prized sensation of affinity with the Keynesian system, yet it was also different enough to generate expectations of eventual independent development for our fledgling branch of economic knowledge.

The affinities were actually quite impressive. As is well known, the Keynesian system took unemployment far more seriously than had been done by traditional economics and had elaborated a theory of macroeconomic equilibrium with unemployment. Similarly, the early development economists wrote at length about the "vicious circle of poverty" – a state of low-level equilibrium – which can prevail under conditions of widespread rural underemployment. Moreover, the equilibrium characteristics of an advanced economy with urban unemployment and those of an underdeveloped economy with rural underemployment were both held to justify interventionist public policies hitherto strictly proscribed by orthodox economics. The Keynesians stressed the task of expansionary fiscal policy in combating unemployment. The early development economists went farther and advocated some form of public investment planning that would mobilize the underemployed for the purpose of industrialization, in accordance with a pattern of "balanced growth."

In these various ways, then, the claim of development economics to stand as a separate body of economic analysis and policy derived intellectual legitimacy and nurture from the prior success and parallel features of the Keynesian Revolution.

The focus on rural underemployment as the principal characteristic of underdevelopment found its fullest expression in the work of Arthur Lewis. In his powerful article "Economic Development with Unlimited Supplies of Labour" he managed – almost miraculously – to squeeze out of the simple proposition about underemployment a full set of "laws of motion" for the typical underdeveloped country, as well as a wide range of recommendations for domestic and international economic policy.

With the concept of rural underemployment serving as the crucial theoretical underpinning of the separateness of development economics, it is not surprising that it should have been chosen as a privileged target by the defenders of orthodoxy and monoeconomics.[4] For example, Theodore W. Schultz devoted a full chapter of his well-known book *Transforming Traditional Agriculture* (Yale, 1964) to an attempt at refuting what he called "The Doctrine of Agricultural Labor of Zero Value."[5] This suggests an interesting point about the scientific status of economics, and of social science in general. Whereas in the natural or medical sciences Nobel prizes are often shared by two persons who have collaborated in, or deserve joint credit for, a given scientific advance, in economics the prize is often split between one person who has developed a certain thesis and another who has labored mightily to prove it wrong.

At the outset of his celebrated article, Lewis had differentiated the underdeveloped economy from Keynesian economics by pointing out that in the Keynesian system there is underemployment of labor as well as of other factors of production, whereas in an underdevelopment situation only labor is redundant. In this respect, my own work can be viewed as an attempt to generalize the diagnosis of underemployment as the characteristic feature of underdevelopment. Underdeveloped countries did

[4] See, for example, Jacob Viner, "Some Reflections on the Concept of 'Disguised Unemployment,' " in *Contribuições à Análise do Desenvolvimiento Econômico* (Essays in honor of Eugênio Gudin), (Rio de Janeiro: Agir, 1957), pp. 345–54.

[5] His principal empirical argument was the actual decline in agricultural output suffered when the labor force suddenly diminished in a country with an allegedly redundant labor force in agriculture, as happened during the 1918–19 influenza epidemic in India. Arthur Lewis pointed out later that the consequences he had drawn from the assumption of zero marginal productivity in agriculture would remain fully in force provided only the supply of labor at the given wage in industry exceeds the demand, a condition that is much weaker than that of zero marginal productivity. See W. Arthur Lewis, "Reflections on Unlimited Labor," in *International Economics and Development: Essays in Honor of Raúl Prebisch* (New York and London: Academic Press, 1972), pp. 75–96.

have hidden reserves, so I asserted, not only of labor, but of savings, entrepreneurship, and other resources. But to activate them, Keynesian remedies would be inadequate. What was needed were "pacing devices" and "pressure mechanisms"; whence my strategy of unbalanced growth.

My generalization of the underemployment argument may have somewhat undermined the claim of development economics to autonomy and separateness. As the work of Herbert Simon on "satisficing" and that of Harvey Leibenstein on "X-efficiency" were to show, the performance of the advanced economies also "depends not so much on finding optimal combinations for given resources as on calling forth and enlisting . . . resources and abilities that are hidden, scattered, or badly utilized" – that was the way I had put it in *The Strategy of Economic Development* for the less developed countries.[6] A feature I had presented as being specific to the situation of one group of economies was later found to prevail in others as well. Whereas such a finding makes for reunification of our science, what we have here is not a return of the prodigal son to an unchanging, ever-right and -righteous father. Rather, our understanding of the economic structures of the West will have been modified and enriched by the foray into other economies.

This kind of dialectical movement – first comes, upon looking at outside groups, the astonished finding of Otherness, and then follows the even more startling discovery that our own group is not all that different – has of course been characteristic of anthropological studies of "primitive" societies from their beginning and has in fact been one of their main attractions. In the field of development economics, something of this sort has also happened to the ideas put forward by Arthur Lewis. The dynamics of development with "unlimited" supplies of labor, which was supposed to be typical of less developed countries, have in fact prevailed in many "Northern" economies during the postwar period of rapid growth, owing in large part to massive immigration, temporary or permanent, spontaneous or organized, from the "South."[7] One of the more interesting analytical responses to this situation has been the dual labor market theory

[6] New Haven: Yale University Press, 1958, p. 5.
[7] C. P. Kindleberger, *Europe's Postwar Growth: The Role of Labor Supply* (Cambridge, Mass.: Harvard University Press, 1967).

of Michael Piore and others. This theory is easily linked up with the Lewis model, even though that connection has not been made explicit as far as I know.

2. *Late industrialization.* I have suggested in the preceding pages that the concept of underemployment achieved its position as foundation stone for development economics because of its affinity to the Keynesian system and because of the desire of the early writers on our subject to place themselves, as it were, under the protection of a heterodoxy that had just recently achieved success. There was, moreover, something arcane about the concept, often also referred to as "disguised unemployment," that served to enhance the scientific aura and status of the new field.

Along with the mysteries, however, the common sense of development also suggested that some rethinking of traditional notions was required. It became clear during the depression of the thirties and even more during World War II that industrialization was going to hold an important place in any active development policy of many underdeveloped countries. These countries had long specialized – or had been made to specialize – in the production of staples for export to the advanced industrial countries which had supplied them in return with modern manufactures. To build up an industrial structure under these "late-coming" conditions was obviously a formidable task that led to the questioning of received doctrine according to which the industrial ventures appropriate to any country would be promptly acted upon by perceptive entrepreneurs and would attract the required finance as a result of the smooth working of capital markets. The long delay in industrialization, the lack of entrepreneurship for larger ventures, and the real or alleged presence of a host of other inhibiting factors made for the conviction that, in underdeveloped areas, industrialization required a deliberate, intensive, guided effort. Naming and characterizing this effort led to a competition of metaphors: big push (Paul Rosenstein-Rodan), takeoff (Walt W. Rostow), great spurt (Alexander Gerschenkron), minimum critical effort (Harvey Leibenstein), backward and forward linkages (Albert O. Hirschman). The discussion around these concepts drew on both theoretical arguments – new rationales were developed for protection, planning, and industrialization itself – and on the experience of European industrialization in the nineteenth century.

In the latter respect, the struggle between advocates and adversaries of monoeconomics was echoed in the debate between Rostow and Gerschenkron. Even though Rostow had coined what became the most popular metaphor (the "takeoff"), he had really taken a monoeconomics position. For he divided the development process into his famous five "stages" with identical content for all countries, no matter when they started out on the road to industrialization. Gerschenkron derided the notion "that the process of industrialization repeated itself from country to country lumbering through [Rostow's] pentametric rhythm"[8] and showed, to the contrary, how the industrialization of the late-coming European countries such as Germany and Russia differed in fundamental respects from the English industrial revolution, largely because of the intensity of the "catching-up" effort on the part of the latecomers. Even though it was limited to nineteenth-century Europe, Gerschenkron's work was of great importance for development economics by providing *historical* support for the case against monoeconomics. As industrialization actually proceeded in the periphery, it appeared that Third World industrialization around mid-twentieth century exhibited features rather different from those Gerschenkron had identified as characteristic for the European latecomers.[9] But for the historically oriented, Gerschenkron's work supplied the same kind of reassurance Keynesianism had given to the analytically minded: he showed once and for all that there can be more than one path to development, that countries setting out to become industrialized are likely to forge their own policies, sequences, and ideologies to that end.

Subsequent observations strengthened the conviction that industrialization in the less developed areas required novel approaches. For example, modern, capital-intensive industry was found to be less effective in absorbing the "unlimited supplies of labor" available in agriculture than had been the case in the course of earlier experiences of industrialization. Advances in

[8] *Economic Backwardness in Historical Perspective* (Cambridge, Mass.: Harvard University Press, 1962), p. 355.

[9] A. O. Hirschman, "The Political Economy of Import-Substituting Industrialization in Latin America," published in 1968 and reprinted in Hirschman, *A Bias for Hope: Essays on Development and Latin America* (New Haven: Yale University Press, 1971), Chapter 3.

industrialization were frequently accompanied by persistent inflationary and balance-of-payment pressures which raised questions about the adequacy of traditional remedies and led, in Latin America, to the "sociological" and "structuralist" theses on inflation, which, interestingly, have now gained some currency in the advanced countries, usually without due credit being given.[10] Also, the vigorous development of the transnational corporation in the postwar period raised entirely new "political economy" questions about the extent to which a country should attract, restrict, or control these purveyors of modern technology and products.

III. The mutual-benefit assumption

The new (far from unified) body of doctrine and policy advice that was built up in this manner was closely connected, as noted earlier, with the proposition that the core industrial countries could make an important, even an essential, contribution to the development effort of the periphery through expanded trade, financial transfers, and technical assistance.

The need for large injections of financial aid fitted particularly well into those theories advocating a "big push." It was argued that such an effort could only be mounted with substantial help from the advanced countries, as the poor countries were unable to generate the needed savings from within. Here the underlying model was the new growth economics, which, in its simplest (Harrod-Domar) version, showed a country's growth rate to be determined by the propensity to save and the capital-output ratio. Growth economics had evolved independently from development economics, as a direct offshoot of the Keynesian system and its macroeconomic concepts. While devised primarily with the advanced industrial countries in mind, it found an early practical application in the planning exercises for developing countries that became common in the fifties. These exercises invariably contained projections for an expansion of trade and aid. Their underlying assumption was necessarily that such enlarged economic relations between rich and poor countries would be beneficial for both. Now this proposition fits nicely

[10] See Chapter 8, this volume.

into orthodox monoeconomics, but it might have been expected to arouse some suspicion among development economists and to mix rather poorly with some of the other elements and assertions of the new subdiscipline. For example, so it could have been asked, why are the countries of the South in a state where, according to some, it takes a huge push to get them onto some growth path? Why are they so impoverished in spite of having long been drawn into the famous "network of world trade"[11] which was supposed to yield mutual benefits for all participants? Is it perhaps because, in the process, some countries have been *caught* in the net to be victimized by some imperialist spider? But such indelicate questions were hardly put in the halcyon days of the immediate postwar years, except perhaps in muted tones by a few faraway voices, such as Raúl Prebisch's. Of that more later.

Action-oriented thought seldom excels in consistency. Development economics is no exception to this rule; it was born from the marriage between the new insights about the sui generis economic problems of the underdeveloped countries and the overwhelming desire to achieve rapid progress in solving these problems with the instruments at hand, or thought to be within reach, such as large-scale foreign aid. A factor in "arranging" this marriage, in spite of the incompatibilities involved, was the success of the Marshall Plan in Western Europe. Here the task of postwar reconstruction was mastered with remarkable speed, thanks, so it appeared at least, to a combination of foreign aid with some economic planning and cooperation on the part of the aid recipients. It has often been pointed out that this European success story led to numerous failures in the Third World, that it lamentably blocked a realistic assessment of the task of development, in comparison with that of reconstruction.

But the matter can be seen in a different light. True, the success of the Marshall Plan deceived economists, policymakers,

---

[11] This was the title of a well-known League of Nations study stressing the benefits of multilateral trade which were being threatened in the thirties by the spread of bilateralism and exchange controls. Its principal author was Folke Hilgerdt, a Swedish economist. In the immediate postwar period, Hilgerdt, then with the United Nations, noted that trade, however beneficial, had not adequately contributed to a narrowing of income differentials between countries. With Hilgerdt coming from the Heckscher-Ohlin tradition and having celebrated the contributions of world trade to welfare, this paper, which was published only in processed form in the proceedings of a congress (I have not been able to locate it), was influential in raising questions about the benign effects of international economic relations on the poorer countries.

and enlightened opinion in the West into believing that infusion of capital helped along by the right kind of investment planning might be able to grind out growth and welfare all over the globe. But – and here is an application of what I have called the "Principle of the Hiding Hand" – on balance it may have been a good thing that we let ourselves be so deceived. Had the toughness of the development problem and the difficulties in the North-South relationship been correctly sized up from the outset, the considerable intellectual and political mobilization for the enterprise would surely not have occurred. In that case, and in spite of the various "development disasters" which we have experienced (and which will be discussed later in this essay), would we not be even farther away from an acceptable world than we are today?

In sum, one historical function of the rise of development economics was to inspire confidence in the manageability of the development enterprise and thereby to help place it on the agenda of policymakers the world over. The assertion of the mutual-benefit claim served this purpose.

IV. The strange alliance of neo-Marxism and monoeconomics against development economics

Predictably, when the path to development turned out to be far less smooth than had been thought, the hybrid nature of the new subdiscipline resulted in its being subjected to two kinds of attacks. The neoclassical Right faulted it for having forsaken the true principles of monoeconomics and for having compounded, through its newfangled policy recommendations, the problem it set out to solve. For the neo-Marxists, on the other hand, development economics had not gone far enough in its analysis of the predicament of the poor countries: so serious was their problem pronounced to be that nothing but total change in their socioeconomic structure and in their relations to the rich countries could make a difference; pending such change, so-called development policies only created new forms of exploitation and "dependency." The two fundamentalist critiques attacked development economics from opposite directions and in totally different terms: but they could converge in their specific indictments – as they indeed did, particularly in the important arena of industrialization. Because the adherents of neoclassical economics and those of various neo-Marxist schools of thought live in quite separate worlds, they were not even aware of acting in unison. In general, that strange de facto alliance has hardly been noted; but it plays an important role in the evolution of thinking on development and its story must be briefly told.

Doubts about the harmony of interests between the developed and underdeveloped countries arose at an early stage among some of the major contributors to the new subdiscipline. There was widespread acceptance of the view that the advanced industrial countries could henceforth contribute to the development of the less advanced, particularly through financial assistance, but questions were raised in various quarters about the equitable distribution of the gains from trade, both in the past and currently. In 1949, Raúl Prebisch and Hans Singer formulated (simultaneously and independently) their famous "thesis" on the secular tendency of the terms of trade to turn against countries exporting primary products and importing manufactures.[12] They attributed this alleged tendency to the power of trade unions in the advanced countries and to conditions of underemployment in the periphery. The argument was put forward to justify a sustained policy of industrialization. Arthur Lewis was led by his model in a rather similar direction: as long as "unlimited supplies of labor" in the subsistence sector depress the real wage throughout the economy, any gains from productivity increases in the export sector are likely to accrue to the importing countries; moreover, in a situation in which there is surplus labor at the ruling wage, prices give the wrong signals for resource allocation in general and for the international division of labor in particular; the result was a further argument for protection and industrialization.

Both the Prebisch-Singer and the Lewis arguments showed that without a judiciously interventionist state in the periphery, the

[12] An account of the emergence of the thesis is now available in Joseph Love, "Raúl Prebisch and the Origins of the Doctrine of Unequal Exchange," *Latin American Research Review* 15 (November 1980): 45–72. See also my earlier essay "Ideologies of Economic Development in Latin America" (1961), reprinted in *A Bias for Hope*, Chapter 13. The latest review of the ensuing controversy and related evidence is in two articles by John Spraos: "The Theory of Deteriorating Terms of Trade Revisited," *Greek Economic Review* 1 (December 1979): 15–42, and "The Statistical Debate on the Net Barter Terms of Trade between Primary Commodities and Manufactures," *Economic Journal* 90 (March 1980): 107–28.

cards were inevitably stacked in favor of the center. On the whole, it looked as though this was the result of some unkind fate rather than of deliberate maneuvers on the center's part. Critics from the Left later took Arthur Lewis to task for viewing unlimited supplies of labor as a datum, rather than as something that is systematically *produced* by the colonizers and capitalists.[13] Lewis was of course fully aware of such situations and specifically notes at one point that in Africa the imperial powers impoverished the subsistence economy "by taking away the people's land, or by demanding forced labour in the capitalist sector, or by imposing taxes to drive people to work for capitalist employers."[14] For Lewis these practices were simply not a crucial characteristic of the model – after all, a decline in infant mortality could have the same effect in augmenting labor supply as a head tax.

It appears nevertheless that the debate among development economists in the fifties included the canvassing of some antagonistic aspects of the center-periphery relation. The theories just noted attempted to show that the gain from trade might be unequally distributed (perhaps even to the point where one group of countries would not gain at all) but did not go so far as to claim that the relationship between two groups of countries could actually be exploitative in the sense that trade and other forms of economic intercourse would enrich one group *at the expense* of another – an assertion that would be unthinkable within the assumptions of the classical theory of international trade. Yet, even this kind of assertion was made at a relatively early stage of the debate. Gunnar Myrdal invoked the principle of cumulative causation (which he had first developed in his *American Dilemma*) in seeking to understand the reason for persistent and increasing income disparities *within* countries; but the notion was easily extended to contacts between countries. Myrdal's argument on the possibility of further impoverishment of the poor region (or country) was largely based on the likelihood of its losing skilled people and other scarce factors, and also on the possible destruction of its handicrafts and industries.

[13] G. Arrighi, "Labour Supplies in Historical Perspective: A Study of the Proletarianization of the African Peasantry in Rhodesia," *Journal of Development Studies* 6 (April 1970): 197–234.

[14] W. Arthur Lewis, "Economic Development with Unlimited Supplies of Labour," published in 1954 and reprinted in A. N. Agarwala and S. P. Singh, ed.; *The Economics of Underdevelopment* (London: Oxford University Press, 1958), p. 410.

Independently of Myrdal, I had developed similar ideas: Myrdal's "backwash effect"–the factors making for increasing disparity–became "polarization effect" under my pen, whereas his
"spread effect"–the factors making for the spread of prosperity
from the rich to the poor regions–was named by me "trickling
down effect." (Optimal terminology is probably achieved by
combining Myrdal's "spread" with my "polarization" effects.)
We both argued, though with different emphases, that the possibility of the polarization effect being stronger than the spread
effect must be taken seriously, and thus went counter not only
to the theory of international trade, but to the broader traditional
belief, so eloquently expressed by John Stuart Mill,[15] that contact
between dissimilar groups is always a source of all-around
progress. Anyone who had observed the development scene
with some care could not but have serious doubts about this
view: in Latin America, for example, industrial progress was
particularly vigorous during the World Wars and the Great Depression when contacts with the industrial countries were at a
low ebb. To me, this meant no more than that *periods* of isolation
may be beneficial and I saw some alternation of contact and
isolation as creating optimal conditions for industrial development.[16] In any event, both Myrdal and I looked at the polarization effects as forces that can be opposed and neutralized by
public policies; and I tried to show that instead of invoking such
policies as a deus ex machina (as I thought Myrdal did), it is
possible to see them as arising out of, and in reaction to, the
experience of polarization.

A strange thing happened once it had been pointed out that
interaction between the rich and poor countries could in certain
circumstances be in the nature of an antagonistic, zero-sum
game: very soon it proved intellectually and politically attractive
to assert that such was the essence of the relationship and that it
held as an iron law through all phases of contacts between the
capitalist center and the periphery. Just as earlier those brought

[15] "It is hardly possible to overrate the value, in the present low state of human improvement, of placing human beings in contact with persons dissimilar to themselves, and
with modes of thought and action unlike those with which they are familiar. . . . Such
communication has always been, and is peculiarly in the present age, one of the
primary sources of progress." J. S. Mill, *Principles of Political Economy*, Book III, Chapter
17, para. 5.
[16] *Strategy*, pp. 173–5, 199–201.

up in the classical tradition of Smith and Ricardo were unable to conceive of a gain from trade that is not mutual, so did it become impossible for the new polarization enthusiasts to perceive anything but pauperization and degradation in each of the successive phases of the periphery's history.[17] This is the "development of underdevelopment" thesis, put forward by André Gunder Frank, and also espoused by some of the more extreme holders of the "dependency" doctrine. Given the historical moment at which these views arose, their first and primary assignment was to mercilessly castigate what had up to then been widely believed to hold the promise of economic emancipation for the underdeveloped countries: industrialization. We are now in the mid-sixties, at which time real difficulties and growing pains were experienced by industry in some leading Third World countries after a prolonged period of vigorous expansion. This situation was taken advantage of in order to characterize all of industrialization as a total failure on a number of (not always consistent) counts: it was "exhausted," "distorted," lacked integration, led to domination and exploitation by multinationals in alliance with a domestic "lumpen bourgeoisie," was excessively capital-intensive and therefore sabotaged employment, and fostered a more unequal distribution of income along with a new, more insidious, kind of dependency than ever before.

At just about the same time, the neoclassical economists or monoeconomists – as they should be called in accordance with the terminology of this essay – were sharpening their own knives for an assault on development policies that had pushed industrialization for the domestic market. In contrast to the multiple indictment from the Left, the monoeconomists concentrated on a single, simple, but to them capital, flaw of these policies: misallocation of resources. By itself this critique was highly predictable and might not have carried more weight than warnings against industrialization emanating from essentially the same camp ten, or twenty, or fifty years earlier. But the effectiveness of the critique was now greater for various reasons. First of all, as a result of the neo-Marxist writings just noted, some of the early advocates of industrialization had now themselves become its sharpest critics. Second, specific policies which in the early stage had been useful in promoting industrialization, though at

[17] This view has been aptly labeled "catastrofismo" by Aníbal Pinto.

the cost of inflationary and balance-of-payments pressures, did run into decreasing returns in the sixties: they achieved less industrialization at the cost of greater inflation and balance-of-payments problems than before. Third, the practice of deliberate industrialization had given rise to exaggeration and abuse in a number of countries, and it became easy to draw up a list of horrible examples that served to incriminate the whole effort. Fourth, a new set of policies emphasizing exports of manufactures from developing countries became attractive, because of the then rapid expansion of world trade, and the possibilities of success of such policies was demonstrated by countries like Taiwan and South Korea. Under these conditions, the neoclassical strictures became more persuasive than they had been for a long time.

The target of the complementary neo-Marxist and neoclassical writings was not just the new industrial establishment, which in fact survived the onslaught rather well; on the ideological plane, the intended victim was the new development economics, which had strongly advocated industrial development and was now charged with intellectual responsibility for whatever had gone wrong. The blows from Left and Right that fell upon the fledgling and far from unified subdiscipline left it, indeed, rather stunned: so much so that the most intrepid defense of what had been accomplished by the postwar industrialization efforts in the Third World came not from the old stalwarts, but from an English socialist in the tradition of Marx's original position on the problem of backward areas, the late Bill Warren.[18]

V. The real wounding of development economics

It would of course be silly – just as silly as the German proverb *Viel Feind, viel Ehr* (many enemies, much honor) – to hold that any doctrine or policy that is attacked simultaneously from both Left and Right is, for that very reason, supremely invested with truth and wisdom. I have already noted that the neoclassical critics made some valid points, just as the neo-Marxists raised a number of serious issues, particularly in the areas of excessive foreign control and of unequal income distribution. But normally

[18] B. Warren, "Imperialism and Capitalist Accumulation," *New Left Review*, no. 81 (Sept.–Oct. 1973): 3–45, and "The postwar economic experience of the Third World," in *Toward a New Strategy for Development*, pp. 144–68.

such criticisms should have led to some reformulations and eventually to a strengthening of the structure of development economics. In fact, however, this was not to be the case. No new synthesis appeared. Several explanations can be offered. For one thing, development economics had been built up on the basis of a construct, the "typical underdeveloped country," which became increasingly unreal as development proceeded at very different rates and took very different shapes in the various countries of Latin America, Asia, and Africa. Lenin's law of uneven development, originally formulated with the major imperialist powers in mind, caught up with the Third World! It became clear, for example, that, for the purpose of the most elementary propositions of development strategy, countries with large populations differ substantially from the ever more numerous ministates of the Third World,[19] just as there turned out to be few problems in common between petroleum exporters and petroleum-importing developing countries. The concept of a unified body of analysis and policy recommendations for all underdeveloped countries, which contributed a great deal to the rise of the subdiscipline, became in a sense a victim of the very success of development and of its unevenness.

But there was a more weighty reason for the failure of development economics to recover decisively from the attacks it had been subjected to by its critics. It lies in the series of political disasters that struck a number of Third World countries from the sixties on, disasters that were clearly *somehow* connected with the stresses and strains accompanying development and "modernization." [20] These development disasters, ranging from civil wars to the establishment of murderous authoritarian regimes, could not but give pause to a group of social scientists, who, after all, had taken up the cultivation of development economics in the wake of World War II not as narrow specialists, but impelled by the vision of a better world. As liberals, most of them presumed that "all good things go together"[21] and took it for granted that if only a good job could be done in raising the national income of

---

[19] This is stressed, for example, by Clive Y. Thomas, *Dependence and Transformation: The Economics of the Transition to Socialism* (New York: Monthly Review Press, 1974), passim.
[20] On this subject, see also Chapters 3 and 5, this volume.
[21] See Robert Packenham, *Liberal America and the Third World* (Princeton: Princeton University Press, 1973), pp. 123–9.

the countries concerned, a number of beneficial effects would follow in the social, political, and cultural realms.

When it turned out instead that the promotion of economic growth entailed not infrequently a sequence of events involving serious retrogression in those other areas, including the wholesale loss of civil and human rights, the easy self-confidence that our subdiscipline exuded in its early stages was impaired. What looked like a failure to mount a vigorous counterattack against the unholy alliance of neo-Marxists and neoclassicists may well have been rooted in increasing self-doubt, based on mishaps far more serious than either the "misallocation of resources" of the neoclassicists or the "new dependency" of the neo-Marxists.

Not that all the large and gifted group of development economists which had in the meantime been recruited into the new branch of knowledge turned suddenly silent. Some retreated from the position "all good things go together" to "good economics is good for people."[22] In other words, rather than assuming that economic development would bring progress in other fields, they thought it legitimate to operate on the basis of an implicit Pareto-optimality assumption: like plumbing repairs or improvements in traffic control, the technical efforts of economists would improve matters in one area while at worst leaving others unchanged, thus making society as a whole better off. Economic development policy was here in effect downgraded to a technical task exclusively involved with efficiency improvements. An illusion was created and sought that, by confining itself to smaller-scale, highly technical problems, development economics could carry on regardless of political cataclysms.

There was, however, another reaction that was to have a considerable impact. Experiencing a double frustration, one over the appalling political events as such, and the other over their inability to comprehend them, a number of analysts and practitioners of economic development were moved to look at the economic performance itself with a more critical eye than before. In a Freudian act of displacement, they "took out" their distress over the political side on the weaker aspects of the economic record. Within countries with authoritarian regimes, the displacement was often reinforced, unintentionally of course, by the official

---

[22] An expression attributed to Arnold Harberger, in an article in the *New York Times* of February 7, 1980.

censorship that was much more rigorous with regard to political dissent than in matters of economic performance.

It was, in a sense, an application of the maxim "all good things go together" *in reverse*. Now that political developments had taken a resoundingly wrong turn, one had to prove that the economic story was similarly unattractive. Some economists were satisfied once the balance between political and economic performance had been restored in this fashion, be it at a wretchedly low level. But others were in a more activist mood. Impotent in the face of political injustice and tyranny, yet feeling a faint sense of responsibility, they were attempting to make amends by exposing *economic* injustice. In doing so, they paid little attention to John Rawls who argued, at just about that time, in *A Theory of Justice* that "a departure from the institutions of equal liberty . . . cannot be justified by or compensated for by greater social or economic advantage."[23] But perhaps it was fortunate – and a measure of the vitality of the development movement – that the disappointment over politics led to an attempt at righting at least those wrongs economists could denounce in their professional capacity.

Here then is one important origin of the concern with income distribution which became a dominant theme in the development literature in the early seventies. Albert Fishlow's finding, on the basis of the 1970 census, that income distribution in Brazil had become more unequal and that some low-income groups may even have come to be worse off in absolute terms, in spite of (because of?) impressive growth, was particularly influential.[24] An alarm based on this and similar data from other countries was sounded by Robert McNamara, the President of the World Bank, in his annual address to the Board of Governors meeting in 1972. A large number of studies followed, and an attempt was made to understand how development could be shaped in accordance with distributional goals, or to formulate policies that would combine the objectives of growth and distribution.

Before long, attention was directed not only to the relative aspects of income distribution, but to the absolute level of need satisfaction among the poorer groups of a country's population. Thus was born the concern with *basic needs* – of food, health,

---

[23] Cambridge, Mass.: Harvard University Press, 1971, p. 61.
[24] "Brazilian Size Distribution of Income," *American Economic Review* 62 (May 1972): 391–402.

education, etc. – that is currently a principal preoccupation of development economics. Just as the construct of the "typical underdeveloped country" gave way to diverse categories of countries, each with characteristics of its own, so did the heretofore unique maximand of development economics (income per capita) dissolve into a variety of partial objectives, each requiring consultation with different experts – on nutrition, public health, housing, and education, among others.

There is of course much to be said for this new concreteness in development studies, and particularly for the concern with the poorer sections. Nevertheless, development economics started out as the spearhead of an effort that was to bring all-around emancipation from backwardness. If that effort is to fulfill its promise, the challenge posed by dismal politics must be met rather than avoided or evaded. By now it has become quite clear that this cannot be done by economics alone. It is for this reason that the decline of development economics cannot be fully reversed: our subdiscipline had achieved its considerable luster and excitement through the implicit idea that it could slay the dragon of backwardness virtually by itself or, at least, that its contribution to this task was central. We now know that this is not so; a consoling thought is that we may have gained in maturity what we have lost in excitement.

Looking backward, the whole episode seems curious. How could a group of social scientists that had just lived through the most calamitous "derailments of history" *in various major economically advanced* countries entertain such great hopes for economic development per se? Here I can perhaps offer some enlightenment by drawing on my recent work in the history of ideas. In *The Passions and the Interests* I showed that the rise of commerce and money-making activities in the seventeenth and eighteenth centuries was then looked upon as promising for political stability and progress; and I stressed that such optimistic expectations were not based on a new respect for these activities, but rather on *continuing contempt* for them: unlike the passionate, aristocratic pursuit of glory and power with its then well-recognized potential for disaster, the love of money was believed to be "incapable of causing either good *or evil* on a grand scale."[25] A similar perception may have been at work in

[25] Princeton: Princeton University Press, 1977, p. 58.

relation to the less developed countries of Asia, Africa, and Latin America of the twentieth century. The Western economists who looked at them at the end of World War II were convinced that these countries were not all that complicated: their major problems would be solved if only their national income per capita could be raised adequately. At an earlier time, contempt for the countries designated as "rude and barbarous" in the eighteenth century, as "backward" in the nineteenth and as "underdeveloped" in the twentieth had taken the form of relegating them to permanent lowly status, in terms of economic and other prospects, on account of unchangeable factors such as hostile climate, poor resources, or inferior race. With the new doctrine of economic growth, contempt took a more sophisticated form: suddenly it was taken for granted that progress of these countries would be smoothly linear if only they adopted the right kind of integrated development program! Given what was seen as their overwhelming problem of poverty, the underdeveloped countries were expected to perform like wind-up toys and to "lumber through" the various stages of development single-mindedly; their reactions to change were not to be nearly as traumatic or aberrant as those of the Europeans, with their feudal residues, psychological complexes and exquisite high culture. In sum, like the "innocent" and *doux* trader of the eighteenth century, these countries were perceived to have only *interests* and *no passions*.

Once again, we have learned otherwise.

Around

National Power and the Structure of Foreign Trade

2

Beyond asymmetry:
critical notes on myself as a young man
and on some other old friends

"Dependency Theory Reassessed" was the title of the plenary session at the 1976 meetings of the Latin American Studies Association. In my remarks as session chairman I presented some of the speakers, such as Fernando Henrique Cardoso and Osvaldo Sunkel who were among the first to discuss "dependencia" in the early or mid-sixties, as the founding fathers of the theory. Then I proceeded to introduce myself as the frequently unacknowledged founding grandfather, on the strength of my book *National Power and the Structure of Foreign Trade* (1945). The point of the present note, however, is not to substantiate this claim; it seems more useful to spell out my present critical perspective on that *Jugendschrift* of some 35 years ago (the manuscript was actually written in 1941–2) and, in the process, to criticize as well some aspects of the dependencia literature.

The historical backdrop of my book was the successful drive of Hitler's Germany to expand its trade with, and its political influence in, Eastern and Southeastern Europe during the thirties. In attempting to explain what had happened, I dwelt not so much on the diabolical cunning of the Nazis, or on Dr. Schacht's technical innovations such as bilateralism, exchange controls, and so on, as on the structural characteristics of international economic relations that, as I wrote, "make the pursuit of power a relatively easy task." The Nazis, according to this point of view, had not

Reprinted by permission from *International Organization* 32 (1) (© 1978 by the Board of Regents of the University of Wisconsin System), pp. 45–50. This essay was also published as part of an introduction to an expanded paperback edition of *National Power and the Structure of Foreign Trade*, reprinted in 1980 by its original publisher, the University of California Press.

The comments on dependency theory in this essay complement other disputations about ideology, particularly in Chapters 5, 6, and 7 of this volume.

perverted the international economic system, they had merely capitalized on one of its potentialities or side effects; for "power elements and disequilibria are potentially inherent in such 'harmless' trade relations as have always taken place, e.g., between big and small, rich and poor, industrial and agricultural countries–relations that could be fully in accord with the principles taught by the theory of international trade" (p. 40).

It is of course this position which accounts for the durability of my book: the political dimensions and side effects of foreign trade and investment are still very much with us–two obvious examples are the relations of the United States with Latin America and of the Soviet Union with Eastern Europe.[1]

In forging a link between international economics and politics I focused primarily on the economic concept "gain from trade" and showed how, in line with the maxim *fortuna est servitus*, this gain can spell dependence of the country that receives the gain on the country that bestows it. Going along with the assumptions of classical theory, I assumed that both countries gain, but emphasized that in a large number of constellations, these gains are asymmetrical: a given volume of trade between country A and B may be much more important for B than for A. A simple quantitative reflection of this asymmetry is present in the frequent case where a small, poor country (B) carries on a large portion of its trade with a large, rich country (A). In that case imports of A from B could well represent 80 percent of B's total exports while accounting for no more than 3 percent of A's total imports. I made a great deal of this and similar asymmetries and disparities and devised various statistical instruments in an attempt to measure them.

So much for my grandfatherhood. Having explained how relations of influence, dependence, and domination arise right out of "mutually beneficial" trade I let matters rest there except for some, in retrospect infinitely naive, proposals to "arrive at an internationalization of the power arising out of foreign trade" (p. 80). In other words, I invoked a *deus ex machina*; I wished away the unpleasant reality I had uncovered instead of scrutinizing it

---

[1] In the latter respect, an explicit use of my conceptual framework is in Paul Marer, "The Political Economy of Soviet Relations with Eastern Europe," in S.J. Rosen and J.R. Kurth, eds., *Testing Theories of Economic Imperialism* (Lexington, Mass.: Lexington Books, 1974), pp. 231–60.

further for some possibly built-in modifier or remedy. In this respect, my treatment had once again a great deal in common with that of many dependencia theorists: they too tend to rest content with the demonstration that dependency relations are deeply entrenched in the structure of the international system; they hardly ever explore whether that system might contain the "seeds of its own destruction" or might otherwise be subject to some changes. If they invoke revolution, it is also as a *deus ex machina*, rather than because they have identified any emerging forces capable of staging that desired event.

It may be instructive to indicate how this common defect of my original treatment and of most dependencia writings could be remedied by taking as point of departure the very situation of asymmetry previously noted: an identical trade flow that represents the bulk of the small, poor country's total trade while occupying only a small percentage of the large, rich country's trade. The straightforward inference from this observation is that the large country, having a much smaller stake in this common trade than the small country, is able to bend the latter to its will by subtle or not-so-subtle hints that the benefits of this trade might otherwise be withdrawn. But the next question is now: how solid or stable is the resulting relation of domination and dependency?

In his recent book, *Beyond Economic Man*, Harvey Leibenstein has reminded us of Tolstoy's critique, in *War and Peace*, of those military experts who predict the outcome of battles by looking only at the quantifiable elements of the strength of the opposing armies, such as the number of men and weapons – Tolstoy stresses fighting spirit and morale as an often more decisive factor. This thought has an obvious relevance here. The ability to inflict deprivation is more easily quantified than the willingness to accept it for the sake of, say, freedom from domination, and in the recent past there have been several important episodes where this willingness has been underestimated, with disastrous results for those who thought that "objectively" they were bound to prevail.

While this factor – the willingness to accept economic (or physical) punishment – must be taken into account in assessing the stability of the dependence relationship, one cannot count on it. To do so would again be tantamount to invoking a *deus ex machina*. What we are looking for is a slightly more reliable relation between the initial asymmetry and some built-in tendency towards its elimination or reduction. Perhaps such a relation can be made to arise out of the following conjecture, based primarily on the observation of United States-Latin American relations. A country whose trade or investment is dominated by ties to a large and rich country is, at some point, likely to devote its attention with single-minded concentration to this uncomfortable situation and to an attempt to loosen or cut these ties. But the large rich country which carries on only a small portion of its international economic relations with the country it dominates is normally preoccupied with its more vital *other* interests, for example, with its relations to the other large powers. Hence our basic economic disparity generates a disparity of *attention*, or at least of high-level attention to use the language of bureaucratic politics, and this disparity now favors the *dependent* country: that country is likely to pursue its escape from domination more actively and energetically than the dominant country will work on preventing this escape. The British Empire is said to have been acquired in a fit of absent-mindedness. However that may be, it seems a more convincing proposition that empires, formal or informal, tend to crumble that way.

In the United States, the lack of attention to Latin American affairs at the highest level of government has often been noted. Generally it has been deplored; it leaves the field by default, so the argument goes, to the interests of those parties – traders, bankers, investors – with a direct, but narrow stake in these countries. Now it is quite correct that occasionally when, in some crisis, Latin American affairs were taken seriously at the highest level in Washington, it was perceived that the national interest of the United States by no means coincided with the short-term interests of individual trading or corporate groups, and actions were then taken that were more responsive than earlier low-level policies to the aspirations of Latin Americans. But it would be totally illegitimate to conclude from these few cases that Latin America would be better off if its affairs were continually handled, like those of, say, China or Russia, at the highest levels of the United States government. From the point of view of Latin America's aspirations, the advantage of day-to-day policy being in the hands of lower-level diplomats heavily influenced by an intrusive business community is precisely that policies so formed are usually short-sighted as well as reasonably predictable. (Occasionally they become so inept and conflictual that they have to be corrected by a salvage operation staged at a higher level of policy-making.) For these reasons they are no match for a determined adversary. In other words, if the efforts of a country to lessen its dependence are to prosper, there is no substitute for that "wise and salutary neglect" on the part of the imperial power which Burke long ago recognized as a basic cause of the growing strength of England's North American colonies. And it is my contention that the likelihood of such neglect – and of correspondingly concentrated attention on the part of the dependent country – is inscribed in the asymmetrical trade percentages just as much as the facts of dependence and domination themselves.

Insofar as U.S.-Latin American relations are concerned, the preceding argument could be criticized by pointing to the numerous interventions of the United States in Latin American affairs, from the early ones in Mexico, the Caribbean, and Central America to the more recent actions in Guatemala, Cuba, the Dominican Republic, and Chile, to mention just the better known cases. What sort of neglect is it, one might well ask, that results in this pattern of conduct? It must be recognized that a dominant power, be it the United States or the Soviet Union, has been able to bring military power to bear, overtly or covertly, when it judges that a country within its sphere of influence is breaking away or is otherwise going "too far." But this does not at all mean that the dependent country never has any room for maneuver. The point I have been making can be reformulated as follows: because of the disparity of attention, dependent countries are in a favorable position to utilize what room for maneuver they have and may be able to widen this room; within limits that are often uncertain and constantly changing, the dominant country is unlikely to pay the attention and make the effort needed to counter or effectively rein in dependent countries straining to achieve a greater degree of autonomy. [A striking confirmation of this proposition is supplied by the Polish events of 1980–81 – no matter what their final outcome.]

The possibility of a dialectical movement which would transform an asymmetrical relation, not into its opposite à la Hegel, but at least into a relation of considerably reduced asymmetry has been suggested here only for a specific variety of dependence – the one based on the sort of asymmetrical trading and investment pattern which was the focus of my book. There are actually a number of more familiar situations where initial domination or dependence activates tendencies in the opposite direction: for example, when a country which dominates the world market of one commodity or product raises its price and thereby eventually loses its monopoly because new producers elsewhere take advantage of the high supply price; or when a country that initially has little bargaining power in relation to a firm wishing to exploit its natural resources increases this power over time both because the firm's installations, once built, are captives of the country where they are located and because the country is likely, in due time, to insist on training its own technologists and other experts – a group that could run those installations in the event of takeover. In general, trade and investment relations between countries A and B may lead initially to dependence of B on A, for reason of the various asymmetries, but to the extent that economic intercourse increases the resources at B's command it becomes possible for B to pursue, by diversification and other means, a policy of lessening dependence, be it at the cost of some of these welfare gains.

It will be noted that the mechanisms through which such counterforces arise are very different from case to case: they range from purely economic reactions, as in the case of monopoly pricing, to purely political considerations as in my attempt to show that an asymmetrical trading pattern will lead to asymmetrical degrees of attention to that pattern. To ferret out such mechanisms is anything but easy, particularly when, as in the latter case, initial asymmetry and dependency relations are grounded in economics while the countertendency relies on a certain kind of political reaction coming into play.

But the failure to discover the countertendencies is not due only to difficulties of crossing interdisciplinary boundaries; to a considerable extent it must be attributed to an intellectual orientation that is both undialectical and what I would call antipossibilist.[2] For many of the countertendencies that can be discovered

---

[2] See my advocacy of a "passion for the possible" (a phrase due to Kierkegaard) in the introduction to *A Bias for Hope: Essays on Development and Latin America* (New Haven, Conn.: Yale University Press, 1971), pp. 26–37.

are possibilities rather than certainties, and social scientists often consider it beneath their scientific dignity to deal with possibility until *after* it has become actual and can then at least be redefined as a probability.

These intellectual attitudes have affected much of the thinking on dependencia. Moreover, one of the main issues around which that thinking arose in the 1960s was the question whether the intensive industrialization Latin America had experienced since World War II was going to change radically its characteristics as a "periphery" that is dependent on a dominant "center." Dependencia theorists answered this question strongly in the negative and argued that an industrialized Latin America was, if anything, *more* dependent on the advanced countries than ever before, although in a different and perhaps more subtle manner. As happens frequently in the social sciences, the success of the theory rested in part on the nonobvious nature of its assertions; part of its success was also due to the naivete of those who had hailed industrialization as the cure-all of Latin America's poverty and backwardness. But the demonstration that hope for escape from domination is doomed over and over again, no matter what happens to the development of the productive forces, can hardly be repeated indefinitely. It would be reminiscent of the absurd Stalinist doctrine in the 1930s – which served of course to justify the purges – that the closer a country approaches the final stage of communism the sharper the class struggle is bound to become and the more relentlessly it must be waged.

Fortunately some Latin American social scientists are recognizing that, in its original form, the dependencia thesis is subject to decreasing intellectual returns and have begun to explore the "contradictory character of social processes." As I hope to have shown here, these are the lines along which the more interesting discoveries are now to be made.

Around
The Strategy of Economic Development

Introductory note

As was pointed out in Chapter 1, the major disappointments of the past two decades over Third World developments have occurred in the political realm. While the economic growth record has been from fair to excellent, at least in terms of aggregate expansion, the political record must be called from barely tolerable to disastrous. To understand the interrelationship between economic and political development, the need for "trespassing" and crisscrossing the traditional disciplinary boundaries of economics and political science should be obvious. Nevertheless, the economists and political scientists of the advanced industrial countries have not been strongly attracted to this sort of activity, perhaps because of their tight unidisciplinary upbringing, and the pioneering contributions are due to such Latin American social scientists as Fernando Henrique Cardoso and Guillermo O'Donnell. Some of my own efforts in this field are contained in the following group of essays.

The political repercussions of economic development are the central focus of two essays in this group (Chapters 3 and 5) and they also are an important theme of the third (Chapter 4). "The Changing Tolerance for Income Inequality in the Course of Economic Development" was written in the early seventies when economists and policymakers had become highly critical of the unequal distribution of the fruits of growth in the less developed countries. One explanation for this somewhat sudden concern has already been put forward in Chapter 1: I suggested that disappointment over the rise of authoritarianism in some important Third World countries led analysts to look at the *economic* performance of these countries with a more critical eye than before (see pp. 21–2). Authoritarianism was thereby seen as the cause of a new preoccupation with the distribution of wealth within developing countries. The inverse causal sequence is of course more familiar: authoritarian regimes are typically installed, so the story goes, in order to repress social protest, which, in turn, is bred by the increasing concentration of income that occurs in the course of growth. There obviously is something to this account, but Chapter 3 attempts to show that the actual sequence is more complicated: the relationship between growth, rising inequality, and political instability is far from straightforward or linear, due to what I call the "tunnel effect." Within the special context of Latin America, the possible causal links between phases or stages of economic growth and the rise of authoritarian regimes are critically explored in Chapter 5, "The Turn to Authoritarianism in Latin American and the Search for Its Economic Determinants." Ideological factors are given special attention in Section II of that chapter.

Both chapters attribute an important role to certain imbalances that arise in the course of development, and are therefore related, albeit somewhat loosely, to the principal theme of *The Strategy of Economic Development* (1958).[1] Chapter 4, "A Generalized Linkage Approach to Development, with Special Reference to Staples," represents a more straightforward extension of *Strategy* where the concept of "forward and backward linkages" had been introduced as a key mechanism in development and industrialization. A number of additional linkage effects are canvassed in this essay, particularly for the primary products (staples) which have long been the principal exports of the countries of the periphery. It is argued that the economic, social, and even political development patterns of these countries can often be illuminated by a close look at the constellation of linkage effects characteristic of these staples.

---

[1] Chapter 5 also represents a further development of my article, "The Political Economy of Import-Substituting Industrialization in Latin America" (published in the *Quarterly Journal of Economics* of 1968 and reprinted in *A Bias for Hope*), which in turn updated and expanded a number of propositions about the process of industrialization that had been put forward in *Strategy*.

3

The changing tolerance for income inequality in the course of economic development

A drastic transvaluation of values is in process in the study of economic and political development. It has been forced upon us by a series of disasters that have occurred in countries in which development seemed to be vigorously under way. The civil war in Nigeria and the bloody falling apart of Pakistan are only the most spectacular instances of such "development disasters."

As a result, one reads with increasing frequency pronouncements about the bankruptcy of the "old" development economics, with its accent on growth rates, industrialization, and international assistance, and about the need for a wholly new doctrine that would emphasize income distribution, employment, and self-reliance.[1]

The present paper is not written with the intention of stemming this tide, which surely represents a wholesome reaction and response to current problems. It is grounded, however, in the strong feeling and insistent recollection of one participant observer that the intellectual enthusiasm for development in the fifties and early sixties reflected elements of real hopefulness that were then actually present in many developing countries. What was not correctly perceived was the precarious and transitory nature of that early hopeful and even exuberant phase. This essay, then, is an effort to understand both where we were right

Originally published in *The Quarterly Journal of Economics* 87 (Nov. 1973): 544–65, with a mathematical appendix by Michael Rothschild not reproduced here, as well as in *World Development* 1 (Dec. 1973): 29–36. © 1973, by the President and Fellows of Harvard College. Reprinted by permission of John Wiley & Sons, Inc.
[1] For a particularly forceful statement of this sort, see Mahbub ul Haq, "Employment and Income Distribution in the 1970s: A New Perspective," *International Development Review* (Dec. 1971): 9–13. See also Chapter 1, this volume, pp. 21–3.

and where we went wrong. It will proceed on a fairly abstract level, reach out into several fields other than economics, and stray, on occasion, from the immediate experience and concern that are at its origin.

I. Gratification over advances of others:
the tunnel effect introduced

I shall start by baldly stating my basic proposition. In the early stages of rapid economic development, when inequalities in the distribution of income among different classes, sectors, and regions are apt to increase sharply, it can happen that society's *tolerance* for such disparities will be substantial. To the extent that such tolerance comes into being, it accommodates, as it were, the increasing inequalities in an almost providential fashion. But this tolerance is like a credit that falls due at a certain date. It is extended in the expectation that eventually the disparities will narrow again. If this does not occur, there is bound to be trouble and, perhaps, disaster.

To make this proposition plausible, I shall first argue by analogy. Suppose that I drive through a two-lane tunnel, both lanes going in the same direction, and run into a serious traffic jam. No car moves in either lane as far as I can see (which is not very far). I am in the left lane and feel dejected. After a while the cars in the right lane begin to move. Naturally, my spirits lift considerably, for I know that the jam has been broken and that my lane's turn to move will surely come any moment now. Even though I still sit still, I feel much better off than before because of the expectation that I shall soon be on the move. But suppose that the expectation is disappointed and only the right lane keeps moving: in that case I, along with my left lane cosufferers, shall suspect foul play, and many of us will at some point become quite furious and ready to correct manifest injustice by taking direct action (such as illegally crossing the double line separating the two lanes).

It is easy to translate this situation into the language of welfare economics. An individual's welfare depends on his present state of contentment (or, as a proxy, income), as well as on his expected future contentment (or income). Suppose that the individual has very little information about his future income, but at some point a few of his relatives, neighbors, or acquaintances improve their economic or social position. Now he has something to go on: expecting that his turn will come in due course, he will draw gratification from the advances of others–for a while. It will be helpful to refer to this initial gratification as the "tunnel effect."

This is a simple and, I believe, immediately persuasive proposition. While it has to be formulated with greater care so as to spell out the conditions under which it does or does not hold, perhaps I shall be allowed to dwell on it and to advertise its novelty. The tunnel effect operates because advances of others supply information about a more benign external environment; receipt of this information produces gratification; and this gratification overcomes, or at least suspends, *envy*. Though long noted as the most uninviting of the seven deadly sins because, unlike lust, gluttony, pride, etc., it does not provide any initial fun to its practitioners, envy is nevertheless a powerful human emotion. This is attested to by the writings of anthropologists, sociologists, and economists, who all have proclaimed, in general quite independently of one another, that if you advance in income or status while I remain where I was, I will actually feel worse off than before because my relative position has declined.

In economics this has been argued as the "relative income hypothesis," according to which the welfare of an individual varies inversely with the income or the consumption of those persons with whom he associates.[2] In sociology the topic has been profusely studied under the heading of "relative deprivation." While this term is sometimes used to denote any lag of

---

[2] James S. Duesenberry, *Income, Saving and Theory of Consumer Behavior* (Cambridge, Mass.: Harvard University Press, 1949), Ch. 3. A clear diagrammatical exposition is in Harvey Leibenstein, "Notes on Welfare Economics and the Theory of Democracy," *Economic Journal*, 72 (June 1962); 300–5. Leibenstein considers three possible ways in which individuals make comparisons between their income and that of others: "(1) *Pure* Pareto comparisons in which each individual takes into account his own income but no one else's; (2) the 'share of the pie' comparisons in which each individual takes into account the income distribution from a relative point of view but not the absolute magnitude of his income; and (3) the 'compromise Pareto comparison' in which individuals take into account both the absolute magnitude of their income and their relative income position" (p. 301).

The "pure Pareto comparison," where an individual's utility is not decreased by the improving fortunes of his neighbor as long as his own income does not change, is a limiting case in this scheme. There is no room in it for the possiblity of a positive interaction between my and my neighbor's utility.

real accomplishments behind expectations, its predominant meaning refers to the feelings experienced by a person or group of persons who are falling behind others or who see others catch up with them in regard to income, influence, and status.[3] Finally, anthropologists, who are less given to using jargon, speak unabashedly of the envy caused by isolated advances of individuals in small, poor communities; they view many institutions, such as fiestas, gift giving, and appointment of the rich to financially burdensome honorary positions, as social mechanisms designed to lessen the potentially destructive impact of envy on personal bonds and social cohesion.[4]

This is no doubt an impressive body of converging writings, and massive data have been gathered in their support. But relentless pursuit of this line of reasoning and research may have led to a trained incapacity to perceive the tunnel effect and its importance in a number of contexts.

A preliminary way of rekindling perception is to reverse the signs of the phenomenon under study. Suppose my neighbor or acquaintance, far from improving his position, experiences a bad setback such as losing his job while I am keeping mine: Do I now experience the opposite of relative deprivation, that is, the satisfaction of relative enrichment? This is unlikely, for one thing, because envy, mortal sin though it may be, is an altogether gentle feeling if compared to *Schadenfreude*, the joy at someone else's injury, which is the emotion that would have to come into play to make me happy in this situation. The more important reason is the tunnel effect in reverse: once again I shall take what is happening to my neighbor as an indication of what the future might

---

[3] For an excellent survey and bibliography, see Thomas F. Pettigrew, "Social Evaluation Theory: Convergences and Applications," *Nebraska Symposium on Motivation, 1967* (Lincoln: University of Nebraska Press, 1967), particularly pp. 261–73. The concept was introduced by S. A. Stouffer and his associates in the well-known monumental study of the American soldier in World War II (*The American Soldier, Vol. 1, Adjustment During Army Life;* Princeton, N.J.: Princeton University Press, 1949). See note 16, p. 48.

For a development of the concept in its narrower and more useful meaning, see W. G. Runciman, *Relative Deprivation and Social Justice* (London: Routledge and Kegan Paul, 1966). The wider meaning, which practically equates relative deprivation with any form of discontent, is extensively used in Ted Robert Gurr, *Why Men Rebel* (Princeton, N.J.: Princeton University Press, 1970).

[4] See Ch. 7 entitled "The Fear of Envy" in George M. Foster, *Tzintzuntzan: Mexican Peasants in a Changing World* (Boston: Little, Brown, 1967); also Frank Cancian, *Economics and Prestige in a Maya Community* (Cambridge, Mass.: Harvard University Press, 1963), p. 135 and passim.

have in store for me, and hence I will be apprehensive and worried – less well off than before, just as he. This reaction is well-known from the onset and spread of depressions.[5]

The opposite reaction wil surely take place when the economy experiences a cyclical upturn. Now the news that someone I know is getting his job back while I am still unemployed gives me a pleasure that overwhelms any possible envy, for the event is hailed as a confirmation that better times are under way for me also. This is close to the situation in countries that experience a vigorous surge of development.

As long as the tunnel effect lasts, everybody feels better off, both those who have become richer[6] and those who have not. It is therefore conceivable that some uneven distribution of the new incomes generated by growth will be preferred to an egalitarian distribution by all members of the society. In this eventuality, the increase in income inequality would not only be politically tolerable; it would also be outright desirable from the point of view of social welfare.

II. Some evidence

But this possible consequence of the tunnel effect is a theoretical curiosity, whereas the effect itself definitely is not. In a number of countries its reality has impressed itself on careful observers. Interestingly enough, it was often stumbled upon by researchers who were looking for the opposite phenomenon, such as seething discontent and revolutionary fervor among the urban poor, and were surprised and sometimes not a little disappointed at what they actually found.

The following comments on a sample survey carried out over a decade ago in the *favelas* of Rio de Janeiro are a first case in point:

One way of testing the favelado's sense of sharing in what goes on in the nation is to ascertain the extent to which he perceives national economic growth as producing real gains to himself. When asked in February of 1961 whether things had improved, had remained about the same, or had become worse for him during the last five years, nearly one out of two favelados replied that his present situation is worse. Another three out of ten found that

[5] See, however, footnote 21, this chapter.
[6] See, however, Section III, this essay.

their situations remained much the same. . . . The general sensation that things have not improved noticeably for themselves has not created any great disillusion among favelados with the idea of industrialization as a road to prosperity. The favelado does not deny that the nation's industrial growth has produced benefits for people like himself; he only states that his own situation has not changed appreciably. Thus, when asked immediately after the above question whether the growth of industry had benefited people like themselves, most answered affirmatively. Their explanation, however, was almost entirely in terms of the expansion of job opportunities *for others* – friends, acquaintances, or simply other Brazilians.[7]

Writing also in the early sixties, a well-known Mexican political scientist coined the term "hope factor" to explain what by then amounted to an astonishingly long record of political stability in his country.[8] Even after this record had been shattered by the events of 1968 and the Tlatelolco massacre, another observer wrote:

> Even though the perspectives of individual advance are limited, there is one reason for which one finds less disappointment with the development process among lower-class persons of all sectors than might be expected. With education spreading rapidly and with migration on the increase, there are a number of relatively easy ways of achieving personal advance. Thus even when an individual has been unable to get a new job or in general has not improved his income or position, it is nevertheless probable that *he knows one or several persons* who have been successful in these respects. . . .[9]

The contrast between the objective situation of low incomes, poor working conditions, and general deprivation, on the one hand, and the subjective mood of hopefulness, on the other, were also found to be characteristic of the Puerto Rico of the late fifties:

> We suggest that Puerto Ricans feel far better off than the objective facts of incomes, education and occupations show. . . . Puerto Ricans perceive the existing marked inequalities. Yet they do not feel particularly depreciated by them, and certainly not overwhelmed by them; indeed, on some counts, their views of life and how good it is have often seemed to ignore the objective situation . . . on every visible count, these people at all levels are full of hopes for the future.[10]

---

[7] Frank Bonilla, "Rio's Favelas: The Rural Slum within the City," *American Universities Field Staff Reports Service* vol. 8 (3) (New York, 1961): 8–9.

[8] Pablo González Casanova, *La democracia en México* (Mexico: Era, 1965, popular edition), p. 133.

[9] David Barkin, "La persistencia de la pobreza en México: un análisis económico estructural," *Comercio Exterior*, Banco Nacional de Comercio Exterior, México, Aug. 1971, p. 673 (my translation and italics).

[10] Melvin M. Tumin with Arnold Feldman, *Social Class and Social Change in Puerto Rico* (Princeton, N.J.: Princeton University Press, 1961), pp. 165–6.

In an article dealing with the continent as a whole, two Latin American sociologists catch the essence of these situations by asserting that ". . . the patterns of deferred social mobility, even though somewhat mythical, are nonetheless effective."[11]

Finally, we shall quote some revealing personal remarks about the general atmosphere of countries where mid-twentieth-century style, capitalist development suddenly "broke out." They come from an American anthropologist who reminisces about her stay in Venezuela, in an article in which she gives a sympathetic account of a recent trip to Cuba:

> I thought about what I had seen in Cuba, and about Venezuela, and about my own country. . . . I thought about how when I went to Venezuela, I felt that for the first time I realized something about my own country which I had not previously seen there: the idealism which is inherent in what I had experienced [in the United States] as materialism and individual self-seeking. I saw that for Venezuelans, for whom economic development had just begun . . . the democratizing of material consumption and the opening up of opportunities – for those able to seize them – was a truly exciting and liberating idea.[12]

This passage is of particular interest, first, because it sensitively renders the feeling of the early exuberant phase of development during which the tunnel effect operates; and, secondly, because it illustrates at the same time the considerable reluctance of social-justice-minded intellectuals to perceive the effect – it just goes too much against the grain of any but the most honest to speak of this deplorable "false consciousness" or of that vulgar frontier atmosphere as an "exciting and liberating idea"! Moreover, social scientists live in an intensely competitive atmosphere in which envy and "relative deprivation" are far more prevalent than hopefulness caused by someone else's advance; and although one hesitates to make these ad homines points, they may help explain why the tunnel effect, though widely noted, has not been dealt with in a systematic way in either economic or sociological theory.

III. Consequences for integration and revolution

A brief digression is in order. The various descriptions of the "hope factor" reported in the previous section strongly suggest

[11] Fernando Henrique Cardoso and Jorge Luis Reyna, "Industrialization, Occupational Structure, and Social Stratification in Latin America," in Cole Blasier, ed., *Constructive Change in Latin America* (Pittsburgh: University of Pittsburgh Press, 1968), p. 51.
[12] Lisa Peattie, "Cuban Notes," *Massachusetts Review* (Autumn 1969): 673–74.

that the subject of this paper shades over into a topic familiar to political sociologists: the effect of social mobility on political stability and social integration. This relationship has usually been examined from the point of view of the reactions of the socially mobile themselves, while our focus has thus far been on those who are left behind. With respect to the upwardly mobile, the economist, with his touching simplicity, would tend to think that there is no problem: being better off than before, these people are also likely to be more content with the world around them. Social history has shown, however, that matters are far more complicated: as Tocqueville already noted, the upwardly mobile do not necessarily turn into pillars of society all at once, but may on the contrary be disaffected and subversive for a considerable time. The principal reason for this surprising development is the phenomenon of partial and truncated mobility: the upwardly mobile who may have risen along one of the dimensions of social status, such as wealth, find that a number of obstacles, rigidities, and discriminatory practices still block their ascent along other dimensions as well as their all-around acceptance by the traditional elites, and consequently they feel that in spite of all their efforts and achievements, they are not really "making it."[13] Only as social mobility continues for a long period, and the traditional system of stratification is substantially eroded as a result, will the upwardly mobile become fully integrated – or "coopted."

Discrimination against *nouveaux riches* by the older elites is by no means the only reason for which the upwardly mobile may be critical of the society in which they live and advance. A more charitable interpretation would point to the possibility that convictions about social justice, once formed, acquire a life and staying power of their own so that they are not necessarily jettisoned when pressing personal problems of material welfare have been solved – not, in any way, until after a decent time interval.

This dynamic of the socially mobile is thus the reverse of the

---

[13] For an excellent survey with particular attention to this problem, see Gino Germani, "Social and Political Consequences of Mobility," in N. Smelser and S. M. Lipset, eds., *Social Structure and Mobility in Development* (Chicago: Aldine, 1966), pp. 371ff. It is also possible, of course, that aspirations, once aroused, will outrun achievements, but this explanation of the discontent of the upwardly mobile is far less convincing than the one mentioned in the text.

one that has been suggested here for those who are left behind: during a first and all-round paradoxical phase, frustration and continued alienation are the lot of the upward bound, while the nonmobile derive satisfaction from the anticipation that matters are bound to improve pretty soon. This earlier conclusion of ours can be maintained as the nonmobile see only the improvement in the fortunes of the mobile and remain totally unaware of the new problems being encountered by them. In a second phase there may then take place a symmetrical switch: the upwardly mobile become integrated, whereas the nonmobile lose their earlier hope of joining the upward surge and turn into enemies of the existing order. It is quite unlikely, however, that the beginning of the second phase will coincide for the two groups. Noncoincidence of these two changeovers will obviously be the norm. The upwardly mobile may become integrated, while the left-behind ones are still experiencing the tunnel effect. Alternatively and more interestingly, the nonmobile may experience the turnaround from hopefulness to disenchantment, while the mobile are still disaffected. This last situation clearly contains much potential for social upheaval. Its possible occurrence might even qualify as a theory of revolution.[14] At this point, however, I shall abandon the matter to the historians for I must return to the tunnel effect and its reversal.

IV. From gratification to indignation

As was pointed out, gratification at the advances of others arises under the tunnel effect not from benevolence or altruism, but strictly from an expectational calculus: I expect that my turn to move will soon come. Nonrealization of the expectation will at some point result in my "becoming furious," that is, in my turning into an enemy of the established order. This change from supporter to enemy comes about purely as a result of the passage of time – no particular outward event sets off this dramatic turnaround. In this respect, the theory of so-

---

[14] It comes close to satisfying the criterion the French historian Ernest Labrousse has suggested for the arising of revolutionary situations: namely, that, "the vast majority of the country is united in a total rejection of existing society and of the reigning order of things." Richard Cobb, *A Second Identity: Essays on France and on French History* (London: Oxford University Press, 1969), pp. 272–3.

cial conflict here proposed is quite distinct from the "*J*-curve" hypothesis, which attributes revolutionary outbreaks to a sudden downturn in economic performance coming after a long upswing.[15] Such a downturn no doubt increases the likelihood of commotion, but it is by no means indispensable. Providential and tremendously helpful as the tunnel effect is in one respect (because it accommodates the inequalities almost inevitably arising in the course of development), it is also treacherous: the rulers are not necessarily given any advance notice about its decay and exhaustion, that is, about the time at which they ought to be on the lookout for a drastically different climate of public and popular opinion; on the contrary, they are lulled into complacency by the easy early stage when everybody seems to be enjoying the very process that will later be vehemently denounced and damned as one consisting essentially in "the rich becoming richer."[16]

Semantic inventions and inversions are perhaps the best portents of the turnaround. To give an example: in the fifties the term "pôle de croissance" (growth pole), coined by François Perroux, was widely used for the growing industrializing cities of the developing countries. At some point during the next decade, this expression, which suggested irradiation of growth, gave way to a new term "internal colonialism," which was now said to be practiced by these same cities with regard to their zones of economic influence.

[15] James C. Davies, "Toward a Theory of Revolution," *American Sociological Review*, 27 (Feb. 1962): 5–19.

[16] It is tempting to suggest a reinterpretation, along the foregoing lines, of the famous and paradoxical findings about the morale in the American armed forces during World War II. While wartime promotions had of course been much more prevalent in the Air Corps than in the Military Police, the survey conducted by Stouffer and his associates found more frustration over promotions in the former than in the latter. This finding has been the origin and one of the mainstays of the theory of relative deprivation. The study argued that Air Corps promotions, though frequent in comparison with those in the other branches, lagged in relation to expectations and aspirations aroused within the Corps by the actual promotions of those who made rapid careers. While other social scientists have later proposed different explanations, not enough attention has perhaps been devoted to the time dimension. The survey was taken rather late in the war, in 1944. Is it not likely that if a similar survey had been taken earlier, the finding would have confirmed the common-sense expectation that promotion morale was higher in the Air Corps than in the Miliary Police? Early in the war the rapid advances of some most probably reinforced morale in line with the tunnel effect; only later on, as the various members of the Air Corps reached their level and failed to achieve quite what they had been led to expect, did frustration take over. See S. A. Stouffer et al., *The American Soldier*, pp. 250ff.

V. The tunnel effect: social, historical, cultural, and institutional determinants of its strength

In what kind of societies does the tunnel effect arise and gather strength? What are the conditions under which it will last for a substantial time period or, on the contrary, decay rapidly and turn into the opposite, namely disappointment, alienation, and outrage at social injustice? Answering this question is crucial for bringing our hypothesis down to earth and for ascertaining its empirical and heuristic usefulness.

For the tunnel effect to be strong (or even to exist), the group that does not advance must be able to empathize, at least for a while, with the group that does. In other words, the two groups must not be divided by barriers that are, or are felt as, impassable. Thus, the fluidity or rigidity of class lines will have an obvious bearing on the intensity of the tunnel effect.

But stratification according to social class is a distinction of limited usefulness for our purpose. However unevenly economic growth proceeds, any strong advance is likely to mean gains or new and better jobs for members of several different classes. One might therefore conclude that the tunnel effect will always come into being as, within each social class, those who are not advancing empathize initially with those who are. But this need not happen if each class is composed of ethnic or religious groups that are differentially involved in the growth process. Hence, the contrast between fairly unitary and highly segmented societies is particularly relevant for our topic. If, in segmented societies, economic advance becomes identified with one particular ethnic or language group or with the members of one particular religion or region, then those who are left out and behind are unlikely to experience the tunnel effect: they will be convinced almost from the start of the process that the advancing group is achieving an unfair exploitative advantage over them. The nonmobile group may thus make the prediction opposite to that implied in the tunnel effect: As a result of another group's advance, it will expect to be *worse* off. The possibility of this reaction will be discussed in the next section. In any event, it appears that highly segmented societies will or should eschew strategies of development that are politically feasible elsewhere because of the availability of the tunnel effect.

More concretely, the capitalist road to development appears to be particularly ill-suited for highly segmented societies; if it is followed there, it will require a far greater degree of coercion than it did in the fairly unitary countries in which capitalist development scored its historic successes. On the other hand, rejection of the capitalist road does not yield a ready proven alternative, for the centralized decision making typical of social- ist systems is unlikely to function at all well in segmented societies.[17]

A variant of a segmented society in which economic progress becomes largely identified with one domestic segment is a soci- ety where most emerging economic opportunities are created or seized by foreigners. Once again, the tunnel effect will not pros- per in such a situation. The greater the role of foreign capital and of foreign skilled personnel in the development process, the less expectation of eventual participation in it will there be on the part of the local population, including large parts of the local elites. Hence, tolerance for the emerging inequalities of income will be low, and the need for coercion to maintain social and political stability correspondingly high, even at an early stage of the process.

In passably homogeneous societies where resources are largely owned domestically, the tolerance for economic inequalities may be quite large as no language, ethnic, or other barrier keeps those who are left behind from empathizing with those who are "mak- ing it." It seems that, once again, "to him who hath shall be given," for the country that enjoys the manifold advantages of a nonsegmented citizenry gains thereby the additional latitude of being able to develop without having to impose the serious and perhaps crippling constraints arising from the need to make all portions of the community advance at a roughly even pace.

On the other hand, the greater tolerance of these more homo- geneous countries for inequality has a real and possibly fearful price. As we know, the greater the tolerance, the greater is the *scope* for the reversal that comes once the tunnel effect wears off (unless the inequalities are corrected in time). In this fashion a somewhat counterintuitive conclusion is reached: the more ho-

---

[17] For a detailed argument, see the case study of centralized vs. decentralized decision making in a segmented society (rail vs. road in Nigeria) in my *Development Projects Observed* (Washington, D.C.: Brookings, 1967), pp. 139–48.

mogeneous the country, the more prone will it be to violent social conflict in the course of development unless its leadership is uncommonly perceptive and able.[18] Once again I must leave it to the historians to ascertain whether any empirical sense can be made out of this purely deductive proposition; it might be mentioned, however, that part of the evidence favoring the hypothesis could come not from actual revolution, or similar civil strife, but from protracted lower class alienation such as is found in Argentina, France, and Italy.

National homogeneity is ordinarily defined in terms of static characteristics such as unity of race, language, and religion. But the most effective homogenizing agent is perhaps an intensive historical experience that has been shared by all members of a group. Wars and revolutions typically can be such experiences, and the tunnel effect is therefore frequently at its most potent in postwar and postrevolutionary societies. The result can be an irony-laden historical cycle: revolutions are often made to eradicate a certain kind of inequality, but after such a revolution and because of it, society will have acquired a specially high tolerance for new inequalities if and when they arise. A particularly apt illustration is the Mexican Revolution and its subsequent "betrayal" through the sharply uneven development of recent decades. Similarly, the egalitarian or, rather, "born equal" heritage of the United States—the collective leaving behind of Europe with its feudal shackles and class conflicts—may have set the stage for the prolonged acceptance by American society of huge economic disparities.

The more or less unitary character of a country is probably the most important single criterion for appraising the likely strength and duration of the tunnel effect. But other distinctions are of interest. It can be argued, for example, that the strength of

---

[18] This point is similar to one that can be made about the economic consequences of the size of countries. While the literature of economic development has – quite properly – stressed the advantages of size, particularly in connection with import-substituting industrialization, large size also means that it is possible for a large backward region to fall cumulatively and hopelessly behind – as the progressive region absorbs for a long time virtually all of the country's industrial growth and develops a modern agriculture to boot. So wide, protracted, and dangerous a cleavage cannot arise as easily in a small country, as, under most circumstances, economic growth there either has to spill over to the poorer regions or will come to a halt. A related distinction with an important bearing on the differential strength of the tunnel effect is that between rapid-growth and slow-growth countries. It is briefly discussed in chapter 5, p. 130.

family bonds has a direct bearing on these matters. In many cases, the advances of others will generate hope not so much for oneself as for one's children. The prediction that my children will have a better life than I did should improve my own welfare in any event, but it will do so with particular force if I expect my grown-up children to be living with me, to share in the expenses of the household, and eventually to support me in my old age. From this point of view, then, traditional family arrangements facilitate the operation of the tunnel effect and turn out to have some development-promoting potential.[19]

Provided it is not highly segmented, "traditional" society is generally in a better position than its modern counterpart to take advantage of the tunnel effect. Members of traditional societies are typically tied to each other by a dense network of obligations that are both mutual and flexible: it is none too clear what it is that is owed nor when it falls due. Hence, when some members of such a society advance, their obligations are apt to expand, and many of those who remain behind expect to be benefited in due course and in some measure as a result of their pre-existing, if imprecise, claims on the former. La Rochefoucauld noted this effect in a maxim that in general is as fine a formulation of the tunnel effect as I have come across: "The immediate feeling of joy we experience when our friends meet with luck . . . is an effect . . . of our hope to be lucky in turn or to gain some advantage from their good fortune."[20]

Next, a distinction may be made between various "theories of success" that typically prevail in different societies or cultures. If individual advances are attributed primarily to chance, the suc-

---

[19] For other arguments along this line, see my *A Bias for Hope: Essays on Development and Latin America* (New Haven: Yale University Press, 1971), chapter 14. The proposition about family arrangements that is put forward in the text is a special case of a more general proposition: the tunnel effect will be the stronger, the weaker is the time preference for present over future income, i.e., the lower is the discount rate.

[20] *Maximes*, 582. The phenomenon in reverse was pointed out at about the same time by Thomas Hobbes: "Griefe, for the Calamity of another, is PITTY; and ariseth from the imagination that the like calamity may befall himselfe; . . . therefore for Calamity arriving from great wickedness, the best men have the least Pitty; and for the same Calamity, those have least Pitty, that think themselves least obnoxious [= exposed] to the same." *Leviathan*, Part I, Chapter 6. La Rochefoucauld and Hobbes both came upon these insights in the course of their search for a rigorous, if unpleasant, science of human nature. Unpleasantness of findings almost became a test of rigor and truth for them. Naturally enough, it did not occur to them that, in the situations at hand, self-centeredness has the virtue of overcoming envy and *Schadenfreude*, respectively.

cess of others will occasion the tunnel effect; for the next time fortune strikes, I may well be the lucky one. Hence, the belief that the world is governed by chance, ordinarily considered so harmful to sustained development, has something to recommend itself to the extent that the tunnel effect is considered a valuable, if somewhat volatile, resource for an economy attempting to achieve growth. If, on the other hand, success of others is likely to be attributed from the outset to nepotism, favoritism, or similar unfair practices, then there will hardly be any initial feeling of anticipatory gratification among those who are not participating in the division of the spoils.

It is also conceivable, though perhaps not very likely, that success of others is attributed to their superior merit and qualities such as hard work. Those who are left out would then blame only themselves for their lack of advance. They could, as a result, either simply defer to the more successful members of their community, or they might envy them for being more richly endowed, or they could try to emulate them by redoubling their own effort. In this case, therefore, the result would be rather indeterminate, and one needs more information.[21]

A further possiblity is that the success of others is attributed not to their qualities, but to their *defects*. One often rationalizes his own failure to do as well as others in the following terms: "I would not want to get ahead by stooping to his (ruthless, unprincipled, servile, etc.) conduct." This sort of attribution of suc-

---

[21] Attribution theory, a relatively new branch of social psychology, has attempted to throw light on this area of human behavior. Experiments have been devised to study the extent to which onlookers pin the blame for accidents on those who have been involved rather than on ill fate. Apparently the onlooker typically resorts to what has been called "defensive attribution": he looks for some good reason why the accident is one of the involved parties' own peculiar fault so as to gain the assurance that the mishap could not possibly happen to himself. (Only if no such good reason can be found, if in other words the person who might be blamed is and behaves very much like the onlooker, then and only then will the latter tend to exonerate the former and blame fate instead.) On the other hand, if another person, rather than being involved in an accident, experiences a lucky break, the onlooker will tend to credit chance rather than merit, thereby gaining some hope that a similar lucky break is in store for him. Besides being unflattering to human nature, these findings introduce an asymmetry into the operation of the tunnel effect: it will be stronger in the forward than in the backward direction; that is, the expectation to share eventually in the advances of others will be more pronounced than the expectation to follow them in their setbacks. For an experimental confirmation of this asymmetry and for references to other research in this area, see Jerry I. Shaw and Paul Skolnick, "Attribution of Responsibility for a Happy Accident," *Journal of Personality and Social Psychology*, 18 (1971): 380–3.

cess is not too dissimilar, in its consequences for the tunnel effect, from the one that concentrates on the merits of those who have risen. It makes it possible, of course, for those who are not advancing to rest content with their own station in life. But it could also happen that the next time around they will change their conduct and be a bit more ruthless, unprincipled, servile, etc., than hitherto. To the extent that it is easier to be servile and unprincipled than gifted and hardworking, attribution of success of others to their faults rather than to their qualities may actually facilitate the operation of the tunnel effect.

A distinction related to these theories of success is based on the various organizational ways in which individual advances are perceived to come about. Such perceptions depend fundamentally on the decision-making system. If decision making is perceived to be largely decentralized, individual advances are likely to be attributed to chance, or possibly to merit (or demerit). When decision making is known to be centralized, such advances will be attributed to unfair favoritism or, again, to merit. To the extent that merit is not a likely attribution, decentralized decision making, which permits success of others to be explained by chance, is therefore more conducive to giving full play to the tunnel effect. It is indeed characteristic of market economies. Centralized-decision-making economic systems have come typically into the world because of excessive inequalities existing in, or arising under, decentralized systems. It is interesting to note that they will strain to be more egalitarian not just because they want to, but also because they have to: centralization of decision making largely deprives them of the tolerance for inequality that is available to more decentralized systems.

Similar considerations apply as a *given* economic system evolves in the direction of greater centralization or decentralization. For example, the tolerance for inequality can be expected to decline when a capitalist economy becomes more oligopolized and bureaucratized. An upsurge in populist sentiment has usually been attributed to the greater concentration of wealth that has sometimes been characteristic of such a period. But the tolerance for inequality may decline even without such concentration, simply because those who are excluded from advances no longer perceive such exclusion as temporary bad luck, but as an inevitable or even calculated effect of the "system."

VI. An alternative reaction:
apprehension over advances of others

It is a basic idea of this essay that changes in the income of B lead to changes in A's welfare not only because A's relative position in the income scale has changed, but because changes in B's fortunes will affect A's prediction of his own future income. The principal case that has been considered so far is the tunnel effect: B advances, and this leads A to predict an improvement in his own position as well. Mention has also been made of the diametrically opposite situation: a deterioration in B's situation leads A to be apprehensive about his own, as is the case in a spreading depression. Is a mixed case conceivable? In other words, could A come to feel under certain circumstances that an advance on the part of B is likely to affect his own welfare *negatively*? Actually this sort of prediction is not too far-fetched: it is likely to be made in a society whose members are convinced that they are involved in a zero-sum game because resources are available in strictly limited amounts. This representation of social reality has been called the Image of Limited Good by George Foster, who claims it to be typical of many peasant societies around the world.[22] Assume the Image prevails in a community and that, at one point, a number of its citizens (group B) improve their position, while the income of the rest of the people (group A) remains unchanged. One conclusion to be drawn from such a development would of course be for both A and B to give up the Image. But suppose the community is strongly committed to it as a result of past experiences: one way of maintaining the Image is then to dismiss what has happened as purely transitory. And if the advance of group B appears to be irreversible, then the Image can be held on to only by the prediction that A's fortunes will soon suffer decline.[23]

[22] *Tzintzuntzan*, chapter 6.

[23] One reason for this prediction could be A's feeling that B, as a result of his increased wealth, will also acquire more power, a good that is generally acquired at the expense of others, and that this redistribution of power, besides being in itself objectionable to A, will have in time an adverse effect on his economic position. Such a feeling is likely to arise particularly if B comes to be *substantially* better off than A. Oskar Morgenstern has pointed to this situation as one limitation to the doctrine of Pareto optimality. See his "Pareto Optimum and Economic Organization," in Norbert Kloten et al., eds., *Systeme und Methoden in den Wirtschafts- und Sozialwissenschaften* (Tubingen: J. C. B. Mohr, 1964), p. 578.

It is in fact possible that we have here come upon a better way of accounting for what has been described by Foster and others as the "prevalence of envy" in peasant societies.[24] It may well be that when B advances, this makes A unhappy not because he is envious, but because he is worried; on the basis of his existing world view, he must expect to be worse off in short order. In other words, A is unhappy not because of the presence of relative deprivation, but because of the anticipation of absolute deprivation.

The reinterpretation of institutionalized envy, which is suggested here, can actually be seen to be closely related to the tunnel effect. In a society without the experience of sustained growth, an initially emerging situation in which one group of people is improving its economic position while another group remains stationary is probably felt as essentially unstable: either available resources have not increased, and in that case group A will necessarily suffer a decline to compensate for B's rise; or some windfall gain has expanded total resources, and in this case group A will soon get its proper share of the windfall. Therefore, one or the other of these two outcomes is likely to be anticipated rather than the continuation of the current situation. Which one will be picked as most likely will of course make a great deal of difference to the course of social conflict in that society. The decision could often be narrowly balanced, as on a knife's edge, depending as it does on A's perception of the causes of B's initial advance. This perception will depend on the factors briefly reviewed in the preceding section. But it now appears that the alternative for those who are left behind is not merely between an expectation of sharing in the advances of others and the status quo, but between expectation of advance and anticipation of decline. This situation and the knife-edge character of the decision between these alternative expectations perhaps explain why the forecasting of social conflict is such hazardous business.

VII. Concluding remarks

The preceding argument suggests a few summary points and concluding remarks.

[24] *Tzintzuntzan*, pp. 153–5.

1. If growth and equity in income distribution are considered the two principal economic tasks facing a country, then these two tasks can be solved sequentially if the country is well supplied with the tunnel effect. If, because of existing social, political, or psychological structures, the tunnel effect is weak or nonexistent, then the two tasks will have to be solved simultaneously, a difficult enterprise and one that probably requires institutions wholly different from those appropriate to the sequential case.[25] To make matters worse, it may be impossible to tell in advance whether a given country is or is not adequately supplied with the tunnel effect: as was argued in the last section, it is conceivable that only development itself will tell.

2. On the basis of the distinction just made, it is possible to speak of two kinds of "development disasters." The first is characteristic of societies that have attempted to develop by means of a strategy implying the arising of new inequalities or the widening of old ones; but, in view of their structure, these societies should never have done so. Nigeria and Pakistan are probably cases in point. The other kind of development disaster occurs in countries in which the above strategy is nicely abetted for a while by the tunnel effect, but where ruling groups and policymakers fail to realize that the safety valve, which the effect implies, will cease to operate after some time. This situation has been increasingly typical of a number of Latin American countries: Brazil and Mexico have already experienced disasters,[26] and there are numerous portents of more to come.

3. In contrast with most conventional representations, the development process is here viewed as being exposed to crisis, and perhaps disaster, even after lengthy periods of forward move-

[25] Political scientists have described the difficulties facing the new states of the twentieth century in these terms. Whereas, so they point out, the countries of Western Europe had centuries to solve, one after the other, the various problems of modernization and nation building – territorial identity, authority, mass participation, etc. – the new nations are faced with all of them at once. See Samuel P. Huntington, *Political Order in Changing Societies* (New Haven: Yale University Press, 1968), Ch. 2; Stein Rokkan, "Dimensions of State Formation and Nation-Building," in Charles Tilly, ed., *The Formation of States in Western Europe* (Princeton, N.J.: Princeton University Press, 1975), pp. 562–600. Various alternative sequential paths are explored in Dankwart A. Rustow, *A World of Nations* (Washington: Brookings, 1967), Chapter 4.

[26] [The reference here is to the installation of an authoritarian regime in Brazil in 1964 and in particular to its highly repressive phase, which started in 1968 (and lasted until about 1975), and to the crushing, by military force, of the Mexican student movement of 1968, also known as the "Tlatelolco massacre."]

ment. The view here proposed necessarily allocates a decisive role to politics. Its implications for the political evolution of countries where the tunnel effect operates are obvious. As long as the effect is strong, the developing country will be relatively easy to govern. It may even exhibit a surprising aptitude for democratic forms, which, alas, is likely to be ephemeral; for, after a while the tunnel effect will decay and social injustice will no longer go unperceived and unresisted. As a first reaction, the coercive powers of the state will then be used to restrict participation and to quell protest and subversion. More constructive programs of responding to crisis are easy to conceive, but seem to be extraordinarily difficult to bring into the world.

4

A generalized linkage approach to development, with special reference to staples

Theorizing on economic development in historical perspective[1]

The career of development economics in the last twenty-five years illustrates one of the crucial differences between the natural and the social sciences. In the natural sciences, as Thomas Kuhn has shown, the formulation of a new paradigm is followed by an extended period in which the paradigm is fully accepted and the labors of "normal science" are devoted to its verification, application, and further extension. In the social sciences, on the other hand, the enunciation of a new paradigm not only gives rise to similar sympathetic labors, but is often followed almost immediately by a persistent onslaught of qualification, criticism, and outright demolition that is very much part of normal social science. This situation explains the distinctive intellectual climate of the social sciences: here the confident belief in a genuine cumulative growth of knowledge, so characteristic of the natural sciences, hardly ever has a chance to arise.

The story of development economics since 1950 is a case in point: it tells of progress on the condition that intellectual progress is defined as the gradual loss of certainty, as the slow mapping out of the extent of our ignorance, which was previously hidden by an initial certainty parading as paradigm. The main purpose of the present paper is not to trace the progressive disintegration of the initial paradigm; it is rather to build on one specific critical approach that was elaborated in the course, and for

Reprinted from *Economic Development and Cultural Change* 25 (Supplement 1977): 67–98, by permission of the University of Chicago Press. © 1977 by the University of Chicago. All rights reserved. The Supplement contains essays in honor of Bert F. Hoselitz.

[1] See Chapter 1 for a broader survey.

the purpose, of this disintegration. Nevertheless, if that approach is to be extended, a brief account of the movement of ideas within which it originated is perhaps a useful prologue.

From the point of view of intellectual history, one of the important, though hardly ever mentioned, dates in the emergence of development economics was the publication, in 1948–9, of two definitive articles by Paul Samuelson on the pure theory of international trade.[2] The articles proved that under certain largely traditional assumptions (no factor movements, zero transport costs, etc.) free trade could be relied on to equalize not the relative but the absolute factor prices in the various trading countries and that trade could thus function as a perfect substitute for the movement of factors of production across national borders. The classical theory of international trade has of course long taught that trade could lead to mutual gains for all trading countries, but Samuelson's results were much stronger and pointed to trade as a potential force toward the equalization of incomes around the world.

This brilliant theoretical capstone of the classical and neoclassical theory was put into place just as consciousness of the persistent and widening international inequality of incomes was becoming acute in the postwar years. While in Kuhn's scientific revolution sequence, the accumulating facts are supposed to gradually contradict the paradigm, here the theory contributed to the contradiction by resolutely walking away from the facts. As a result, Samuelson's findings – even though they have been put forward with all due warnings about the unrealistic and demanding nature of the assumptions on which they rested – acted as a devastating boomerang for the traditional theory and its claim to usefulness in explaining the problems of the real world. The challenges put forward at around the same time by Raúl Prebisch and Hans Singer were far less polished than Samuelson's theory and were immediately contested on statistical and analytical grounds, but they achieved a degree of credibility both because they took these problems seriously and because of the self-inflicted wound from which the classical theory was now suffering.

But Western economics avoided the charge of being incompe-

[2] Paul A. Samuelson, "International Trade and the Equalization of Factor Prices," *Economic Journal* 58 (June 1948): 163–84, and "International Factor-Price Equalisation Once Again," ibid., 59 (June 1949): 181–97.

tent to deal with the problems of underdevelopment by advances in another one of its branches. The fledgling growth theory, in its Harrod-Domar version, jumped into the breach and supplied for a while a much-needed paradigm for the purpose of understanding and, hopefully, remedying the poverty of Asia, Africa, and Latin America. It became an article of faith, reinforced by the rapid postwar recovery and growth (as then understood) of both Western and Eastern Europe, that growth depended critically on the injection of an adequate amount of capital, domestic or foreign. A generation of planners and foreign aid officials came to believe in the reality and manipulability of the Propensity to Save and the Capital-Output Ratio, and they stuck to this faith over an astonishingly long period of time for the good reason that the representation of the world in terms of these concepts was essential to their status as experts – it was "the only game in town."

A revolutionary or radical variant of the same theory made its appearance not long after the elaboration of the Harrod-Domar growth model and its first application to underdeveloped countries. In an influential article published in 1952, Paul Baran argued that, without social revolution, growth in these countries was impossible: foreign private capital was exploitative, parasitic or *comprador* local elites were unable and unwilling to invest productively, and foreign aid only had the effect of shoring up the existing growth-defeating power structure. This representation of reality did not reject the logic of the orthodox paradigm which had installed productive capital investment as the prime mover. But it argued that the sociopolitical characteristics of the poor countries and their relations to the centers of capitalist-imperialist expansion were such as to make capital investment there both inadequate and unproductive.[3]

Between the thesis, which sees development as certain provided capital is injected in the right amounts, and the antithesis, which views development as impossible given the social and political status quo, there was a great deal of room for intermediate positions. In fact, once evidence accumulated on actual economic developments in the periphery, the two extreme positions looked unsatisfactory.

[3] Paul A. Baran, "On the Political Economy of Backwardness," *Manchester School of Economics and Social Studies* 20 (January 1952): 66–84.

The first attempts at moving away from the excessive simplicities of the paradigmatic growth model took the form of showing that the amount of investment depended not only on the total income earned during the preceding period but also on the distribution of income, a concept almost as familiar to economists as that of aggregate income flow. What is remarkable – though it has remained unnoticed – is that the two major contributions that were made along these lines in 1955 and 1956 reached opposite conclusions. One paper, by Walter Galenson and Harvey Leibenstein, argued that the greater the capital intensity of new production the greater would be the share of profits in the ensuing income stream and therefore the higher the reinvestment out of profits in the next period. The other article, by Robert Baldwin, suggested that an equalitarian distribution of income would make for rapid growth because domestic markets would then more easily reach the size necessary for the establishment and profitable operation of consumer goods industries.[4] Clearly, the two sets of authors had different circumstances in mind: Galenson-Leibenstein wrote in terms of an industrialization process that is already powerfully under way, whereas Baldwin was assessing the comparative ability of countries operating at a much earlier stage to attract basic consumer goods industries. Looked at in this way, the two theories are no longer contradictory, for it is possible and even likely that the patterns of income distribution that are supportive of rapid growth are different at different stages of development. In fact, the economic history of the United States during the nineteenth century outside of the South bears considerable resemblance first to the Baldwin and then to the Galenson-Leibenstein pattern, moving from a comparatively egalitarian to a highly concentrated income distribution, with industrial development proceeding apace throughout.

The articles just noted were valuable in puncturing the ruling paradigm and its excessive aggregation, but they continued to emphasize the income side of the economy. The pace of economic development was made to depend, not on total income,

---

[4] Walter Galenson and Harvey Leibenstein, "Investment Criteria, Productivity and Economic Development," *Quarterly Journal of Economics* 69 (August 1955): 343–70; Robert E. Baldwin, "Patterns of Development in Newly Settled Regions," *Manchester School of Economics and Social Studies* 24 (May 1956): 161–79.

but on the way in which income was divided among different groups. A more radical break with the paradigm came through suggestions that a determining influence on growth may issue from the production side of the economy. Sociologists like Bert Hoselitz and others took this point of view when they focused on the conditions for the emergence of entrepreneurship. As an economist, I preferred to simply assume an insufficiency of entrepreneurial motivation and then to systematically search for such constellations of productive forces as would move private or public decision makers to "do something" through special pressures – pressures that are more compelling than those that are expected to move the rational decision maker of received economic theory.[5]

One suggestion along this line was that development is accelerated through investment in projects and industries with strong forward or backward linkage effects.[6] I argued that entrepreneurial decision making in both the private and the public sectors is not uniquely determined by the pull of incomes and demand, but is responsive to special push factors, such as the linkages, emanating from the product side.

Backward and forward linkages have become part of the language of development economics. Looking at this success from the point of view of the sociology of knowledge, I suspect that it owes much to my having presented the linkages as intimately tied to input-output analysis, that is, to the existing technical corpus of economic knowledge. As such they seemed more operational, less fuzzy than, for example, Perroux's propulsive industry or Rostow's leading sector. Actually, of course, input-output analysis is by nature synchronic, whereas linkage effects need time to unfold. This basic difference has bedeviled various ingenious attempts at comprehensive, cross-section measurement of linkage effects and at thereby "testing the linkage hy-

[5] For an exploration of similar "extra" pressures in the area of technological change, see Nathan Rosenberg, "The Direction of Technological Change; Inducement Mechanisms and Focusing Devices," *Economic Development and Cultural Change* 18 (October 1969): 1–24. [Another early "supply-side" dissent from mainstream analysis is implicit in the structuralist thesis on inflation, as pointed out in Chapter 6, Section I.]

[6] See my *Strategy of Economic Development* (New Haven, Conn.: Yale University Press, 1958), Chapter 6. The first rough outline of the idea is in a paper written in 1954 and republished as Chapter 1 in *A Bias for Hope: Essays on Development and Latin America* (New Haven, Conn.: Yale University Press, 1971), pp. 59–61.

pothesis."[7] The more illuminating uses of the concept are perhaps to be found in a number of historically oriented studies
which paid close attention to the sequence of development in
individual countries.[8]

I now wish to propose some extensions and generalizations of
the linkage concept along several lines. First I shall consider
processes that, because of their similarities to the backward and
forward variety, also deserve to be called linkages and have
indeed been so labeled already. Then I shall suggest a more
inclusive linkage concept and use it to look at selected development sequences. Finally, in the course of some methodological
observations, I shall discuss, among other things, the relation of
the generalized linkage approach to the staple and development-
of-underdevelopment theses as well as its affinity to what I shall
call micro-Marxism.

A brief personal comment on how this essay came to be written is in order here. For a number of years I have assembled
notes, references, and ideas on the topics to be discussed and
have taught seminars around them. All along I felt that to deal
with them adequately required a vast amount of further research
eventually to be incorporated in a book. Yet that research and
that book were postponed from year to year as new interests
claimed increasing portions of my time or as the task seemed too
formidable. Then came the invitation to contribute a paper for a
special occasion. At that point I decided to write an article rather
than a book about the matters I have been carrying around with
me. Thus the following pages should be read as an outline and
preview of what the book might have been or may yet be.

[7] Werner Baer and Isaac Kerstenetzky, "Import Substitution and Industrialization in
Brazil," *American Economic Review* 54 (May 1964): 411–25; Pan A. Yotopoulos and Jef-
frey B. Nugent, "A Balanced Growth Version of the Linkage Hypothesis," *Quarterly
Journal of Economics* 87 (May 1973): 157–72. The latter article has led to a regular symposium on linkage effect measurement, with contributions by Prem S. Laumas, Michel
Boucher, James Riedel, Leroy P. Jones, and a reply by Yotopoulos and Nugent in
Quarterly Journal of Economics 90 (May 1976): 308–43. The paper by Jones is particularly
noteworthy for solving, at last, the problem of how to measure total (direct and
indirect) forward linkage effects.

[8] Albert Fishlow, *American Railroads and the Transformation of the Ante-Bellum Economy*
(Cambridge, Mass.: Harvard University Press, 1965); Judith Tendler, *Electric Power in
Brazil: Entrepreneurship in the Public Sector* (Cambridge, Mass.: Harvard University
Press, 1968); Michael Roemer, *Fishing for Growth: Export-led Development in Peru, 1950–
1967* (Cambridge, Mass.: Harvard University Press, 1970); Scott R. Pearson, *Petroleum
and the Nigerian Economy* (Stanford, Calif.: Stanford University Press, 1970). See also
Richard Weisskoff and Edward Wolff, "Linkages and Leakages: Industrial Tracking in
an Enclave Economy," *Economic Development and Cultural Change* 25 (July 1977): 607–28.

I. Linkage effects – some further varieties and some interactions

I have defined the linkage effects of a given product line as investment-generating forces that are set in motion, through input-output relations, when productive facilities that supply inputs to that line or utilize its outputs are inadequate or nonexistent. Backward linkages lead to new investment in input-supplying facilities and forward linkages to investment in output-using facilities.

A. Consumption and fiscal linkages

The linkage concept was put forward with industry and industrialization primarily in mind because here it was possible to conceive of linkages of considerable variety and depth in both the backward and forward directions. Nevertheless, the concept has also had useful applications to primary production, where its close connection with the staple thesis soon became evident. The staple thesis, as originated by Harold Innis and further developed by Canadian economists and economic historians, has attempted to show how the growth experience of a "new" country is concretely shaped by the specific primary products which it successively exports to world markets. It is an attempt to discover in detail how "one thing leads to another" through the requirements and influence of the staple, from transportation facilities and settlement patterns to the establishment of new economic activities. The original linkage concept captures of course only one aspect of this overall process, the one that is most directly tied to the procurement and elaboration of the staple itself. But some important additional aspects can be encompassed by the concept once it has been appropriately stretched by bringing the income side into the picture. For one thing, the new incomes earned in the process of staple production and export may be spent initially on imports, but these imports, once grown to a sufficient volume, could eventually be substituted by domestic industries. The somewhat roundabout mechanism through which certain import-substituting industries are called into life by the staple in this manner has been aptly called consumption linkage,[9] in contrast,

[9] By Melville H. Watkins in his well-known paper, "A Staple Theory of Economic Growth," *Canadian Journal of Economics and Political Science* 29 (May 1963): 141–58. In Chapter 7 of *Strategy*, I had described the same phenomenon – the "swallowing up" through industrialization of successive categories of expanding imports in the course of export-led growth – but had not characterized it as a linkage.

the more direct backward and forward linkages might be sub-
sumed under the name of production linkages. A notable characteristic of the consumption linkages is that they can be outright negative rather than merely weak or nonexistent. It is
now widely recognized that during the first phase of export
expansion in the countries of the periphery an important effect
is, not the creation of new industries to satisfy rising consumer
demand, but the destruction of established handicraft and arti-
san activities as labor is withdrawn from them for staple production and as new imports of consumer goods compete successfully against them.[10] It is at this point, among others, that
the linkage approach and the staple thesis make contact with
the development-of-underdevelopment thesis which will be discussed briefly below.

Another important way in which one thing may lead to another
is through the ability of the state to tap the income stream accruing from the staple to various parties, particularly to the owners
of the mines and plantations. If the state levies taxes on these
incomes and channels the proceeds into productive investment, it
is possible to speak of fiscal linkages of the staple to be contrasted
with the, again, more direct physical (or production) linkages
described in my *Strategy of Economic Development*.[11]

A comparative appraisal of the existence, strength, and reliabil-
ity of these various linkage effects for different staples in various
socioeconomic settings is one way toward an understanding of
the growth process in the countries of the periphery, during the
period of export-led growth. A considerable advantage of this

---

[10] Staffan B. Linder, *Trade and Trade Policy for Development* (New York: Praeger Publishers, 1967), pp. 143–9 and 171–2; Stephen H. Hymer and Stephen A. Resnick, "A Model of an Agrarian Economy with Non-agricultural Activities," *American Economic Review* 59 (September 1969): 493–506; Stephen A. Resnick, "The Decline of Rural Industry under Export Expansion: A Comparison among Burma, Phillipines, and Thailand, 1870–1938," *Journal of Economic History* 30 (March 1970): 51–73.

[11] See Pearson, *Petroleum*, pp. 46–50 and passim. When the incomes from the staple accrue primarily to domestic parties who save a substantial portion of these incomes, a centralized national banking system can accomplish a redirection of the income stream that would be similar to that achieved by fiscal linkage. According to a communication from Juan Linz, in Spain this "banking linkage" has been of some importance and has served to channel funds from the citrus-fruit and mineral-ore exporters toward the industrial sector. Another note: the opposition between fiscal and physical linkages is not absolute, for it is perfectly conceivable that a government would use the revenues accruing from a given economic activity to establish an industry that is linked, in backward and forward fashion, to that activity.

approach is that it points from the outset to the possibility of characteristically different experiences in line with different linkage constellations.

B. Conditions favoring fiscal linkage

The most favorable constellation would of course be one in which a staple was simultaneously endowed with strong production, consumption, and fiscal linkages. Unfortunately, this ideal situation is not likely to occur: a little reflection suggests that one kind of linkage is often to be had only at the expense of another. For example, the fiscal linkages have made a strong showing in those mining and petroleum activities that had all the earmarks of the "enclave." But the enclave is defined by the absence of involvement with the rest of the economy, that is, by the absence of other kinds of linkages. It is precisely because of this absence of links that the enclave becomes an obvious and comparatively easy target of the fiscal authorities. Being a foreign body, often owned by foreigners to boot, the enclave has few defenders of its interests once the state acquires the will and authority to divert toward its own ends a portion of the income stream originating therein.

Let us consider, on the other hand, a productive activity with many direct links to the rest of the economy, either because of strong backward and forward linkages or, more simply, because it is carried on in the central region of a country by producers with intimate ties to a dense network of traders and townspeople. Clearly, with so many friends in court this activity is not likely to be subjected to significant special taxation. The situation that is brought to mind here is that of coffee-growing countries such as Brazil and Colombia. In both countries, coffee has been crucial for the creation of settlement patterns, transportation networks, and consumption linkages, but it has yielded a fiscal contribution only quite late in its history as an export staple, and then only as the unintended result of economic policies originally directed to quite different and sometimes even opposite ends. In both Africa and Latin America, policies that had been adopted for the purpose of helping the growers of coffee, cocoa, and other staples by insulating them from depressed world market prices later turned into instruments that permitted taxation of the same growers, and these tax proceeds were then partly devoted to the financing of development ventures.[12]

If it is correct that fiscal linkages are usually associated with the lack of physical and consumption linkages and vice versa, the question of which set of linkage endowments is more favorable arises. The answer is complex, as it depends on the speed and strength with which the various linkages are likely to make their appearance. Only a few of the factors relevant to such a comparison can be discussed here.

Fiscal linkage depends on the willingness and ability of national governments to tax, or otherwise to claim participation in, the incomes originating in mining and similar enclave-type enterprises. This propensity to tax – and to own – has of course grown spectacularly since decolonization and other political developments have established the state in Asia, Africa, and Latin America as an actor with some autonomy. As a result, the development prospects of countries with nonrenewable natural resources are now very different from what they were under colonialism and earlier capitalist expansion.

As I have already hinted, fiscal linkage has a better chance to emerge if the enclave resources are owned by foreigners, for the same reason that an enclave is taxed more readily than an activity with a dense linkage network: taxing a foreign company comes more easily than assessing nationals who, besides owning the resources, are likely to run or "own" the government as well. The foreign-owned nitrate and copper mines of Chile, for example, yielded substantial revenues to the Chilean state during the early decades of the century, while the large, locally owned cocoa plantations of Ecuador created a bonanza that profited primarily a handful of Guayaquil families who controlled the Ecuadorean government from Paris, where they had settled to spend their fortunes pleasantly and rapidly.[13]

But the Chilean part of this story brings to mind that the ability to tax the enclave is hardly a sufficient condition for vigorous economic growth. For the fiscal linkage to be an effective

[12] See also, pp. 82–3.
[13] The history of this episode remains to be written. My sources are conversations with Professor Frank Fetter and with some descendants of the cocoa planters in Guayaquil – their fathers and grandfathers had to return to Ecuador after having been ruined by the witches' broom disease that destroyed the cocoa plantations, as well as by the depression of the thirties.

development mechanism, the ability to tax must be combined with the ability to invest productively. Here lies precisely the weakness of fiscal linkage in comparison with the more direct production and consumption linkages. In the case of the latter, existing production lines or imports to be substituted point to the tasks to be undertaken next, whereas no such guidance is forthcoming when a portion of the income stream earned in the enclave is siphoned off for the purpose of irrigating other areas of the economy. Hence the possibility of either faulty investment or a great deal of leakage on the way – for example, the siphoned-off funds may simply lead to an enlarged bureaucracy. The pre-1930s Chilean experience with nitrates and copper has been analyzed in the latter terms,[14] while a reexamination of Peru's abortive mid-nineteenth-century guano boom has pointed to ill-considered railroad investments as the main culprit.[15] No matter how adept governments have become at taxing the income stream originated by the export staple, the success of fiscal linkage continues to be daunted by similar difficulties. This is so, to repeat, not because funds in the hands of governments are always "wasted," but because the tasks taken on by governments through fiscal linkage are intrinsically more difficult than those that are assumed, frequently by private capital, in conjunction with physical and consumption linkages.

As long as the ability to tax and the ability to invest productively are both required for fiscal linkage to qualify as an effective mechanism, it would be easy to make a pronouncement to the effect that both of these abilities must be acquired by the state pari passu. Having stressed both the likelihood and the uses of unbalanced growth, I would rather refrain from that sort of advice and examine instead the comparative problems and

[14] Aníbal Pinto, *Tres ensayos sobre Chile y América Latina* (Buenos Aires: Solar, 1971), pp. 71ff.; that nitrate mining led to substantial nonfiscal linkages is demonstrated and stressed in a paper by Carmen Cariola and Osvaldo Sunkel, "La expansión salitrera y sus repercusiones sobre la economia agraria en el período 1880–1930" (October 1974), written for the Economic History Project of the Joint Committee on Latin American Studies (Social Science Research Council and American Council on Learned Societies).

[15] See Shane J. Hunt, "Growth and Guano in Nineteenth-Century Peru" (discussion paper no. 34, Research Program in Economic Development, Princeton University, February 1973). This paper is written in part in rebuttal of the earlier view, put forward in Chapter 2 ("Peru in the Guano Age") of Jonathan V. Levin, *The Export Economies* (Cambridge, Mass.: Harvard University Press, 1960), that the revenues from guano were largely dissipated through luxury imports and profit remittances.

advantages of the more likely unbalanced growth paths. It is possible to distinguish, as I did in *Strategy*, between an orderly, or permissive, and a disorderly, or compulsive, sequence.[16]

The unbalanced path can be said to be more orderly when the ability to tax develops ahead of the ability to invest: fiscal revenue is collected before the authorities have prepared a well-considered and commensurate shelf of investment projects. In extreme cases of this imbalance much of the revenue accumulates as foreign exchange, as is currently happening in small countries that are large petroleum producers. In less affluent cases, such as that of Chile earlier in the century, the disproportion between the accruing revenue and the ability to invest it productively in the domestic economy is likely to be reflected by an enlarged bureaucracy, by more plentiful and frequently unrealistic social services, by spending on armaments and other wasteful investments, and, in the balance of payments, by an increase in the imports of consumer goods. The trouble with this imbalance is that it is not self-correcting: bureaucracy, social services, and even unproductive public investments can go on expanding for a considerable time, and little pressure is brought on the government to develop its entrepreneurial capabilities instead. Insofar as the expansion of the bureaucracy and of social services is concerned there is at least the possibility that the increased imports of consumer goods which this expansion is likely to bring will eventually result in some consumption linkages. In this manner, spending of the tax proceeds for such "unproductive" purposes can be a lesser evil than their expenditure for supposedly productive investment projects that turn out to be failures.

In the opposite model, the government's motivation to develop some sector of the economy other than the staple outpaces its ability to extract taxes from the exporting interests. The obvious outcome of this situation is inflation induced by deficit spending or credit expansion. Although fraught with social and political dangers, this sort of disequilibrium situation contains at least some stimulus in the direction of balance at a higher level: the inflation itself can act as a powerful argument for the generation of more fiscal resources and for the procurement of foreign finance. This more compulsive unbalanced path is characteristic of countries where the export staple is owned by nationals that

[16] Hirschman, *Strategy*, pp. 78–83, 86–96, and passim.

are proficient at resisting taxation. It finds indeed a prototypical illustration in the Brazilian experience of the fifties.

As discussed so far, fiscal linkage is restricted to the direct participation of the state in the income stream generated by the export sector. A more roundabout way for the state to extract revenue is through the levying of customs duties on the manufactures that are imported into a country with an expanding export trade in primary products. This indirect extraction has been the more common way for the state to raise revenue and has in fact been the mainstay of public finance at the early stage of export-led growth whenever the state has been too weak, vis-à-vis the staple producers, to insist on direct fiscal linkage. On the whole, the revenues raised by means of the indirect route have paid for an expansion of government functions and services. They also have often served to provide infrastructure investments for the further expansion of primary exports; in this manner they have accentuated the colonial character of the economies concerned, whereas direct fiscal linkage investments have typically been undertaken for the opposite purpose, that is, to diversify the economy away from the dominant export staple.[17]

C. Forward linkages as handicaps

Though less problematic than fiscal linkages, production and consumption linkages are by no means wholly straightforward and uniformly reliable. In my original treatment of the subject, the relation between market size and the economic size of plant was singled out as the key variable that would trigger the private or public entrepreneurship needed to take up opportunities for backward- and forward-linkage investments as well as for import substitution. Further reflection and observation have made it clear, however, that other variables are also at work and help explain the differential speed with which these investments come into being.

One such variable is the degree of technological "strangeness" or "alienness" of the new economic activities in relation to the ongoing ones. In an environment in which backward linkages originate primarily among the owner-operators of the ongoing

[17] See Thomas B. Birnberg and Stephen A. Resnick, *Colonial Development: An Econometric Study* (New Haven, Conn.: Yale University Press, 1975).

activity, such linkages can be expected to be rather weak if the required input comes from an industry whose process and technique is totally unfamiliar to these operators. The linkage dynamic may thus be held back by the difficulties of making a technological leap whose size differs with different industries – it is bigger in the case of textiles, for example, than in metalworking and chemicals.[18]

In the case of agricultural and industrial raw materials, the size of the technological jump is almost always big for backward linkage since, under modern conditions, the technique of growing wheat or coffee or sugarcane has very little in common, except for the seeds or cuttings, with the technique of fabricating the tools or synthetic fertilizers that are used as inputs by the growers. The same is true for many of the forward linkages that are potentially so significant for staple-based economic development. The milling, refining, and other processing industries are usually technological strangers to the staple. Perhaps the principal reason why it is difficult to establish backward and forward linkage industries around the staples is not so much that, as I argued originally, there are fewer linkage effects in agriculture than in industry, but that they largely point to industries whose technologies are alien to the grower of the staple.[19] Hence, for a very long time these industries are carried on abroad, where, moreover, they are usually protected through the well-known tariff pattern making for stiff effective rates.

Processing industries have of course been established near the growing areas when they were indispensable to preparing the harvested product for world markets. The existence of forward linkages of this sort has depended more on compelling technical characteristics of the product than on entrepreneurial choice. An obvious example is sugarcane which, in the interest of maximizing sugar yield, must be crushed as soon as possible after cutting, and which is far too bulky to be transported for any distance. An

---

[18] I have explained this matter at greater length in "The Political Economy of Import-substituting Industrialization in Latin America" (1968), reprinted in *Bias for Hope* (see p. 114). In the case of agriculture, technological strangeness is often combined with other obstacles to backward or forward linkages being taken up by the producers themselves; among those obstacles are the need for large amounts of capital due to scale requirements and the lack of marketing access and knowledge.

[19] There are exceptions, of course: in many areas where coffee is grown the bags in which the beans are shipped are made from the fibers of the agave family of plants which are grown by the coffee farmer along the borders of his coffee plantings.

even better example is the shipping of bananas in cardboard cartons, which was begun during the sixties. Previously the fruit had always been shipped on the stem, making the banana the export staple with possibly the smallest added postharvest value. Shipping in cartons turned out to be a considerable convenience in terms of speed of loading and unloading; it also saved on shipping space and weight, partly because the weight of the useless center stalk alone comes to about 15 percent of the total. In addition, the packaging of bananas in cartons provided employment to the exporting countries, and the need for cartons meant a stimulus for their pulp and paper industries. But the decision to go to cartons was exclusively dictated by the need to find a way of avoiding bruising the fruit during transport after the tough Gros Michel had been widely replaced by the more delicate Cavendish variety. The switch to the latter had in turn been made necessary by the destructive Panama disease, against which the Gros Michel proved to be defenseless in spite of protracted and expensive efforts at control.[20]

The normal and quite justified reaction to this story is to lament the developing country's inability to exploit such simple, obvious, and useful opportunities for forward linkages except under conditions of utter technological necessity and to look for institutional arrangements and economic incentives that would facilitate the perception and grasping of such opportunities. But the earlier example of sugarcane points to a rather different moral: because processing operations and forward linkages in general tend to be technological strangers to the staple, these operations, when they do come into existence because of compelling requirements of the staple's export technology, tend to be undertaken and controlled by groups distinct from the grower of the staple, who is thus relegated more firmly to his agricultural role. The sugarcane grower or rice farmer who delivers his crop to the sugar refinery or rice mill owned and operated by "others" is effectively cut off from any further economic activities on behalf of his product. From this point of view, it begins to appear paradoxically that the less of these forward

---

[20] See R. E. Evenson, J. P. Houck, Jr., and V. W. Ruttan, "Technological Change and Agricultural Trade: Three Examples – Sugarcane, Bananas, and Rice," in *The Technology Factor in International Trade*, ed. R. Vernon (New York: Columbia University Press, for the National Bureau of Economic Research, 1970), pp. 442–51.

linkages exist in the case of staples, the better. Conditions for the development of entrepreneurial initiative on the part of the staple grower may be more favorable if the staple requires only a few simple operations such as drying and bagging to prepare it for the market and if it does not have to rely on alien transportation. For example, the higher the staple's value per unit of weight the more worthwhile it is for the grower or a member of his family to take it to market. In the absence of elaborate forward linkage industries based on alien technology and probably run by alien entrepreneurs, the grower of the staple may himself become involved in the more accessible nonindustrial forwarding operations, such as transportation, commerce, and finance; he or a member of his family may become specialized in these functions; and from a strong base here he can eventually contribute to industrial development through the exploitation of opportunities for consumption linkages that may appear in the wake of the staple boom. This corresponds substantially to the history of commercial, urban, and eventual industrial expansion via import substitution following upon coffee exports in the São Paulo and Antioquia regions of Brazil and Colombia. The lack of cumulative development that has marked the career of such staples as sugarcane, groundnuts, and cotton also fits into the picture: in these cases the alien forward linkage industries of refining and ginning, or the need for specialized – hence alien – transportation because of distance and bulk of the staple (groundnuts), cut off the producer of the staples from any further involvement with them.[21]

I have shown that fiscal linkage has the best chance of coming into play when a staple is a true enclave and is therefore poor in other linkages of whatever kind. Now it appears similarly that the absence of one linkage – technologically complex, hence alien, forward linkage – creates favorable conditions for another, more diffuse kind of linkage as staple growers develop the entrepreneurial initiative needed for the cumulative growth of commerce and other economic activities around the staple. Forc-

---

[21] During earlier discussions, some observers noted that in many underdeveloped areas specialization in the production of staples for exports led to "onceover," noncumulative development. This intermediate possibility – a reality in many countries – has been lost sight of as the discussion has centered on the alternatives: immiserization or cumulative development. See, in particular, H. Myint, *Economic Theory and the Underdeveloped Countries* (London: Oxford University Press, 1971), Chapters 3 and 4 (originally published as articles in 1954).

ing matters only a little, one might say that both fiscal and consumption linkages are more likely to appear if some other linkages are absent.

II. Linkages – a broader definition and a new subdivision

By now, the various linkages and their interaction have taken on a new character and importance. They appear to constitute a structure that is capable of generating alternative paths toward development or underdevelopment for the different staple exporters. In other words, some of the principal features of a country's development in the period of export-led growth can be described in terms of linkages deriving from its staple. The question arises, therefore, why this is so and how the structure can be further developed.

The linkages capture much of the development story for a reason that has already been given; development is essentially the record of how one thing leads to another, and the linkages are that record, from a specific point of view. They focus on certain characteristics inherent in the productive activities already in process at a certain time. These ongoing activities, because of their characteristics, push or, more modestly, invite some operators to take up new activities. Whenever that is the case, a linkage exists between the ongoing and the new activity. All our previous linkages fall within this definition.

With this generalization of the linkage concept a new subdivision may be suggested. On the one hand, there are situations in which the same economic operators who are already engaged in the ongoing activity are impelled to undertake the additional activity; this is linkage due to insiders or "inside linkage." On the other hand, the push to take up new activities may be felt not so much by those who are involved in the ongoing activity as by other parties. For example, the ongoing activity might be carried on by indigenous economic operators, while the new activity would be taken up by foreigners or by the state. This is linkage through outsiders or "outside linkage."

Except for fiscal linkage, which is outside linkage by definition, the new subdivision cuts across all previous linkage categories. Forward and backward linkages, in particular, can be either outside or inside. In the latter case, one is in the presence of vertical integration. With this new terminology, it is possible to give a compact formulation of various propositions about development patterns and to generate new hypotheses in the process. To illustrate: (*a*) if the new activity is technologically alien to the ongoing activity, inside linkage will meet with special difficulties; (*b*) twentieth-century latecomers tend to have a particularly marked preference for inside over outside linkage; hence the conjecture arises that (*c*) the industrialization process of those latecomers is subject to special problems and perhaps discontinuities whenever the next steps of the development process require, or are believed to require, a massive injection of alien technology.[22]

A more general use of the new linkage categories is to look at the developmental advantages and drawbacks that may be associated with each. Thus, outside linkage has the advantage of mobilizing new agents and of preventing an excessive concentration of economic wealth and power, while the advantage of inside linkage is that it develops the entrepreneurial initiatives of the older agents and permits them to break out of their existing pursuits. The balance of these advantages and corresponding disadvantages in each case is likely to reveal a great deal about different development profiles and about missed or captured opportunities. In the following discussion, some further varieties of inside and outside linkages will be reviewed.

A. Inside linkage: invitation to spatial mobility

A linkage exists whenever an ongoing activity gives rise to economic or other pressures that lead to the taking up of a new activity. But how is newness to be defined? Until now, as in the cases of forward and backward linkage, newness has been understood as a new kind of productive activity and, specifically, as one yielding a new product. With the broader linkage concept, a new activity could also be defined as one that yields the

---

[22] Proposition (*a*) was put forward earlier in this essay; proposition (*b*) is in my "Political Economy of Import-substituting Industrialization in Latin America"; and proposition (*c*) plays an important role in Guillermo O'Donnell's analysis of the economic foundations of bureaucratic authoritarianism in Latin America. See his "Reflexiones sobre las tendencias generales de cambio en el Estado Burocrático-autoritario," mimeographed (Buenos Aires: CEDES, August 1975). A somewhat different English version is in *Latin American Research Review* 13 (1978): 3–38.

same product as before but is carried on in a new place. An inside linkage can therefore be said to exist when some characteristics of the ongoing activity compel or invite some or all of its operators to move to another place even though they may not plan, at least initially, to undertake a new activity.

A considerable contribution to the analysis of this kind of process is made by Clifford Geertz in his observations on Indonesia.[23] The Javanese rice farmer, living in the midst of paddies that have been carefully terraced over many generations, clings to his parcel of land with the utmost tenacity. Geertz has contrasted the resulting immobility of the Javanese farmer with the mobility of the cultivators on the Outer Islands who typically engage in slash-and-burn agriculture. Two very different patterns of colonial exploitation resulted: in Java it was possible to force the rice farmer to devote some of his land to the cultivation of sugarcane for delivery to Dutch-owned refineries, whereas in the Outer Islands the colonizers were unable to take advantage of this convenient system of indirect production. Instead, they established and managed their own plantations of coffee, tea, and rubber. The preexisting mode of agricultural production thus had important consequences for the form of colonial exploitation: in Java the colonizer penetrated virtually every peasant household, whereas in the Outer Islands he made his presence felt through the creation of enclaves. These differences also determined differences in decolonization: in Java it took the form of letting most of the land in sugarcane revert to paddy; the plantations of the Outer Islands, on the other hand, were expropriated, but continued to produce the same crops, mostly for export, as before.

While primarily helpful for the understanding of the specific patterns of colonization and decolonization, the characteristics noted by Geertz also have importance for gauging development perspectives. The tenacity with which the Javanese rice farmer clings to his land is due in part to his expectation that some extra care in maintaining the terraces, irrigation ditches, and bunds, as well as special efforts at weeding and other labors, will produce increases in yield sufficient to feed his growing family. While the rice plant, with its elaborate infrastructure, has received over the centuries and still receives and needs "tender,

---

[23] Clifford Geertz, *Agricultural Involution: The Processes of Ecological Change in Indonesia* (Berkeley: University of California Press, 1963).

loving care," it also responds to such care almost indefinitely. In economic terms this amounts to saying that the marginal productivity of labor used in paddy rice farming declines only very slowly and is probably perceived as having an even smaller downward slope than turns out to be the case in fact. These characteristics have contributed to the immobility of the Javanese rice farmer and to the enormous accumulation of population in the countryside. They also help understand the ease with which opportunities for trade and other services on the island have been appropriated by foreigners, mostly Chinese.

A product or staple with the opposite characteristics would be one whose output per unit of labor input would fall off rapidly as more labor is supplied. In the case of such a product, a population increase in the countryside cannot be absorbed in the existing area of settlement and is likely to lead rapidly to migration to the cities or to the opening up of new lands. An example is the tree crops such as coffee and cocoa which, once planted, require, besides harvesting, only a moderate and not highly variable amount of pruning and weeding (fertilizer being primarily a capital input).

In some cases, moreover, coffee has led to soil exhaustion, which causes the productivity of labor to decline unexpectedly without any increase in labor input. In Brazil, there is a striking contrast between the soil exhaustion of the coffee plantations in the Paraíba Valley near Rio de Janeiro in the second half of the nineteenth century and the century-long undiminished productivity of the cane lands in the *zona da mata* of the northeast. It explains, in part, why the sugar barons of the northeast never became involved in other economic activities, while the coffee planters near Rio, in spite of their expectation and full intention to turn into sedentary plantation owners leading a life of leisure, were forced to look farther afield, to found new plantations in the state of São Paulo, and in the process to become involved in tasks of transportation, communication, and commerce.[24]

The lesson implicit in these examples is not that erosion is good for development – although it can work out that way if fertile lands remain to be opened up fairly close to the eroded ones.

---

[24] Pedro Calmon, *História do Brasil* (São Paulo: Companhia editora nacional, 1947), 4: 384–6, cited in Warren Dean, "The Planter as Entrepreneur: The Case of São Paulo," *Hispanic American Historical Review* 46 (May 1966): 146.

Rather it is that the deeply rooted Western value judgment which sees sedentary agriculture as a huge step forward from more mobile ways of life must be questioned when it is applied outside of its original context, the neolithic revolution. At the very least, it certainly is not true that the more sedentary, the better. This is shown by the comparison of the migrant coffee and cocoa farmers of Colombia, Brazil, Nigeria, and Ghana with situations where the staple fitted right into the existing mode of agricultural production.[25] The latter condition is characteristic of sugarcane in Java, as just mentioned, as well as of cotton in Egypt, groundnuts in northern Nigeria, perhaps coffee in Uganda, and so on. In these situations the staple is grown by an already well-settled peasantry that makes a place for it on land previously uncultivated or devoted to food crops, and techniques of cultivation are rather similar to those that are already in use.[26] The staple fits into the existing production, settlement, and skill pattern with a minimum of disruption, and also with a minimum of cumulative development. Depending on the social, demographic, and political circumstances, the result for the cultivators ranges widely, from the Javanese pattern of impoverishment to "once-over" development. Whatever the actual outcome, the initiative for cumulative development, if any, has to originate elsewhere, that is, in outside linkage.

B. Outside linkage: provision of public goods by the state

At first sight, it may seem that it is asking too much of our approach to make a contribution to this topic. How specific char

---

[25] This is the factor stressed by Robert Baldwin in an article in which he examines the question, primarily for Africa, of why export staples have not led to cumulative growth. The alternative – or rather the dilemma – he describes is that between the mineral enclaves, where a skill ladder exists but is available only to a very small population group, and the agricultural staples, which do not provide for the acquisition of new skills. In my view, Baldwin overrates the importance of the acquisition of specific skills and overlooks the increase in overall competence, versatility, and entrepreneurial drive that can result from migration and geographical mobility. With mobility rather than skill acquisition as the crucial factor, the outlook for development looks somewhat more hopeful (see Robert E. Baldwin, "Export Technology and Development from a Subsistence Level," *Economic Journal* 73 [March 1963]: 80–92).

[26] For the evidence from Ghana and Nigeria, see Polly Hill, *Migrant Cocoa Farmers of Southern Ghana* (Cambridge: Cambridge University Press, 1963), and Sara S. Berry, *Cocoa, Custom, and Socio-Economic Change in Rural Western Nigeria* (London: Oxford University Press, 1975), which, on pp. 75–8, spells out a number of advantages migrants have over local farmers.

acteristics of export staples can contribute to the propensity and ability of the staple growers themselves to engage in further development moves is easy enough to see. But how could such characteristics be related to the behavior of other actors, such as the commercial and industrial classes, foreign investors, or the state? Actually, it will be recalled that one type of developmental behavior on the part of the state, its propensity to tax the staple, has already been related to such characteristics of staples as lack of direct linkages to the rest of the economy. Taxing is of course not all that one wants a development-minded state to do. As I have shown, a state that only knows how to tax a staple may be very far from making an effective contribution to development.

It is in fact conceivable that the opposite kind of involvement is a better way for the state to acquire an ability to promote development. In other words, instead of taxing the staple growers, the state may somehow be pushed into assisting them. If this happens, a new actor comes onto the development stage. This could be yet another case of once-over development: it is conceivable that the state will undertake a specific job which it is uniquely suited to perform and that this will be the end of the story. But it is also possible, and in certain circumstances probable, that the state, as a result of having intervened successfully in one sector of the economy, will acquire the capability and the appetite to tackle advances for other sectors or for the economy in general.[27]

What are the conditions, then, under which the state will be impelled into such assistance activities? This is most likely to occur in connection with services that the staple growers need, but find it difficult or impossible to supply individually or even cooperatively. These conditions point to the domain of public goods that must be supplied by the state if they are to be supplied at all.

There are many well-known public or semipublic goods of this sort, from power, transportation, and irrigation to education and public health. Often designated as "infrastructure," as though they were preconditions for the more directly productive activities, these goods have more usually been provided in response to urgent demands emanating from such activities and from

---

[27] See Judith Tendler, "Technology and Economic Development: The Case of Hydro vs. Thermal Power," *Political Science Quarterly* 80 (June 1965): 236–53.

their need for consolidation, greater profitability, and further expansion.[28]

For staples, the more important of such public goods are transportation and irrigation, as well as disease and pest control. The latter is particularly typical of the linkage phenomenon here described: a characteristic of the staple – that is, its susceptibility to disease and infestation – combined with the fact that success in eradication or control requires remedial action over a large area, means that whenever many producers are involved such action can be undertaken only by an authority with coercive powers. This was precisely the situation that led to an expansion of the role of government in Egypt during the late nineteenth century when cotton, the country's principal staple, was threatened by cotton-worm infestation. According to a recent study, this expansion in the role of government took place even though it went "much against the inclination of many of the British administrators, particularly Lord Cromer. . . ."[29] Naturally, when the expansion of the role of the state takes place under colonial conditions with the colonizers having a set image of their responsibility and its limits, the cumulative effects otherwise to be expected from such a new involvement of the state in the economy will be severely stunted.

In the case of irrigation, the hypothesis that the state may become more development oriented and public serving as a result of practice in providing certain useful public services for staple producers runs up against the well-known Wittfogel thesis which sees state-organized irrigation works as a determinant of "Oriental despotism" in its various forms.[30] This conflict of hypotheses makes it possible to appreciate that the Wittfogel thesis has plausibility only under very special circumstances: that is, when irrigation is essential to the growing of basic food crops, so that state and society come into being jointly as a result of the state's assuming the life-giving function of building, managing, and maintaining the irrigation works. On the other hand, in the numerous situations in which the state has long been in existence as an administrative-bureaucratic entity and then

---

[28] A particularly striking demonstration that railroads in the United States were built piecemeal in this fashion and not "ahead of demand" is in Fishlow (n. 8 above).

[29] E. R. J. Owen, *Cotton and the Egyptian Economy, 1820–1914* (London: Oxford University Press, 1969), p. 215.

[30] Karl Wittfogel, *Oriental Despotism* (New Haven, Conn.: Yale University Press, 1957).

comes to undertake an irrigation activity with the comparatively modest aim of improving the incomes of the staple growers, this new activity on the part of the state may well mean that an otherwise largely parasitic bureaucracy will acquire a development-minded component. While this component may come to exhibit some technocratic traits, it is unlikely to have either the propensity or the power to develop an autocratic style.[31]

A particularly interesting linkage, leading from the staple and its characteristics to state action designed to provide a service which producers are incapable of supplying themselves, is that of price stabilization. Through exchange-rate policy or the institution of marketing boards, the state can, within limits, divorce the international price of a staple from its domestic price; it even can manipulate the staple's international price if the country produces a sufficiently large share of total supplies so as to hold some monopoly power in world markets. In the case of staples grown by many producers, a special need and clamor for this type of state intervention will arise whenever the staple is subject to violent price declines. These conditions point to tropical tree crops such as coffee and cocoa. Because of the 5-year delay between planting and first full crop, supply is particularly likely to be out of phase with demand in cobweb-like fashion. Also, the trees, once in place, keep yielding a crop even if no fertilizing, pruning, or weeding is practiced, so that supply response to lower prices is small in the short run. Finally, the fact that the number of producers is usually quite large makes it unlikely that they will engage in organized remedial action except to join in an interest group that will insistently invoke help from the state.

These characteristics and the resulting special vulnerability of coffee and cocoa prices to world-market disturbances have long been thought of as a liability. They are now seen to have some compensating advantages because of the state action they predictably trigger. The help proffered by the state through the various arrangements just mentioned is in a sense the exact obverse of the extraction of revenue from the staple that has been called fiscal linkage. (Indeed, the staples most likely to elicit fiscal linkage – minerals and petroleum enclaves – are least likely to be the recipients of stabilization assistance as they usually respond to price

[31] See Albert O. Hirschman, *Development Projects Observed* (Washington, D.C.: Brookings Institution, 1967), pp. 166–8.

declines through swift cuts in ouput.) Yet, ironically and dialecti-
cally, once the state has provided stabilization assistance it has
also established the institutional framework and perhaps acquired the frame of mind which will enable it to extract fiscal
revenue from the staple at some future time when prices will have
recovered. And at that point the staple will be just as defenseless
against state taxation, because of its low price elasticity of supply,
as it was earlier against drops in world market prices.

Price stabilization assistance is therefore a particularly interesting variety of state intervention from the point of view of how
one thing leads to another. Whereas assistance categories such
as disease control and irrigation may give the state a new taste
for developmental activities, price stabilization supplies both the
taste and, at some future time, the institutional mechanism to
indulge it.

III. Further observations, mostly methodological

A. On the nature of the generalized linkage approach

Not long ago a new theory of consumption attempted to look
behind the individual consumable commodities which had long
stood in the center of traditional theory. The new theory considered each commodity as a bundle of qualities (say, sweetness,
juiciness, peelability, and appearance in the case of oranges) and
each consumer as demanding various combinations of such
qualities.[32] A number of interesting new results were obtained
by this approach. Similarly, metallurgists have long given up
thinking of metals as discrete, nature-given materials. They have
identified each metal as a bundle of properties (such as hard-
ness, porosity, conductivity, etc.) and have systematically fash-
ioned alloys and substitutes for the purpose of supplying combinations of such properties that happened to be in demand for
various industrial purposes.[33]

The focus on linkages to delineate the development prospects
of different staple exporters has something in common with

---

[32] Kelvin Lancaster, *Consumer Demand: A New Approach* (New York: Columbia University
Press, 1971).

[33] Anthony Scott, "The Development of the Extractive Industries," *Canadian Journal of
Economics and Political Science* 28 (February 1962): 81.

these approaches. It is an attempt to look behind such staples as sugarcane, coffee, rice, or tobacco and to identify some general characteristics of these products that influence and condition the kind of development experienced by the countries specializing in them. Such an attempt at finding meaningful classification criteria is not new. Economic geographers and others have sometimes grouped staples into various natural or botanical categories for the purpose of showing that differences in economic and sociopolitical destinies can be made intelligible in this way.

This sort of scheme – mineral products, tropical agricultural products, temperate agricultural products – has been adopted in an influential essay by Fernando Henrique Cardoso and Enzo Faletto on the economic and political development of Latin America.[34] The integration of economic with sociological and political analysis and the demonstration that characteristic differences could be established between the development or underdevelopment experiences of different groups of Latin American countries made this into a pathbreaking work. Nevertheless, in searching for general properties of staples that are likely to impart distinctive characteristics to the development process, the appropriate method is not to borrow these properties from some alien field, such as botany or climatology, but to look for properties that arise out of the development process itself and then to conduct the analysis in terms of these properties. For appraising a country's development prospects, the knowledge that its export staple is endowed with a certain constellation of linkages is obviously more revealing than the information that the staple is a tropical agricultural product.

The system laid out here makes it possible to translate technical information into a language that points directly toward development possibilities. For example, both the availability of tubewells and the addition of a highway to a rail link tend to make for substitution of inside for outside linkage as farmers install

---

[34] Fernando Henrique Cardoso and Enzo Faletto, *Dependencia y desarrollo en América Latina* (Mexico City: Siglo XXI, 1969), available in English as *Dependency and Development in Latin America* (Berkeley: University of California Press, 1979). A further important development of this typology is in Osvaldo Sunkel and Pedro Paz, *El subdesarrollo latinoamericano y la teoría del desarrollo* (Mexico City: Siglo XXI, 1970), pp. 317–43. For a good survey of the related literature, see Norman Girvan, "The Development of Dependency Economics in the Caribbean and Latin America: Review and Comparison," *Social and Economic Studies* 22 (March 1973): 1–33.

their own tubewells and ship their produce to market in their own trucks instead of having to rely on state-managed irrigation and railroad systems.[35] A number of possible consequences can immediately be visualized as a by-product of these substitutions: they could enhance private entrepreneurship, concentrate income, and complicate the extraction of fiscal revenue. So far so good; but there remains much room for enriching this language and for substantially modifying the hypotheses thus far generated in the process. A good example of a modification that has already taken place is found earlier in the present essay: in the case of staples, forward linkages that imply considerable industrial processing were shown to act as developmental handicaps rather than as propellants because they tend to be technologically alien and therefore lock the producers of the staple into their agricultural activity.

A major general caveat follows: the various characteristics of staples and ensuing linkages, however neatly arranged in an apparently comprehensive system, have been extracted from the observation of actual experience. They therefore constitute no more than a useful arrangement of our present knowledge of development mechanisms. The way in which linkages have proliferated since the concept was first proposed makes it likely that this process of knowledge gathering is by no means at an end. It is therefore most important to consider the preceding schemes as open-ended and to use them primarily for heuristic purposes while remaining receptive to new information.

B. Relation to the staple and development-of-underdevelopment theses

The approach set out here has several points of contact with other attempts to account for the development experience of the countries of the periphery in the period of export-led growth.

The close relation of the linkage approach to the staple thesis will be evident by now. The former is essentially an attempt to supply the somewhat scattered insights of the latter with a conceptual framework that makes a more systematic exploration possible, with the just-noted proviso that the framework here proposed is not to be taken as an exhaustive explanatory scheme.

[35] For this and other development-related contrasts between road and railroad (in Nigeria), see my *Development Projects Observed*, pp. 139–48.

The question remains of how the approach set out here relates to another interpretation that has been put forward in recent years and that is perhaps best referred to as the "development-of-underdevelopment" thesis. At first sight, it seems difficult to conceive of a greater contrast than that between the linkage approach and the neo-Marxist writings of, say, André Gunder Frank who is responsible for the above phrase.[36] For "development of underdevelopment" means essentially that one thing did *not* lead to another in the countries of the periphery; that, in fact, things there have constantly been going from bad to worse. The impact of capitalism and imperialism on the periphery has been to extract surplus and, in the process, to impoverish the people, destroy local industry, deplete the soil and subsoil, and emasculate and corrupt the local elites. To the extent that a certain amount of capitalist development in the form of industrialization cannot be denied, it is attributed exclusively to lack of contact with the imperialist center on the part of certain privileged regions and during certain exceptional periods.[37]

From the point of view of the linkage approach, some of the assertions of this kind of writing are not particularly shocking. It is implicit in what has been said that contact with the capitalist center through exports of staples may well result for the countries of the periphery in an impoverished population with exhausted natural resources. This would be the case as long as the particular staple is not activating fiscal linkage, is endowed only with technologically alien forward linkage, and leads to the competition of imported consumer goods driving local industry and handicraft out of existence, rather than to consumption linkages. Even when fiscal linkage is present, but the state is unable to invest productively the revenue it extracts, the ensuing situation may not be better than if the revenue generated by the staple were largely accruing to absentee owners. Many of the proposi-

---

[36] André Gunder Frank, "The Development of Underdevelopment," *Monthly Review* 18 (September 1966): 17–31, and *Capitalism and Underdevelopment in Latin America* (New York: Monthly Review Press, 1967); see also Samir Amin, *L'Accumulation à l'échelle mondiale* (Paris: Anthropos, 1971).

[37] For critiques of these views from within the left and/or the periphery, see Fernando Henrique Cardoso, *As contradições do desenvolvimento associado*, Estudos CEBRAP (São Paulo: CEBRAP, April–June 1974); also published as chapter 1 of his *Autoritarismo e democratização* (Rio de Janeiro: Paz e Terra, 1975); and Bill Warren, "Imperialism and Capitalist Industrialization," *New Left Review*, no. 81 (September/October 1973), pp. 3–45.

tions of this essay point to the possibility of particularly unfortunate combinations of circumstances: while fiscal linkage is predicated on the absence of forward and backward linkages, it is perfectly conceivable that during a prolonged period neither physical nor fiscal linkages will put in an appearance. In this manner the present approach, while admittedly originating in the attempt to understand how development can happen, is equally able to account for lack of development or for periods of "development of underdevelopment." It has no blind spot with respect to the possibility of immiserization and is in this respect quite unlike the classical theory of international trade which can at worst conceive of a zero gain from trade for any country participating in world commerce.

At the same time, of course, the present approach is fully alive to the possibilties of development, particularly to those that may be wholly unintended on the part of exploitative operators and authorities who are responsible for the development of underdevelopment. Most of the linkages that were reviewed here – consumption linkages, the extraction of revenue from the staple, or the provision of pest control and price stabilization by the state – are in the nature of events that are originally unintended on the part of those who got staple production under way. The present approach makes it possible to understand such potentially positive events as already contained in a preceding exploitative phase. Therefore, it has a claim to being more truly dialectical than the development-of-underdevelopment thesis, which misses altogether the intimate connection between the various phases of what ought to be understood as a dynamic process.[38]

One of the great merits of the development-of-underdevelopment thesis has been the devastating and definitive critique of the concept of "traditional society," an unhistorical construct endemic in much of the previous development literature, that supposedly prevailed wherever dynamic development had not

---

[38] There is no intention here to suggest that the development story always has a happy end, that after a period of exploitation development's turn may surely be expected to come. For one thing, the opposite sequence, from a spurt of development to a period of stagnation and exploitation, can frequently be encountered, as I have attempted to show in discussing the positive and negative effects of foreign investment (see "How to Divest in Latin America, and Why," in *Bias for Hope*, Chapter 11). The need is for an analysis that can account for turnarounds of either kind. See also Chapter 2, this volume.

yet taken hold.[39] It is too bad that some of the critics have substituted for this construct the equally unhistorical notion of a uniform downward slide which all countries outside the capitalist-imperialist center are supposed to have experienced or to be experiencing until such time as they throw off the imperialist or neo-imperialist yoke.

C. From linkages to micro-Marxism

Having taken my distance from contemporary neo-Marxist theorizing about the periphery, I shall now claim for my own approach a degree of intellectual kinship with the Marxian system. To this end something must first be said about the nature of the properties or characteristics of staples that have been singled out as giving rise to linkages.

Some of the linkages, such as the backward and forward ones, are directly tied to the technical conditions of production of the staple. Technological change will of course affect the number and kinds of such linkages, but they are invariant to social and political change. If attention is focused instead on, say, the fiscal linkages, the importance of the political context is immediately manifest. For fiscal linkage actually to happen the state must have evolved the will and ability to stake a claim, for purposes of reinvestment elsewhere in the economy, on the resources that are being exploited in its territory. Fiscal linkage does not therefore inhere in petroleum like a certain percentage of sulphur; it becomes associated with that product in certain historical circumstances. Nevertheless, the point is that fiscal linkage does not happen just because the state becomes modern, autonomous, development oriented, or anti-imperialist. For a number of rea-

---

[39] The argument that the backwardness and poverty of the periphery is not a "state of nature," but is closely related to the development and enrichment of the center, is of course much older than the development-of-underdevelopment thesis of A. G. Frank, and is in fact implicit in Marx's theory of primitive accumulation. Even without plunder or exploitation, close economic contact between advanced and less advanced regions or countries can make for cumulatively divergent paths of development and impoverishment because of "backward" or "polarization" effects, as was shown in Gunnar Myrdal, *Economic Theory and Under-developed Regions* (London: Duckworth, 1957) and in my *Strategy*, Chapter 10. An early criticism of the concepts of "traditional society" and "modernization" is in Fernando Henrique Cardoso, *Empresário industrial e desenvolvimento econômico* (São Paulo: Difusão Européia do Livro, 1964), pp. 65–72. See also Chapter 1, Section IV, this volume.

sons tied to its mode of production – lack of physical linkages plus the likelihood of foreign ownership at a certain historical period – the presence of petroleum predisposes the state to develop the propensity to tax far more than if its staple consisted of some agricultural product grown by many local farmers on their own land in the central region of the country. In this manner it is after all possible to trace influences that go from the product and its technology – that is, from the "productive forces" – to a specific shape of economic development and to certain sociopolitical happenings, like nationalism and taxation, which define that shape.

There is obviously something here that has a considerable affinity with Marxism and historical materialism, but the difference is also striking. Marxist thought has traditionally focused on a very few constellations of productive forces – such as the feudal or capitalist modes of production – that are dominant over wide geographical areas and persist over long periods of time; social and political configurations are seen as deriving from these macromodes. The linkage approach also takes characteristic features of technology and production processes as points of departure for understanding social events, but it does so on a much smaller scale, in much more minute detail, and for a much more limited time frame. Hence, "micro-Marxism" might be a good term for this attempt to show how the shape of economic development, including its social and political components, can be traced to the specific economic activities a country takes up.

Marx and the more perceptive Marxists moved themselves in the micro direction when they were dealing with specific events and country experiences. Marx in particular oscillated between the grand generalization with which to characterize an entire epoch or process and the discriminating analysis of events which made differences between countries and subperiods stand out in richly textured detail. An example that is relevant for present purposes is in the preface of *Capital*, where at first we meet with the frequently cited phrase, "the industrially most developed country does nothing but hold up to those who follow it on the industrial ladder the image of their own future." Here Marx seems to suggest that capitalist industrial development is bound to exhibit uniform features and stages in all countries no matter how late they will step on the "ladder." But one only needs to read on in order to realize that Marx had a very acute sense of small and critical differences. For in the very next paragraph (which is apparently never read by those who quote the above sentence), Marx predicts a very different path for Germany and continental Europe in relation to England because of the absence of factory laws and in general because of a variety of social and political residues from feudalism that did not exist in England. In this manner Marx presents elements for a comparative analysis that considerably qualifies and in effect contradicts the generalization with which he starts out.[40]

It is remarkable – and characteristically un-Marxist – that Marx differentiated between England and Germany on the basis of certain elements in Germany's juridical institutions and historical heritage. In projecting likely differences in historical outcome he thus appeals to differences in the "superstructure" while apparently perceiving the infrastructure – industrial development under capitalism – as being identical for England and Germany. In this respect later students of comparative capitalist development were to be more Marxist than Marx. In explaining differences between the development pattern of England and that of latecomers such as Germany and Russia, Gerschenkron, for example, did not invoke residues from the previous historical experiences of the latter two countries; rather, he concentrated on the different rates of development of agriculture and industry during the period of industrial expansion and on the different roles of consumer goods and capital goods production.[41] In looking at countries of even more recent industrialization, I have similarly attempted to show that the "tightly staged" pattern of import-substituting industrialization, the importance of foreigners in the process, and the long-continued absence of any industrial production for export could explain much about some outstanding features of political development in these countries, such as the weakness of the national bourgeoisie.[42]

It is characteristic of this micro-Marxist approach to derive important differences in sociopolitical development from comparatively small and initially difficult-to-perceive differences in the structure of the "productive forces" within what had generally

---

[40] See also Chapter 1, Section I.

[41] Alexander Gerschenkron, *Economic Backwardness in Historical Perspective* (Cambridge, Mass.: Harvard University Press, 1962).

[42] "The Political Economy of Import-substituting Industrialization in Latin America," in *Bias for Hope*.

been considered a uniform historical phase or a homogeneous mode of production. Much more can be done along these lines for the period of industrialization.[43] But micro-Marxism comes particularly into its own when one deals with the development of the countries of the periphery during the so-called period of export-led growth which for most of these countries occupies the second half of the nineteenth century and the first 2 or 3 decades of the twentieth, but goes on even today in some cases. The countries of the periphery were cast by the capitalist center in the role of providers of agricultural and mineral raw products, and most of them specialized along one or a very few individual product lines. With substantial differences existing between the characteristics and linkages of different staples, the productive forces prevailing in these countries were probably more hetero- geneous during the stage of export-led growth than at any other preceding or subsequent historical period. Little wonder, then, that the micro-Marxist approach is particularly suitable and re- vealing for that stage.

D. A final puzzle

There exists a literature that has much in common with the gener- alized linkage or micro-Marxist approach as presented here. In addition to the writings of Harold Innis and other contributors to the staple thesis, this literature consists of a fairly scattered and often impressionistic group of writings that focuses on one or, more often, two products, generally of a single country, in order to derive a great deal of the country's fortunes, misfortunes, and general history from these products and their properties. The archetypical representative of this genre is Ortiz's *Cuban Counter- point,* [44] where the contrast between the beneficent tobacco and the pernicious sugarcane is lyrically portrayed from every con-

---

[43] See, for example, Cardoso, "As contradições"; O'Donnell, "Reflexiones"; and James R. Kurth, "The Political Consequences of the Product Cycle: Industrial History and Politi- cal Outcomes," *International Organization* 33 (Winter 1979): 1–34.

[44] Fernando Ortiz Fernández, *Contrapunteo cubano del tabaco y el azúcar* (Havana: Jesus Montero, 1940); the English version, with a foreword by B. Malinowski, is entitled *Cuban Counterpoint: Tobacco and Sugar* (New York: Knopf, 1947). The Spanish work was reedited by the Consejo Nacional de Cultura in 1963. A related treatment, primarily centered on sugar, is in Ramiro Guerra y Sánchez, *Sugar and Society in the Caribbean,* foreword by Sidney W. Mintz (New Haven, Conn.: Yale University Press, 1964). The original Spanish edition of this influential work was published in 1927.

ceivable angle. Such comparisons of the contrasting performances of two staples have proven to be intellectually attractive; similar, if less baroque, portrayals have been attempted for sugarcane versus coffee in Brazil, tobacco versus coffee in Colombia, and sugarcane versus tree crops in Indonesia.[45]

As will be obvious, I have taken a great deal from this literature and its insights. It has, nevertheless, one fairly pervasive characteristic that arouses intellectual suspicion: in almost all of these pairwise comparisons one staple is assigned the role of all-around villain, while the other is the all-around hero (the exception is Geertz's treatment of cane versus tree crops in Indonesia, where the former is the villain all right, but there is no true hero). In Cuba sugarcane is the villain and tobacco the hero, in Colombia tobacco is the bad guy while coffee is the good guy, and in Brazil sugarcane is once again the villain while coffee is the good guy (note that as a result of these three pairwise comparisons, the ordering of the three staples is actually transitive!). In all of these comparisons the staples are looked at from a wide variety of angles, and one of the two staples scores consistently over the other. The same kind of convergence of pluses in one direction and minuses in the other is observed when economic activities other than staples are looked at from the point of view of their indirect, other-than-output contribution to economic development. Judith Tendler's studies of thermal energy versus hydropower and of generation versus distribution of power in Brazil and Argentina accumulated an impressive number of arguments demonstrating the all-around superiority of hydropower over thermal power and of generation over distribution. Similarly, my own observations on the comparative suitability of road and railroad to postindependence Nigeria resulted in singling out highways and trucking as being consistently superior to railroads, on a large number of diverse counts.[46]

[45] Celso Furtado, *The Economic Growth of Brazil* (Berkeley: University of California Press, 1963), pp. 123–26; Luis Eduardo Nieto Arteta, *Economia y cultura en la historia de Colombia* (Bogotá: Ediciones Tercer Mundo, 1962; first edition in 1942), and particularly his *El café en la sociedad colombiana* (Bogotá: Breviarios de orientación colombiana, 1958); William Paul McGreevey, *An Economic History of Colombia, 1845–1930* (Cambridge: Cambridge University Press, 1971), Chapter 9; Geertz, *Agricultural Involution*.

[46] Tendler, *Electric Power in Brazil* and "Technology and Economic Development: The Case of Hydro vs. Thermal Power", and my *Development Projects Observed*, pp. 139–48.

It is of course possible that this strange convergence is due to some selective perception of reality, with the latter being caused in turn by the underlying questions that are being asked. To give an example: the nineteenth-century coffee boom in Brazil led without any doubt to the rise of São Paulo and eventually to the preeminence of that city as an industrial center, while the growing of sugarcane in the country's northeast ever since the sixteenth century left little behind but the most populous depressed area of Latin America. This contrast impels one to find numerous reasons for pinning praise on coffee and blame on sugarcane.

Nevertheless, we must allow for the possibility that the convergence phenomenon is not just something that is forced by our minds upon a recalcitrant reality for the reason just given: it is illegitimate to discard the hypothesis that the phenomenon may truly "exist in nature" just because we can think of good psychological reasons for which we may want to believe in its existence.

That the convergence phenomenon *may* exist is obvious. The properties which have been found relevant to the analysis of development effects – say, absence or presence of elaborate, technologically alien forward linkage, high or low price per unit of weight, gradually or steeply declining marginal productivity of labor, rapid or slow supply response to price changes – all of these could be so combined in a staple as to make for a cumulation of either pluses or minuses. For example, the botanical-economic nature of many tropical tree crops is such that they score along each of the above dimensions. From many points of view coffee cultivation has resulted in the stimulation of development in a number of countries: it has encouraged the individual cultivators to migrate or to undertake entrepreneurial tasks outside of coffee cultivation, it has led to the formation of strong pressure groups of cultivators and to the consequent intervention of the state to stabilize prices, because of the slow supply response to price it has eventually been possible to tax the coffee farmer during a prolonged period in favor of industry, and so on.

There is, then, nothing intrinsically inconceivable in one particular commodity acting as a multidimensional conspiracy in favor of or against development within a certain historical and sociopolitical setting. But how likely is it that such conspiracies have really existed? For an answer to this question, a brief excursion into a different historical period and event, the emergence of massive slavery in the New World, is revealing. It seems evident that a number of characteristics of sugarcane cultivation – the heavy, largely unskilled work in tropical climates, the availability of free land close to the plantations, the need to keep the labor force together during the slack season, and the possibility of using that force, including women and children, in minor tasks – conspired with the "sugar hunger" in post-Renaissance Europe to create a special affinity between sugarcane and slavery.[47] Obviously it was not sugarcane that created slavery, but it is fairly safe to suggest that slavery would not have become as extended as it did after the sixteenth century without that particular staple and its peculiar bundle of characteristics. A confirmation of the hypothesis is supplied in a way by the absence of slavery from New England, which was surely due in large part to lack of opportunity to engage in slavery, that is, to the poor soils and harsh climate of that region which made it unfit for the introduction of any slave-grown staple and relegated it to small-scale, owner-operated subsistence agriculture.

Generalizing from this historical example, it is possible to conjecture that the emergence of a new mode of production is more intimately tied to the availability, at the proper time, of a specific economic activity with a strong affinity for that mode than is realized later on when the mode has become ubiquitous and dominant and therefore appears to be and has in fact become independent from the activity. This sort of relationship, where a specific economic activity is, to paraphrase Marx, the midwife of a new mode of production, can probably be shown to have prevailed also between the textile industry and the Industrial Revolution. If our conjecture is correct, then the appearance of a new mode of production is prima facie evidence that an activity with that special, intellectually suspect multiple affinity for the

[47] H. J. Nieboer, *Slavery as an Industrial System* (The Hague: Martinus Nijhoff, 1900), pp. 420–2; Sidney W. Mintz, "Foreword," in Guerra; *Cambridge Economic History of Europe* (Cambridge: Cambridge University Press, 1967), 4: 290–1, 311–14; Evsey D. Domar, "The Causes of Slavery or Serfdom: A Hypothesis," *Journal of Economic History* 30 (March 1930): 18–32; Keith Aufhauser, "Slavery and Technological Change," *Journal of Economic History* 34 (March 1974): 36–50, and passages from Ortiz and Tocqueville there cited.

mode must have been around—the new mode could not have made it otherwise.

Having made the case for the possible existence of the convergence phenomenon, I must qualify it in two quite different ways. In the first place, it is easy to claim too much for the connection between the characteristics of a specific staple and the sociopolitical environment. Depending as it does on the exact technical conditions of production, that connection is closely bound up with a particular time and place. It has already been noted that relatively small changes in technique—for example, the substitution of tubewell irrigation for a centrally managed system—may substantially change existing social roles and relations. One of the merits of the generalized linkage or micro-Marxist approach is that it invites the analyst to be constantly on the lookout for technological "news" that may have considerable economic and sociopolitical repercussions. In short, coffee production today in Colombia may have an entirely different social and developmental meaning from coffee production tomorrow in Uganda.

On the other hand, there is not necessarily a one-to-one correspondence between a staple and "its" sociopolitical environment. Strangely enough, a staple that has played an important reinforcing role in relation to a given social and political environment could come to perform this role once again in a very much changed environment. A striking example of such a repeat performance under drastically changed circumstances has been supplied in recent years by sugarcane cultivation in Cuba: some of the same characteristics that once created the affinity between cane and slavery—the large incidence of unskilled labor and the seasonal nature of the demand for labor—now made out of sugarcane the ideal economic activity for the periodic demonstration of community spirit and of the dignity of physical labor as young men and women leave their city pursuits during the cutting season to help out in the fields for short periods. Just as sugarcane magnified the extent of slavery, so it was now enhancing socialism in Cuba as it enabled that country to engage in experiments and pursue directions that are not nearly as readily available to other socialist countries.

"The flax looks just as before. Not one of its fibers is changed, but a new social soul has slipped into its body." This phrase from *Capital* seems nicely to the point, but the somewhat puzzling aspect of the matter is brought out, in a very different context, by Pascal: "Just as all things tell of God to those who know Him and just as they reveal Him to those who love Him, so these same things hide Him from those who do not know Him."[48] In other words, the same factual evidence may fit and even foster opposite interpretations of the world. Analogously, the same staple, its characteristics, and mode of production, may unexpectedly lend strength to two totally different social arrangements and political regimes. At this point, then, my micro-Marxism takes a rather un-Marxist turn. For in Marxist terminology I have just been saying that an identical set of productive forces could not only be compatible, but could entertain a collusive, mutually reinforcing relationship with more than one set of relations of production.

Actually this finding is all to the good, for I am very far from wishing to lay down a new kind of reductionism or determinism. My point has been, not that a staple will determine the sociopolitical environment in any unique and exhaustive way, but that each time it will imprint certain patterns of its own on whatever environment happens to be around and that it is possible and worthwhile to study the imprinting process. A related point is that there are different degrees of affinity or compatibility between specific economic activities, on the one hand, and varieties of sociopolitical environments on the other. At one end of the scale, we have discussed activities that stand in the just-noted collusive and mutually reinforcing relationship with such an environment. And while it is possible for the same activity to entertain such a relationship with more than one sociopolitical environment, there exist at the other end of the scale economic activities that have a very low degree of compatibility with certain sociopolitical frameworks; for example, certain fruits and vegetables that require tender loving care appear to be poorly suited to collectivist agriculture.

But the argument in defense of the convergence phenomenon has carried me too far. To explore these matters systematically would require a much longer work. The present essay has had

---

[48] Karl Marx, *Das Kapital* (Vienna: Verlag für Literatur und Politik, 1932), 1:785; Blaise Pascal, letter to his sister dated April 1, 1648, in *Oeuvres complètes* (Paris: NRF-Pléiade, 1969), p. 484.

as its principal aim to explore lines of compatibility of staples, not with sociopolitical regimes, but with economic development at a given historical period and within the social and political patterns characteristic of that period. And even this topic has barely been opened up for discussion here, as I warned in the opening section.

5

The turn to authoritarianism in Latin America and the search for its economic determinants

Introduction: eighteenth-century hopes and twentieth-century realities

"Economic development of underdeveloped areas" emerged as a new field of studies in the late 1940s and early 1950s. The task was truly formidable, but the promise of tackling it with success was held out by two concurrent developments. Theoretical advances in the economics of growth, together with a number of new insights into the specific nature of underdeveloped economies, provided economists, so it was thought, with the tools they needed to give effective advice to governments wishing to steer their countries onto a path of rapid economic expansion. Secondly, the success of the Marshall Plan in Western Europe seemed to confirm the possibility of rapid economic transformation of nonsocialist economies provided two conditions were present: (1) appropriate amounts of foreign aid would supplement domestic capital formation and (2) beneficent, "indicative" planning would supplement market signals in making sure that available capital resources would be productively invested.

Some twenty-five years later, that early optimism has largely evaporated, for a number of reasons. Growth, while substantial, has by no means overcome the division of the world into the rich "north" and the underdeveloped "south." In the south itself, moreover, the fruits of growth have been divided more unevenly than had been anticipated. And there is another, often unacknowledged, reason for the disenchantment: it looks in-

Originally published in David Collier, ed., *The New Authoritarianism in Latin America* (© 1979 by Princeton University Press), pp. 61–98. Sponsored by the Joint Committee on Latin American Studies of the Social Science Research Council and the American Council of Learned Societies. Reprinted by permission of Princeton University Press.

creasingly as though the effort to achieve growth, whether or not successful, brings with it calamitous side effects in the political realm, from the loss of democratic liberties at the hand of authoritarian, repressive regimes to the wholesale violation of elementary human rights. Many economists, cozily ensconced in their ever-expanding discipline, were unconcerned about the possibility of such connections between economic and political events.[1] Others gave vent to their dismay over political developments by looking for weak points in the economic performance of the disliked regimes, such as alleged "structural stagnation" or regressive income distribution.[2] Only a few were so troubled by the course of events that they were anxious to probe whether it was the quest for economic development that had wrought political disaster, but they found that they lacked the conceptual tools needed to investigate the problem.

My own reaction was to withdraw into history, and more specifically into the history of ideas. Since little light had been shed on the connections between economic growth and political disaster by my contemporaries, I decided to dwell for a while among the political philosophers and political economists of the seventeenth and eighteenth centuries, to find out what they had to say about the likely political consequences of the economic expansion then taking place under their eyes. This retreat into the past resulted in my book *The Passions and the Interests: Political Arguments for Capitalism before Its Triumph* (Princeton, 1977). The most surprising, almost bizarre, idea I came across – and whose intricate genealogy is traced in the book – was the speculation that the expansion of commerce, of industry, and of the market economy would serve to restrain, for various reasons and through various mechanisms, the "passions" of the sovereign and would therefore result in less arbitrary and more humane government. Economic growth would bring constraints that would put an end to abuses of power, to unjust exactions – in short, to "despotism." Put positively, a thriving market economy would be the basis for a political order in which the exercise of individual rights and freedoms would be insured. Or, as Tocqueville was to express it

---

[1] An exception must be made for John Sheahan's thoughtful paper "Market-Oriented Economic Policies and Political Repression in Latin America," *Economic Development and Cultural Change* 28 (January 1980): 267–91.

[2] For an extension of this point, see Chapter 1, Section V.

epigrammatically: "A close tie and a necessary relation exist between these two things: freedom and industry."[3] Yesterday's hopeful doctrine and today's dismal reality could not be farther apart and Tocqueville's sentence would seem to be more applicable to the current Latin American experience if it read instead: "A close tie and a necessary relation exist between these two things: torture and industry." This contrast between the two statements, or between expectation and reality, can usefully serve as a starting point for our discussion.

First of all, it should be noted that the contrast is not so much between European hopes and Latin American disappointments. Not only were there plenty of disappointments in Europe, but hopes similar to those expressed by European thinkers from the seventeenth to the early nineteenth century can be found in late nineteenth- and early twentieth-century Latin America. The idea that an expanding and industrialized economy would discipline the excesses of power-seeking and of passionate politics in general appears in a classic work on Colombian economic history which comments in the following terms on the period of political consolidation and economic expansion subsequent to the termination of the Thousand-Day Civil War in 1902:

> The ultimate foundation of this policy [of industrial protection] was not really or mainly economic. The stimulus (*fomento*) given to industrial firms was an element, and a very important one, in the change of direction which Reyes and the group around him wanted to impart to the political and social life of the country. What mattered was to find a way of reducing the intensity of political infighting which had become unbearable, of making sure that politics would not absorb all of the nation's energies and attention. . . . The formula of the Radicals was being inverted: no longer was liberty to bring us progress; to the contrary, progress was expected and was supposed to bring us liberty.[4]

The idea that an expanding economy and its insertion into the world market would serve as a check against political passions is strongly affirmed, by another Colombian writer, not only for a

---

[3] Through this synthetic formulation, Tocqueville actually paid only lip service to the prevailing doctrine, which he then proceeded to criticize. See *Passions and Interests*, pp. 122–4.

[4] Luis Ospina Vásquez, *Industria y protección en Colombia, 1810–1930* (Medellin: E.S.F., 1955), pp. 326–27. The author goes on to say that industrial development, with its favorable political consequences of "order and liberty," was also expected to make the country less vulnerable to attacks against its territorial and political sovereignty, obviously a matter of great concern to Colombia after the loss of Panama.

growing industrial establishment, but in reference to the increased production of an export staple such as coffee:

> [In the precoffee era, policymakers] are lyrical and romantic because they cannot yet defer to a product whose output is constantly on the increase. It is a time of childhood and play. Coffee will bring maturity and seriousness. It will not permit Colombians to continue playing fast and loose with the national economy. The ideological absolutism will disappear and the epoch of moderation and sobriety will dawn. . . . Coffee is incompatible with anarchy.[5]

It is particularly interesting that the participation of Colombia in the world economy through the coffee trade is viewed here quite positively, as a way of imposing a much-needed discipline on domestic politics and on policy making, rather than as a threat to the country's autonomy, and as a manifestation of its "dependencia."

History has of course largely disappointed the hopes expressed in these eloquent passages. In my book I have tried to explain some of the reasons why the identical optimistic expectations of such eighteenth-century figures as Montesquieu and Sir James Steuart have remained unfulfilled in the advanced industrial countries.[6] By drawing on some of the critics of their ideas, such as Adam Ferguson and Tocqueville, I showed that the very characteristics of the "modern economy" which were supposed to constitute a bulwark against "despotism" could, from an only slightly different perspective, *justify* something close to that abhorred form of government. For the principal point and insight of Montesquieu and Steuart, as of the just cited Colombian authors, was that a more complex economy is a delicate mechanism with exigencies of its own that must not be tampered with. In the mind of a Montesquieu (or of Nieto Arteta) this tampering could emanate only from the government or its head, the capricious sovereign. But the argument cuts several ways; to quote myself, "If it is true *that the economy must be deferred to*, then there is a case not only for constraining the imprudent actions of the prince but for repressing those of the people, for limiting participation, in short, for crushing anything that could be interpreted

---

[5] Luis Eduardo Nieto Arteta, *El café en la sociedad colombiana* (Bogotá: Breviarios de orientación colombiana, 1958), pp. 34–5. This posthumously published essay was written in 1947.

[6] *Passions and Interests*, pp. 117–28.

by some economist-king as a threat to the proper functioning of the 'delicate watch.' "[7]

The principal "economic" explanations of authoritarian rule in Latin America today run along these same lines. The economy and its growth, so it is said, have certain intrinsic exigencies, which are sometimes blatantly ignored by the rulers or ruled, or both. When this happens, regime change becomes likely, and lately such change has meant a move in the direction of a more authoritarian government.[8]

The emphasis of these explanations – which shall soon be examined at greater length – is on the structural characteristics of the economy and on the complex and imperative conditions for its continued growth. These are the to-be-deferred-to exigencies: the *deferenda*. The problem arises from the clash between these deferenda and those who are supposed to do the deferring, but sometimes refuse to abide by the disciplines of the "delicate watch." In this fashion, the differential *propensity to defer* of the policymakers could be an important element in the story we are trying to understand. Latin American policymakers have on occasion shown a particularly low propensity to defer. Sometimes they seem to revel in violating the most elementary constraints of the economic system. The best expression of this attitude is the well-known 1953 advice Perón gave to Carlos Ibáñez, then President of Chile:

> My dear friend:
> Give to the people, especially to the workers, all that is possible. When it seems to you that already you are giving them too much, give them more. You will see the results. Everyone will try to scare you with the specter of an economic collapse. But all of this is a lie. There is nothing more elastic than the economy which everyone fears so much because no one understands it.[9]

A similar refusal to believe in the existence of the "delicate watch" and a similar impatience with any of its constraints were evident in the more ill-considered – and ill-fated – economic and monetary policies of a number of Latin American countries in

---

[7] P. 124. The watch metaphor was repeatedly used by Sir James Steuart in his analysis of the expanding modern economy.

[8] Regime change in the opposite direction has been known to occur and has often been explained along similar lines; important examples are the overthrow of Perón in 1955 and of Rojas Pinilla in 1957.

[9] Quoted from Alejandro Magnet, *Nuestros vecinos argentinos* (Santiago de Chile: 1956), p. 14, by Fredrick B. Pike, "Freedom or Reform in Latin America," Occasional Paper, Graduate Center for South American Studies, Vanderbilt University, Nashville, Tennessee, August 1963, p. 3.

recent decades. So perhaps it is not, after all, that the economy poses at some point particularly difficult problems for the policymakers at certain moments. Rather, the policymakers may be given, every once in a while, to testing the "elasticity" of the economy with utter recklessness and simply to revolting against the constraints in which Sir James Steuart as well as Nieto Arteta had deposited their hope for an end to despotism and to *mal gobierno* (a term whose meaning ranges from poor administration to misrule).

Actually Sir James Steuart gives us a clue as to why such a revolt is almost to be anticipated. He notes the contradiction between the increasing power that is expected to accrue to the sovereign as the economy expands and the simultaneous increase in the constraints on the *use* of that power, with the constraints originating precisely in the increasing vulnerability of the economy, that is, in the nonexistence of that elasticity which Perón had affirmed. Sir James Steuart says that the statesman, faced with this disconcerting situation, "looks about with amazement," but concludes that in the end he will submit to the unexpected and irritating constraints because "he finds himself so bound up by the laws of his political economy, that every transgression of them involves him into new difficulties."[10] Obviously, Sir James Steuart did not foresee the modern Latin American sovereign or policymaker, who, meeting with the same contradiction, will refuse to be "bound up by the laws of his political economy" and will not be deterred by the prospect of "new difficulties."

To put the accent on the nature of the policymaker rather than on the nature of the problems he has to deal with seems a personalistic and therefore rather old-fashioned interpretation. But it can readily be given a more modern social scientific flavor. The policymakers' recurrent illusion about the "elasticity" or nonvulnerability of the economy could be related to a number of characteristics of "late late" industrialization in Latin America. In the first place, industrialization was expected, not just to increase income and employment, but to reduce dependence, to "transfer decision centers" from abroad and thus to lead to greater autonomy for the policymakers. Moreover, while *desarrollo hacia afuera* – development based on the export of primary products – had taken place under the aegis of laissez-faire, that phase, together with the

[10] For references and a more extended treatment, see *Passions and Interests*, pp. 81–7.

ideology that had presided over it, was now considered to have come to an ignominious end. The new phase of industrialization, in contrast, was supposed to require a great deal of guidance and intervention from an activist state. Thus the "statesman" – to use Sir James Steuart's term – was not only expecting to become more powerful; he also felt justified by the newly prevailing ideology in using his power to the hilt. Finally, the unexpected early successes of the "easy" phase of import-substituting industrialization may have led to an overestimate of the economy's "elasticity." This was the hypothesis I put forward in an earlier paper:

> . . . the "exuberant" phase of import substitution was accompanied by flamboyant public policies which badly overestimated the tolerance of the economy for a variety of ventures, be they income redistribution by fiat, the building of a new capital, or other extravaganzas . . . it may be conjectured that in their very different ways, Perón, Kubitschek, Rojas Pinilla, and Pérez Jiménez could all be considered victims of the delusions of economic invulnerability fostered by the surprising early successes and rapid penetration of industry into a supposedly hostile environment.[11]

The point of view here presented can be related to Guillermo O'Donnell's paper on the economic phenomena underlying the rise of authoritarianism in Latin America.[12] This paper, whose principal thesis is to be discussed in the next section, makes a great deal of the unpredictability of policy making in Latin America prior to the establishment of authoritarian regimes, and views it as an important obstacle to accumulation and long-term investment planning. O'Donnell connects the "higher" phase of industrialization in which intermediate inputs and capital goods are to be produced with a greater need for predictability. But it is obvious that some degree of predictability is needed for any sort of development in countries where a large portion of savings, investment, and production decisions are made by private economic agents. To the extent, then, that O'Donnell identifies the lack of minimal predictability of economic policy as an important factor in the retardation of development and in the establishment of authoritarian regimes, he invites us to seek out the reasons for this lack – something that, coming from a rather different perspective, I have attempted to do here.

[11] "The Political Economy of Import-Substituting Industrialization in Latin America," *Quarterly Journal of Economics* 82 (February 1968), reprinted in my *A Bias for Hope: Essays on Development and Latin America* (New Haven: Yale University Press, 1971), p. 100.

[12] Guillermo O'Donnell, "Reflexiones sobre las tendencias generales de cambio en el Estado Burocrático-autoritario," mimeographed (Buenos Aires: CEDES, August 1975). A

Perhaps I can claim by now that my recent absorption in seventeenth- and eighteenth-century thought was not entirely a matter of escaping from an unpleasant reality. That expedition into the ideological past has yielded at least one contribution to the understanding of Latin America's turn toward authoritarianism. It has led me to stress the low propensity of the policy-makers to defer to *normal* economic constraints. This is in contrast to the more common explanations, which have emphasized the *unusually* difficult economic tasks that were encountered. But I certainly do not wish to imply that the latter explanations are all wrong. In fact, a discussion along the lines of the traditional explanations will occupy the larger part of this essay. Toward its end, I shall return briefly to the argument just presented.

I. Economic arguments: specific exigencies of industrialization as determinants of authoritarianism

The "deepening" conjecture of O'Donnell

Over a century after Marx, the *general* proposition that important political change can best be explained by economic factors is neither particularly novel nor wholly convincing. Nevertheless, considerable intellectual excitement is still apt to be generated – quite legitimately so – when a *specific* turn of the political tide is shown or alleged to originate in a *precise* feature of the underlying economic terrain. Guillermo O'Donnell's just-mentioned paper is a good example. Its principal thesis is that the emergence of authoritarian regimes in the major Latin American countries since the 1960s is largely, if indirectly, due to the difficulties of "deepening" (*profundización*) that are apt to beset the industrialization process. "Deepening" is defined as the putting into place, through backward linkage, of the intermediate input and capital goods industries once the "last-stage" industries turning out consumption or final demand goods are established.[13] Written in 1974–75 and presented to a variety of audiences in the course of

---

somewhat different English version is in *Latin American Research Review* 13 (1978): 3–38.
[13] I shall use "deepening" throughout this paper as a translation of O'Donnell's "profundización." Economists should be put on notice that the meaning of "deepening" in O'Donnell's sense is distinct from that of "capital deepening," which refers to an expansion of production achieved in conjunction with an increase in the capital-labor ratio, in contrast to "capital widening," which achieves such an expansion without stepping up capital intensity.

1975, this thesis succeeded in dominating the discussion within a very short span of time. Naturally, the intellectual terrain was well prepared for the O'Donnell thesis by the notion of "exhaustion of import substitution," a phrase that had been more or less current in economic discussions for over ten years.[14] It took only one further step to relate the alleged difficulties of import-substituting industrialization (ISI) in Latin America to the rise, in several countries, of authoritarian regimes. The bare bones of the idea can indeed be found elsewhere, without much explanation and as though it needed none.[15] But O'Donnell's formulation, which he had foreshadowed in his earlier work,[16] was particularly rich, timely and persuasive.

Since I have been a participant in the debate on the industrialization process, I naturally have some feelings about the O'Donnell thesis.[17] These feelings are ambivalent. What is worse, I now realize that my own writings have been ambiguous.

On the one hand, the central purpose of my 1968 article was to question the notion of "exhaustion" of ISI. I therefore have an immediate critical reaction to a thesis which attributes a most momentous political outcome to an economic phenomenon about whose very existence I tried to raise some doubts.

Yet, while arguing that ISI was not necessarily bound to grind to a halt all over Latin America in the absence of profound structural change, I also pointed out: (*a*) that industrialization in Latin America was more of a sequential, "tightly staged" affair than it had been among the earlier industrializers; (*b*) that there are a number of resistances to the backward linkage dynamic, that is, to "deepening" (as well as several ways of overcoming them);

[14] That is, at least since the well-known article of Maria da Conceição Tavares on "Rise and Decline of Import Substitution in Brazil," *Economic Bulletin for Latin America*, 9 (March 1964): 1–65.

[15] A good example is Celso Lafer's analysis of the Brazilian political system, where the "exhaustion of the import-substitution model" is invoked several times to explain the crisis of the "populist republic" and the installation of a new political regime. See Lafer, *O sistema político brasileiro* (São Paulo: Perspectiva, 1975), pp. 69–76.

[16] Already in his *Modernización y autoritarismo* (Buenos Aires: Paidós, 1972), pp. 170ff., O'Donnell related the difficulties of achieving "vertical integration" and of establishing "basic industries" to the trend toward authoritarianism.

[17] O'Donnell generously refers to my work at the start of his own inquiry, "Reflexiones," p. 11. My article "The Political Economy of Import-Substituting Industrialization in Latin America," built on Chapters 6 and 7 of *The Strategy of Economic Development* (New Haven: Yale University Press, 1958; New York: Norton, 1978) and the concepts of backward and forward linkages there introduced. Further thoughts are in Chapter 4, this volume.

and (c) that there is such a thing as an "exuberant" or "particularly easy phase of import substitution when the manufacturing process is entirely based on imported materials and machinery while importation of the article is firmly and effectively shut out by controls."[18]

Jointly, these observations could lend support to the idea that the deepening of industrial structure in the direction of intermediate inputs and capital goods represented some crucial threshold after all.

I have now bared the intimate reasons for which I may either like or dislike the O'Donnell thesis. But the question is obviously not whether the thesis conforms to ideas and opinions previously expressed by me, but whether it is true or false; or, more modestly, whether it is a sustainable generalization considering the historical evidence so far before us.

Attempts to answer that crucial question are made elsewhere by Robert Kaufman and José Serra.[19] Their work raises doubts about the empirical foundation of O'Donnell's thesis with respect to crucial countries such as Brazil and Chile. Only in Argentina is it at all plausible that difficulties of deepening the industrial structure, and the need to do so by bringing in complex foreign technology through multinational firms, have been experienced as real problems before the first, unsuccessful (Onganía) attempt in 1966 to implant an authoritarian regime.[20] But similar correspondences are difficult to establish elsewhere.

It appears, therefore, that O'Donnell's attempt to explain political developments on the basis of economic phenomena is running into trouble. His thesis must be either discarded or reformulated. I would like to advocate the second course: O'Donnell's search should be widened rather than abandoned. As everyone knows, purely political factors, and in particular the reactions to the Cuban revolution – the "great fear" of the Latin American ruling groups, the spread of guerrilla tactics on

---

[18] *Bias*, p. 99.

[19] See their essays in David Collier, ed., *The New Authoritarianism in Latin America*, where this chapter was originally published.

[20] In Chapters 14 and 15 of his well-known book *La economía argentina* (Mexico-Buenos Aires: Fondo de Cultura Económica), first published in 1963, Aldo Ferrer spoke of the "lack of integration" of Argentine industry as one of the major obstacles to a satisfactory growth experience for the country. The meaning of Ferrer's "industrial integration" is very close to that of O'Donnell's "deepening."

the Left, and the determination of the United States to prevent a "second Cuba"—have contributed mightily to the installation of authoritarian regimes in one Latin American country after another since 1958. Nevertheless, the quest for economic development has been so dominant a theme during the last thirty years throughout Latin America that the existence of a systematic connection between the course of this quest—its successes and disappointments, on the one hand, and major political trends, on the other—has an inherent intellectual appeal. The reason for the wide acceptance of O'Donnell's thesis is precisely that appeal. I shall now discuss some alternative ways of establishing such a connection.

But first a methodological point. To establish the connection of some puzzling events—say, regime change in the authoritarian direction in a number of countries—to some underlying causal factor, such as the difficulty of "deepening" the productive structure, it is not enough to show that the latter systematically preceded the various regime changes. There is a need to demonstrate a plausible, meaningful connection between the two series of events. In the case at issue here, this need is particularly strong because, as a result of the Marxian thinking of our time, the appeal to economic causes for noneconomic phenomena carries an excessive aura of a priori plausibility. O'Donnell is clearly aware of these matters: he does not tie the installation of authoritarian regimes directly to the "exhaustion" of ISI, as is done in the more "vulgar" presentations. Instead, he brings in as an intermediate link of the causal chain the already mentioned lack of and need for predictability. At one point, moreover, he attempts to show that his cause became an actual motive for the actors by affirming that the various military coups proceeded (*a*) from an understanding that the political and social disturbances which had to be quelled were in part caused by the recurring inflationary and balance-of-payments crises; *and* (*b*) from the awareness that these crises in turn derived from the lack of vertical integration of national industrial structures.[21] The fact that this sort of statement came under O'Donnell's pen shows that he felt—quite appropriately—the need to prove his thesis by more than just establishing the existence of a temporal sequence leading from his alleged cause to the establishment of authoritarian regimes.

[21] "Reflexiones," p. 16.

Now proposition (*a*) is certainly correct: high inflation rates and recurrent balance-of-payments crises are widely understood as both symptoms and propellents of sociopolitical disintegration; perhaps the policy and coup makers traced these ills even farther, but if they did so they could not have attributed them to the lack of a deepening process that did not even exist as a problem in a number of the countries in question.

This is a good point of departure for the previously announced effort to widen the O'Donnell search. If the deepening thesis does not hold, is there anything, within the sphere of economic development, that can be put in its place? Which, if any, are the economic problems and the ideologies through which such problems were interpreted that have, directly or indirectly, made a number of countries "ripe" for the installation of authoritarian regimes? If the question is asked in this form, one is inquiring both about economic problems as such and about the way in which they have impinged on the consciousness of various social and political groups. In the following I shall touch on both these matters.

The transition to more orthodox economic policies

There does exist a serious alternative candidate for the role that O'Donnell has attributed to deepening. This is the need for a set of more orthodox economic policies after ISI has been pursued for some time through the well-known, but quite unorthodox, combination of inflation, overvaluation of the currency, tight quantitative import controls, and some foreign finance in the form of both aid and private capital.[22] As has often been pointed out, this combination of policies had the virtue of achieving a transfer of income from traditional exporters of primary products to the expanding industrial sector, and of doing so indirectly,

---

[22] In the English literature, the two phases have frequently been labeled "outward-looking" and "inward-looking," respectively. I dislike this terminology because of the positive value judgment "outward-looking" carries in comparison to the supposedly deleterious "inward-looking" phase (note that in Spanish *desarrollo hacia adentro* has a positive connotation because, instead of autarchy and introversion, it evokes the image of opening up the interior and the domestic market). My own value judgments about these two phases will become apparent in the course of the next few pages. But, quite apart from this point, "outward-looking" refers only to one aspect of the new policies, that is exchange rates, tariffs, etc., and disregards the new fiscal and interest-rate policies that can be just as important.

even deviously, without actually taxing the exporters. From the point of view of the state, the arrangement worked better and longer in some countries (such as Brazil) than in others (such as Argentina), largely because the ability of the traditional exporters to fight back by shifting into nonpenalized activities differed considerably from country to country – that ability was much greater for breeders of cattle in Argentina than for growers of coffee in Brazil and Colombia, for the simple reason that cattle, unlike coffee trees, can be slaughtered, whereupon the proceeds from their sale can be invested in nonpenalized activities.[23] But eventually this particular pattern of promoting industrialization ran into trouble everywhere because one or another of the several conditions essential for the functioning of the pattern as a whole came to falter: traditional exports lost ground (some sooner and some later, as just noted); inflation proved difficult to keep within reasonable bounds; resources that had originally been devoted to industrialization were diverted to other purposes (e.g., building of Brasilia); and, partly as a result of these various developments, the providers of foreign capital and aid became skittish.

The slowing down of industrialization that occurred in various countries at different times during the 1950s and 1960s was occasioned more by such difficulties than by any "exhaustion" of ISI, that is, by some intrinsic barrier to further industrial expansion. What happened was that ISI was carried forward under an institutional pattern which at one time represented a brilliant social invention to get around structural obstacles, such as the difficulty of directly taxing the exporters of primary products and the weakness of the domestic bourgeoisie. As frequently happens, the invention was the more brilliant the less conscious or planned it was – that is, during its first phases – and lost in efficacy soon after policymakers realized what had been happening. As in the myths that demonstrate the dangers of wresting secrets from the gods, the policymakers abused their newly discovered knowledge and applied to excess the magic formula that had paid such handsome early dividends.[24]

Moreover, while the original institutional pattern for the pro-

---

[23] See *Bias for Hope*, pp. 11–12, for an elaboration of this point.

[24] See, for example, "The Goldfish" in *Russian Fairy Tales*, collected by A. Afanas'ev (New York: Pantheon, 1973): 528–32.

motion of ISI declined in effectiveness, a number of new opportunities arose as a result of the intervening industrialization, though they went often unnoticed for a considerable time. With the world economy in rapid expansion, export possibilities emerged for some of the new manufactures (as well as for nontraditional primary products), but they were hidden from view by the overvalued exchange rate which made domestic prices appear noncompetitive.[25] Secondly, industrial investment could increasingly be financed out of the profits earned by the new industries, so that the intersectoral transfers that had originally served this purpose became dispensable. Finally, and particularly in the larger countries, industrialization and the expansion of the domestic market laid the economic basis for broadening income taxation, and for borrowing by the state and state agencies from an incipient capital market.

As a result of these new developments and opportunities, it actually became promising to dispense with the deteriorating original pattern for the promotion of ISI. This meant the establishment and maintenance of a nonovervalued exchange rate, combined with greater reliance on direct taxation for public expenditures, on realistic prices for public services, and on capital markets, rather than on inflationary finance and profits from foreign exchange operations.

This sort of transition to a more orthodox, market-oriented set of policies – in the following I shall on occasion just use the term "transition" – was by no means easy to achieve, because of a large number of vested interests that had a stake in the old arrangements. In some cases, in Latin America and elsewhere, the transition came about in a discontinuous way, by combining devaluation with the rapid dismantling of certain exchange controls as well as through enactment, within a brief span of time, of various reforms in the fields of taxation, public service pricing, and capital markets. Because of these characteristics of the transition – opposition to it from various powerful quarters and possible need for discontinuous policy decisions – it *seems* an excellent candidate for taking the place of "deepening" as the un-

[25] Marcelo Diamand and Daniel Schydlowsky have called attention to this situation. See Diamand, *Doctrinas económicas, desarrollo e independencia* (Buenos Aires: Paidos, 1973), Chapters 10 and 11; Schydlowsky, "Latin American Trade Policies in the Seventies: A Prospective Appraisal," *Quarterly Journal of Economics* 86 (May 1972).

derlying economic problem that led to the installation of authoritarian regimes.

Before this hypothesis is considered, it is of interest to examine how it differs from the O'Donnell conjecture. In "Reflexiones . . ." O'Donnell speaks repeatedly of the need for exports of manufactures, as though such exports were part and parcel of "deepening" (for example, p. 17). But this is hardly legitimate, at least without a great deal of further explanation. The turn toward exports of manufactures means first of all that some *existing* industries acquire new outlets for their products – it represents widening rather than deepening. And, as Serra shows, this widening took place in Brazil *after* the advent of authoritarianism, along with an increase in the import coefficient for a number of basic industrial products, that is, just the opposite of deepening. Finally, the transition I have been talking about involves a number of other policies besides export promotion, and these other policies – tax and capital market reform, among others – have once again very little to do with deepening.

From one point of view, it can nevertheless be argued that deepening and the export of manufactures are closely related: an overvalued exchange rate penalizes not only export of manufactures but also the backward linkage or deepening process. The reason is simple. Overvaluation of the domestic currency means that what imports are let in by the control machinery carry an attractively low price tag. With imports of capital goods being given priority in the allocation of scarce foreign exchange, the low domestic cost of imported machinery is apt to act as a deterrent to the domestic manufacture of capital goods, just as overvaluation discourages exports. The establishment of a realistic exchange rate can therefore be important for the development, in due course, of a domestic capital goods industry. But this is an unintended (and usually much delayed) *effect* of the transition.

The economic problems and resulting turning point in economic policy here delineated become even more distinct from deepening once ideological matters are taken into account. As was mentioned earlier the economic problems of which the "policy and coup makers" were most conscious were, first, inflation and, second, balance-of-payments disequilibrium, especially when foreign exchange reserves were threatening to run out. Those who have been responsible for turning Latin American politics in the authoritarian direction, partly under the impact of these twin crises, had some notions about the political and economic problems that were in turn responsible for the immediate emergency. But, as far as I am aware, the lack of deepening played only a very minor, if any, role in such notions except perhaps, once again, in Argentina.

Inflation was first of all attributed to the incompetence, profligacy, and incapacity to resist populist pressures of the precoup governments. But a belief in deeper, more "structural" factors was also at work. In all authoritarian regimes the top economic policymaking positions were first occupied by a certain type of person–one who professed a greater trust in market forces and who denounced, and set out to correct, some of the more serious distortions in relative prices that were the usual legacy of inflation, particularly with regard to exchange, interest, and public utility rates. The ideological influence to which these policymakers were primarily responding was an antiplanning, anti-ISI, and anti-ECLA backlash. As is well known, the most absolutist component of this movement was a group of Latin American economists who had received graduate training at the University of Chicago, in whose department of economics strict neo-laissez-faire views had long been dominant.

But other, seemingly less doctrinaire, influences worked in the same direction. In the middle to late 1960s, the policies that had served to promote ISI were criticized in detail by a group of economists, primarily from the developed countries and with the influential support of such organizations as the Brookings Institution, the World Bank, and the Organization for Economic Cooperation and Development.[26] The principal technical concept developed in these various reports, accompanied by a large out-

---

[26] See Harry G. Johnson, *Economic Policies Toward Less Developed Countries* (Washington, D.C.: Brookings, 1967). This book was written as a critical analysis of the first UNCTAD conference in 1964. The OECD sponsored a large multi-country research project on industrialization and trade policies covering Brazil, India, Mexico, Pakistan, the Philippines, and Taiwan. The principal outcome of the project was *Industry and Trade in Some Developing Countries* by Ian Little, Tibor Scitovsky, and Maurice Scott (published for the OECD by Oxford University Press in 1970). This general report was often far more critical of ISI than the country studies on which it was supposed to be based. This is particularly evident when it is compared with the study by Joel Bergsman, *Brazil: Industrialization and Trade Policies* (OECD-Oxford University Press, 1970). Another large-scale study, sponsored by the World Bank and the Inter-American Development Bank, is by Bela Balassa and Associates, *The Structure of Protection in Developing Countries* (Baltimore: The Johns Hopkins University Press, 1971).

pouring of articles in the professional journals, was that of the "effective protection rate," which can differ substantially from the nominal rate defined by customs duties.[27] By relating the duty to value added rather than to the total value of the protected article, the effective rate expresses the *actual* protection granted by customs duties to the local producer—that is, the extent to which the costs of his own manufacturing operation may exceed world competitive standards. Given the typical phasing of industrialization in the developing countries, with import substitution of consumer goods occurring long before that of intermediate and capital goods, which were imported and paid low duties, the effective protection rates for consumer goods in these countries were often a multiple of the already high nominal rates.

There are two principal ways of bringing down the effective rate: one is to slash the nominal rates on domestically produced consumer goods; the other is to *increase* the rates on intermediate inputs and machinery—as long as these goods are not produced locally but are needed by domestic industry, they usually pay low or zero rates. An increase in such rates is a foregone conclusion once domestic production of these items gets underway. Deepening of the industrial structure is thus another way of bringing down effective protection rates. It is, to be sure, more roundabout than the straightforward cutting of nominal rates. Nevertheless, one might have expected at least some of the numerous publications on the subject to pay attention to it. But, except for an important early article that did make the point,[28] no such suggestion can be found, and the whole weight of the criticism of ISI was in one direction only: if you want to reduce the allocative inefficiences (including such horrors as "negative value added") resulting from high levels of effective protection, you must reduce your nominal rates. Through this unilateral policy advice, the effective protection literature revealed its anti-industrialization bias. It also becomes apparent that deepening was not part of the ideological climate that prepared the ground for transition policies: logically the effective protection analysts

[27] The actual calculation of effective rates required input-output statistics which by the mid-1960s were becoming available for a number of developing countries.

[28] See Max Corden, "The Structure of a Tariff System and the Effective Protection Rate," *Journal of Political Economy* 74 (June 1966): 229.

should have recommended, at least occasionally, deepening of the industrial structure, but they never did so because such a recommendation did not fit their ideological premises and intent. Quite clearly, that literature attacked industrialization, not because it had accomplished too little, but because it was thought to have been carried too far.

Is it, then, in order to proclaim that the rise of authoritarian regimes in Latin America was linked to the need for accomplishing, at a certain phase, the transition to a set of more orthodox economic policies? At first sight, this explanation seems in line both with some of the observed facts and with the declarations and ideologies of the policymakers. In fact, the authoritarian governments that have come to power have often adopted the new set of policies with considerable fanfare and have stuck to them with extraordinary obstinacy even when they were far from successful. In this way the impression has been created that it takes an authoritarian government to accomplish the transition. On a closer look, however, considerable doubts arise on this score.

The fact is that in various cases the transition has been or is being achieved without the presence of an authoritarian regime. Colombia is perhaps the clearest illustration. Here, a number of measures typical of the transition have been taken. First export subsidies and later mini-devaluations have successfully promoted new agricultural and industrial exports; the average level of protection has been lowered; interest rates have been raised substantially, so that the bulk of credit transactions no longer takes place at negative real interest rates; and a substantial income tax reform has been enacted. All of this occurred without the prior establishment of an authoritarian regime. In pre-Allende Chile, similarly, transition policies, particularly with respect to the establishment of more realistic exchange rates through mini-devaluations and export subsidies, made their appearance in the 1960s during the Frei Administration. Brazil is obviously the country whose recent history best fits the hypothesis that it takes an authoritarian regime to accomplish the transition. But this is so only, it now appears, because authoritarianism came so early to Brazil. Policies which look in Brazil as though they are due to the regime change that took place in 1964 were subsequently adopted elsewhere under diverse political auspices.

Accelerating industrial growth through increased income inequality

I shall deal briefly with a third possible connection between economic development and the installation of authoritarian regimes. It can be pieced together from a number of writings, mostly by Brazilian authors.[29] Put as succinctly as possible, here is the thesis: when industrializing countries with the income distribution typical of Latin America move into the phase of stressing the domestic manufacture of automobiles and other durable consumer goods, their politics is likely to move in the authoritarian and repressive direction.

That sectoral patterns of growth have some relation to the nature of the political regime is not really a new idea. The following statement, for example, sounds both familiar and plausible: a government that wishes to pour all of its investment resources into armaments and capital goods for heavy industry must keep consumption down and is therefore likely to be more repressive than a government that lets part of the economy's growth take the form of increased consumption. This sort of reasoning has often been used in explaining the maintenance of authoritarian policies in the Soviet Union; and, at one time, many analysts tied the prospects for political liberalization in that country to changes in economic policies that would favor the long-delayed expansion of consumer goods industries. Events have not precisely confirmed these conjectures, as more consumer goods are now being produced in the Soviet Union, while the authoritarian nature of the Soviet regime is not noticeably on the wane. As a result, not too much has been heard along these lines lately.

For Latin America, an interesting variant of the idea has been proposed. Here it is not the compression of aggregate consumption, designed to make room for an expansion of the capital goods sector, that is held responsible for repressive and authoritarian politics. Rather, the accent is on the *uneven expansion of consumption*, uneven with respect to both kinds of articles and categories of consumers.

The argument goes about as follows. At one stage of Western-style industrial development, the easiest way to foster rapid growth is through an expansion of the automobile and consumer

[29] Parts of the argument are due to Celso Furtado's *Análise do "Modelo" brasileiro* (Rio de Janeiro: Civilização brasileira, 1972).

durable industries, with the latter being aided by a boom in the construction of middle- and upper-income housing, which can itself make a fine contribution to overall growth. As long as it is primarily oriented to the domestic market, this sort of expansion can take place only if there is an adequate block of middle- and upper-income receivers who will want to sustain the consumer durables (and housing) boom through new purchases. Since only the better-off people are in a position to acquire the automobiles, houses, or apartments, and many of the consumer durables, the increase in income that comes with economic expansion must be channeled to them. The poorer sections are at a hopeless distance from being customers of the expanding industries and would merely "waste" any increased earnings on rice and beans; their income must therefore be kept from increasing, the more so as the latter items are in inelastic supply. But in order to achieve that sort of consumption profile (also designated as "excluding and concentrating development" – *desarrollo excluyente y concentrador*), political repression and authoritarianism are required.

There is something intriguing about these propositions. But two critical observations are immediately in order:

1. None of Latin America's authoritarian regimes were established *in order to* pursue the growth strategy that has just been outlined. As with deepening, the idea of that sort of strategy never became an actual motive for the generals and politicians who ushered in those regimes.

2. As in the case of the transition to more orthodox policies, booms or boomlets of automobile and consumer durable industries have taken place in a number of Latin American countries over the past twenty years or so, before as well as after the establishment of authoritarian regimes and also in their total absence.

The argument just presented has nevertheless its convincing side, for it describes rather well what has been going on for a number of years in Brazil, the country with the most spectacular boom in automobile and consumer durable production. From the mid-1960s to about 1973, Brazilian economic policy has indeed funneled massive amounts of consumer credit for automobile and consumer durable purchases to anyone who could claim to be a serious customer, has widened wage and salary differentials, and has held down wages at the low end of the scale, at least until 1974. It is likely that these policies could not have been pursued so consistently in the absence of a "strong" government.

What we have here, therefore, is not an economic explanation of authoritarianism, but a political explanation of a turn in Brazilian economic development: prior existence of an authoritarian government facilitated the shaping of economic policy strongly oriented toward the expansion of a special category of consumption. Much else could be said about the economic and economic-policy *consequences* of authoritarian regimes, but this does not happen to be the subject of the present essay, which deals with their economic *determinants*.

II. Stress on ideology: an overdose of proposed problems?

Having found fault with O'Donnell's "deepening" conjecture and also with the two alternative hypotheses, am I returning empty-handed from the expedition of the preceding section? I do not think so. Rather, on the basis of that expedition, it is possible to suggest that the relationship between unsolved economic problems and regime change is of a somewhat different nature. The search for a single, specific structural economic difficulty underlying the rise of authoritarianism in Latin America seems to me unpromising. But there is obviously a relationship between the rise of authoritarian regimes and the generalized consciousness that the country is facing serious economic problems (which may differ from country to country) without being able to solve them.[30] The greater and more widespread the feeling of incapacity to solve problems, the greater will be the propensity to undertake regime change as well as the readiness on the part of large groups to accept and perhaps hail it. And the greater the number of real or alleged unsolved problems at the moment of the establishment of an authoritarian government, the greater will be the temptation and justification for that government to install itself in power for a long period of time, and the greater are the chances for such a government to legitimate itself, provided some of these problems are capable of being solved or ameliorated. If the matter

---

[30] The process through which some state of affairs comes to be defined as a *problem* that ought to be solved or ameliorated by public policy is discussed in my *Journeys Toward Progress: Studies of Economic Policy-Making in Latin America* (New York: Twentieth Century Fund, 1963, and The Norton Library, 1973), pp. 229–38.

is put in this general way, it is possible to salvage something from the various hypotheses that have been examined. Awareness of the problems of deepening, say in Argentina, and of transition, say in Brazil, may well have contributed in both countries to the regime change in the authoritarian direction and even more to the determination of the new authoritarian regimes to stay in power and to their potential for legitimation. But with this formulation our inquiry changes in nature, as attention is focused not so much on the *hidden* problems to be detected by the penetrating eye of some social scientist as on the tasks that are *openly* and loudly proposed to a society by influential spokesmen from within or without.

This leads me in a new direction. Often it is taken for granted that there is some strict proportionality between the problems a society experiences and the problems proposed to it by its intellectuals, policymakers, and other influentials. But this assumption can be questioned. It is conceivable for the articulation of problems and the elaboration of proposals for their solution to increase at times quite independently of what actually goes on in economy and society. Such an autonomous increase in problem-and-solution proposing could obviously have important political consequences, and I am now going to argue, as an antithesis to the preceding section, that a phenomenon of this sort was strikingly in evidence in Latin America during the past decades.

Some years ago I professed to see considerable value in the structuralist school of thought in Latin America and in its search for the "deep" problems – such as certain land tenure conditions – that were believed to underlie the surface problems of inflation and balance-of-payments disequilibrium. My argument was that in this way the surface problem acts like a searchlight and helps in the early detection of social ills that, if neglected for too long, might be much more difficult to cure.[31] From the point of view of the present essay it appears, however, that the structuralist strategy of problem solving can be and probably has been overdone: in recent decades Latin American societies have been subjected to an unceasing and unprecedented barrage of proposed structural reforms. It is as though the inflation of the price level has produced in the ideological realm an inflation in the generation of "fundamental remedies." When the policies that

[31] For further comments on the structural thesis, see Chapter 8, Section I.

are thus proposed are considerably beyond the capabilities of a society, a pervasive feeling of frustration is easily generated.

We are dealing here with the counterpart of the remarkable ferment, excitement, and creativity that has been so notable a feature of the Latin American intellectual scene during the last thirty years. It was in this period that Latin American social science, while not quite achieving the triumphs of contemporary Latin American literature, gained wide recognition for its vitality. New ideas were constantly generated and often became dominant themes in international discussions. The outstanding contribution of Latin Americans to the analysis of the problems of the poorer countries was recognized, for example, in the nomination of Raúl Prebisch as first Secretary of the United Nations Conference on Trade and Development (UNCTAD).

But there was a counterpart to these achievements that can only now be perceived in retrospect, somewhat similar in nature to that of other such periods of intellectual ferment, from the French Enlightenment to the extraordinary cultural flowering in Vienna at the turn of the nineteenth to the twentieth century. This counterpart was the frustration resulting from the widening gulf between the reality of Latin American societies and the tasks proposed to them.

As we look back at the sequence of these tasks, it appears that they were proposed in order of increasing difficulty. The task proclaimed a few years after World War II was industrialization, when efforts in this direction were already well underway. As an ongoing activity, industrialization was an undertaking clearly within the reach of Latin American societies. But this relatively easy task was soon supplemented, in the 1950s, by the call for planning; it came not only from ECLA but, powerfully backed by loanable funds, from such unimpeachable "establishment" quarters as the World Bank. Planning for economic development was supposed to set targets for the economy as a whole and for the balanced growth of its various sectors, and to indicate how these targets could be achieved by coordinated investment on behalf of both the public and the private sector. This was a more complex undertaking and one that went against the grain of much of the institutional structure of Latin American government and society. Attempts to set up planning agencies and to produce planning documents were duly made in many countries, but the extent to which these efforts had any bearing on the course of governmental action and of economic development differed widely among countries and fluctuated wildly from one period to another, even within those countries where there was an impact. Strangely, the planning agencies which had been set up to impart greater stability to governmental action in the economic field were themselves subject to considerable instability, swinging from hectic bursts of activity and real influence to near total somnolence and impotence. Eventually a certain consolidation of the new bureaucratic structures was achieved; but their accomplishments were decidedly modest in comparison with the ambitious notions which had inspired their creation.

The next task to be proclaimed – in the early 1960s – was for a yet more ambitious undertaking: the economic integraton of the various Latin American economies. Plausibly enough, it was pointed out that efficient and full industrial development could not be achieved by the Latin American countries in isolation because of limited markets and economies of scale. Enormous intergovernmental negotiations were launched, and full-fledged international machineries and bureaucracies were established. The framers of the agreements were not satisfied with the goal of a customs union, but felt that, because of differences between Latin America and Western Europe, it was imperative to attempt the difficult task of apportioning industries to various countries on a complementary basis. Ten to fifteen years later, the various efforts that were undertaken – the Central American Common Market, the Latin American Free Trade Association, and the Andean Pact – had very unequal achievements to their credit, but all of them had fallen far short of their original goals.

Roughly speaking, the tasks of industrialization, planning, and integration can be considered as comparatively "nonantagonistic." As policy goals, they do not explicitly threaten any important class or sector of society, and can be presented as being in the long-run interest of all. But having made an increasingly poor showing at these successively proclaimed tasks, Latin America was summoned by its intellectuals in the middle and late 1960s to do battle on the terrain of *antagonistic* tasks that involved quite another order of difficulty: now it was widely proclaimed, in a final escalation, that Latin America must solve its problems by redistributing wealth and income domestically and by overcoming "dependence," that is, by reordering its international economic relations in what could only be a conflictive process with the major powers, and particularly with the United States. Unsurprisingly, the response to this latest, most demanding, call to action has not been overly impressive.

An ancient myth must be appealed to once again, this time to convey how odd the process just described really was. Everyone is familiar with the story of the wanderer or pretender to the hand of the king's daughter who is given increasingly difficult questions to answer or increasingly complex tasks to accomplish before he is granted access to the coveted prize. In these stories, the easier questions must be *solved* before the next more difficult question is posed. In Latin America, on the other hand, new, more difficult tasks were continuously presented to the state and society *whether or not* the previous task had been successfully disposed of. Indeed it would almost seem that the less satisfactorily a previous task had been grappled with, the bigger was the jump in difficulty of the next task and the sooner was it introduced.

This strange process of ideological escalation may well have contributed to that pervasive sense of being in a desperate predicament which is a precondition for radical regime change. Some Latin American countries were more exposed to this sense than others during the recent past. Among the larger ones, Colombia and Venezuela were probably least affected by the ideological climate just described. In Colombia, there is a tradition of self-conscious intellectual isolation from outside ideological currents and a conviction that the country's problems can somehow be handled by home-grown, savvy members of the country's political elite. Venezuela, with its petroleum wealth, was evidently a special case and ideas elaborated in countries (and by citizens of countries) permanently subject to inflationary and balance of payments pressures were here prima facie suspect.[32] Interestingly, these two countries are also the ones that have so far proved most resistant to the authoritarian wave.

It is with some reluctance that I have put forward the thoughts of the preceding pages, if only because they may of-

---

[32] It is perhaps significant in this connection that the ECLA group of political economists who gathered around Raúl Prebisch and elaborated the various ECLA doctrines in the 1950s did not contain a single Colombian or Venezuelan of stature. For some remarks on the comparative isolation of Colombia from the currents of social science thinking in Latin America, see Francisco Leal Buitrago, "Desarrollo, subdesarrollo y ciencias sociales" in F. Leal Buitrago et al., *El agro en el desarrollo colombiano* (Bogotá: Punta de Lanza, 1977), pp. 27–8.

fend some of my closest friends. Nevertheless, when a series of disastrous events strikes the body politic, everyone's responsibility must be looked at, including that of the intellectuals.[33] Having done just that, I must promptly add some caveats. To begin with, it is not easy to say what, if any, policy conclusions should be drawn in consequence. Obviously it would be folly to wish that the flowering of Latin American social thought of recent decades had not taken place, because this thought may have contributed to an ideological climate of frustration which in turn may bear some responsibility for certain deplorable political events. In other words, it would be ludicrous to draw the conclusion that intellectuals should stop being intellectuals and refrain from analyzing the problems of their countries. One might suggest, however, that they ought to be more fully aware of their responsibility, which is the greater because of the considerable authority they are apt to wield in their countries. Because of this authority, the process that in the realm of science and technology is known as the protracted sequence from invention to innovation often takes remarkably little time in Latin America with respect to economic, social, and political ideas. With social thought turning so rapidly into attempted social engineering, a high incidence of failed experiments is the price that is often paid for the influence intellectuals wield.

My second caveat relates to the weight that ought to be given to the preceding observations. In stressing developments in the ideological realm, I have no wish to claim that they ought to wholly supersede those explanations of the turn to authoritarianism that focus on some soft spot in economic structure or policy. It seems likely, in fact, that behind the occurence of the remarkable intellectual activity of the last decades there lurk in turn "real" economic and political factors that might be encompassed by a more general analysis. An attempt in this direction is made in the next and last section of this essay.

III. A more general framework: the entrepreneurial and reform functions and their interaction

The following notes are exploratory and fragmentary. Their intent is to suggest that the conceptual framework to be proposed has promise.

[33] For further comments on this theme, see Chapters 6 and 7, this volume.

So as not to have to think up everything *ex nihilo,* I shall start out with the by now almost obvious-sounding observation that growth creates imbalances and inequalities. It does so in many dimensions: in *The Strategy of Economic Development* I had stressed the sectoral and geographical imbalances, but increasing social and income inequalities are an important part of this picture. In time, pressures will arise to correct some of these imbalances, both because the continuation of growth requires such correction at some point and because the imbalances bring with them social and political tensions, protest, and action. This formulation leads immediately to the definition of the two principal tasks or functions that must be accomplished in the course of the growth process, and also, as will soon be apparent, to an appreciation of several typical ways in which the process as a whole may run into economic or political trouble.

The first of the two tasks is the unbalancing function, or the *entrepreneurial* function, or, as James O'Connor calls it in *The Fiscal Crisis of the State,*[34] the *accumulation* function. It can be performed by private domestic enterprise, foreign capital, the state, or by any combination thereof. At some point after this function has had its run there will be efforts at catching up on the part of lagging sectors and regions, at social reforms to improve the welfare and position of groups that have been neglected or squeezed, and at redistribution of wealth and income in general. This is the "equilibrating," distributive, or *reform* function. Like the entrepreneurial function, it can be performed by different actors, that is, by the interested parties themselves through collective action or by the state ("reform from above").[35]

---

[34] New York: St. Martin's Press, 1973. For my definition of the disequilibrating and equilibrating functions, see the section "The Two Functions of Government" in *The Strategy of Economic Development,* pp. 202–5.

[35] The term *legitimation function* used by O'Connor seems unnecessarily restrictive since it refers only to such performances of this function as are carried out by the state. Moreover, the term is misleading: it implies something about the objective which actors aim at when they engage in reform activity; quite often, however, nothing could be further from their minds than to seek "legitimation" for the state even when that is the outcome. And now a brief note on my own terminology: I chose *entrepreneurial function* in preference to *accumulation function* because, in talking about those who perform it, the term *entrepreneurs* is less awkward than *accumulators* (or *capitalists*), especially in a developmental context. As to the term *reform function* I chose it in preference to *distributive* (or *redistributive) function* because the latter, like O'Connor's legitimation function, implies that the state alone can perform it. The term *reform function* is not totally satisfactory to me, since it does not seem to include those corrective actions or policies that are designed to help a lagging economic sector catch up

How well these two functions are performed and coordinated is crucial for both economic and political outcomes of the growth process. Some of the trouble that can arise is no doubt traceable to characteristics of the two functions taken in isolation.[36] But the present formulation intends to draw attention to their perhaps more crucial interaction.

From a somewhat Olympian point of view, it is easy to see that the reform function has an essential role to play in making it possible for growth to be sustained after a powerful, yet disequilibrating, push by the entrepreneurs. This is borne out by the famous historical examples of comparatively successful reform experiences – such as the 1832 Reform Act in England, the New Deal in the United States, and the accomplishments of Lázaro Cárdenas in Mexico. But these examples also illustrate that, with the possible exception of sectoral imbalances,[37] those who are performing the entrepreneurial function are ordinarily not only unaware of the emerging need for complementary action but are often strongly opposed to the reform function being performed at all. That function, whether undertaken from below or above, has of course its own interested carriers, performers, or protagonists, but their appearance on the stage at the right time and with the right strength is not in any reliable fashion coordinated with the entrepreneurial function and its performance. In fact, while the performance of both functions (in some

with the others in the process of growth. However, a more inclusive term, such as "corrective," would have been too flat. Also, the term *reform function* has the advantage that its performers can simply be referred to as "reformers." However, use of this term in the text is not meant to imply that these people are "reformists" in the sense of having foresworn any idea of revolution; to my mind, they include anyone determined to correct imbalances and inequities that have arisen in the course of growth, no matter what the consequences; in other words, they can be entrepreneurs, state agencies, reformists, reform-mongers, or revolutionaries.

[36] With respect to the entrepreneurial function (in isolation), see Fernando Henrique Cardoso, *Empresario industrial e desenvolvimento econômico* (São Paulo: Difusão Européia do Livro, 1964) and "The Industrial Elite" in S. M. Lipset and A. Solari, *Elites in Latin America* (New York: Oxford University Press, 1967), pp. 94–116. For case studies of the reform function (in isolation), see my *Journeys Toward Progress*.

[37] Sectoral imbalances come to the attention of entrepreneurs through emerging shortages and relative price rises and, if capital markets function properly, the manifestation of this kind of imbalance is the beginning of its cure, *with the participation in that cure of the entrepreneurs responsible for the imbalance.* With regard to regional disequilibrium, correction is less prompt and predictable and much more political. In the absence of strong, state-sponsored incentives, the imbalance is here unlikely to be redressed by those who caused it. What holds for regional disequilibrium applies even more strongly to social or income inequalities arising or widening in the course of growth.

proper sequence) may be "objectively" essential for the growth process, their protagonists are more often than not determined adversaries, and perhaps must be just that up to a point if they are to accomplish their respective purposes.

I shall now try to spell out some characteristics of the entrepreneurial and reform functions in Latin America, and of their interplay, in comparison to the advanced industrial countries. Later some important differences among Latin American countries will be discussed.

Take, first, the strength of the entrepreneurial function. Here we are on fairly familiar terrain. That strength depends both on the pull of opportunities for profitable investment and on the push of ideological forces. For the European latecomers the powerful impetus of ideology, with its borrowings from diverse sources such as Saint-Simonism in France and Marxism in late-nineteenth-century Russia, has been memorably brought out by Alexander Gerschenkron.[38] Moreover, the effort to build up industries with which one would then proceed to conquer leading positions in world markets for manufactures was often advocated, viewed, and sensed as part and parcel of the competition for national power; just as the desire to recoup such positions after a military defeat had overtones of a national crusade. While the loss of the northern provinces by Mexico and that of Panama by Colombia had a somewhat similar "mind-concentrating" impact on these two countries, the ideological forces propelling industrialization in Latin America were on the whole not nearly as potent. Finally, though, as a result of the Great Depression and then of World War II, there arose considerable unhappiness and soul-searching in Latin America about its economic role in the world. This travail culminated after the war in the Prebisch manifesto of 1949 and its call for industrialization. The subsequent calls for planning and integration can (with some qualification) be considered additional ideological props for industrial development. In Brazil, a particularly determined and temporarily successful attempt to fashion a national ideology for development and industrialization was spearheaded by Kubitschek and a number of his ideological, political, and institutional allies in the 1950s.

But now comes another peculiarity of the Latin American se-

[38] *Economic Backwardness in Historical Perspective* (Cambridge, Mass.: Harvard University Press, 1962), pp. 22–6.

quence: the postwar push for industrialization lasted a mere decade or so and was followed by a very different ideological phase during which pleas for redistribution predominated. What is most interesting is that these pleas came from essentially the same quarters which had issued the earlier calls for a vigorous assertion of the entrepreneurial function. These quarters had become convinced that development now required redistribution rather than continued accumulation along traditional lines.

The ideological forces behind the entrepreneurial function, then, were weaker in Latin America than in Europe. But from the point of view of political outcomes, it is perhaps more important that in Latin America major intellectual voices which had at one time come out in support of the entrepreneurial function rallied soon thereafter behind the reform banner. The older aims of development and industrialization were now denounced and the term *desarrollismo* ("developmentalism"), previously a badge of honor and progress, was strangely but effectively turned into a term of opprobrium![39] A number of reasons can no doubt be found for this reversal – a particularly important one was probably the leadership assumed by foreign capital in the course of the industrialization process. In any event, this sort of reversal has no counterpart in Europe or North America – at least not during the early stages of industrialization – where the support for the entrepreneurial function was far from evaporating when the reform function made its appearance. Here the two functions had distinct ideological constituencies. At most, as more recently with a certain type of Keynesianism, there was simultaneous support for both.

In Latin America the ideological mutation just discussed – the

---

[39] The same reversal can be noted with respect to industrialization, which, after a brief period of praise, was surrounded by terms that conveyed either contempt or impending trouble. A series of extravagant metaphors, with derogatory or pessimistic connotations, came into use. Again and again, industrialization is alleged to have reached an "impasse," to have come to a "dead end" (*callejón sin salida*), even a "chromium-plated (*cromado*) dead end," and is said to suffer from both "exhaustion" (*agotamiento*) and "strangulation" (*estrangulamiento externo*, a term routinely used for the balance-of-payments difficulties typically accompanying a strong industrial spurt). Take even "import-substituting industrialization," a term that is consecrated by now and sounds almost value-free. Obviously all industrializations, with the exception only of England's, were import-substituting to a degree. Why, then, was this term picked to characterize Latin America's industrialization? Could it be because it subtly downgrades that effort? A substitution or *Ersatz* is, as we all know, never quite as good as the real thing. Moreover, the term *import-substituting industrialization* implies, quite

withdrawal of intellectual support from one function and its shift to the other—was particularly evident in Chile, Argentina, and Brazil. Strongly entrenched social groups were left in these countries without any ideological fig leaf, an uncomfortable and perhaps precarious position. In this manner it may be possible to account for the readiness of these groups to use force, which served to make up, as it were, for the lost ideological support. For, as Rousseau pointed out long ago in his *Essay on the Origin of Languages*, force is a substitute for "eloquence" and "persuasion."[40]

Various points can be made about typical differences, among Latin American countries, with regard to our two functions and their interplay. It is apparent, for example, that the reform function arises at widely different dates and with very different lags behind the emergence of the entrepreneurial function.

An obvious way of beginning to account for these differences is to look at the ownership of the economic activities and resources that are shouldering the bulk of the entrepreneurial function. If that ownership is foreign, ideological support for the entrepreneurial function can be expected to be particularly weak, and demands for reforms and redistribution ought to be heard sooner and more powerfully than if ownership of the dynamic economic sector were in domestic hands. In Chile, for example, foreign ownership of the nitrate (and later copper) mines led to early demands on the part of middle-class groups for taxation of the foreign investors and for a consequent strengthening of the state apparatus.[41] On the other hand, an even earlier and more determined attempt at redistribution in the wake of export-led economic development took place in Uruguay, where important

wrongly in the case of most newly established industries no matter which product they turn out, a total absence of creative adjustment and problem-solving.

It is worth noting that the criticism of ISI from within Latin America and from the Left came at about the same time as the criticism of "inward-looking industrialization" that originated primarily within the developed countries, as has been reported (pp. 109, 113). On the conjunction of criticisms of industrialization from Left and Right, see Chapter 1, Section IV.

[40] "In ancient times, when persuasion took the place of public force, eloquence was necessary. What would it be good for today when public force is substituted for persuasion?" (Chapter 20). Rousseau saw force driving out eloquence. But it is also possible that the departure of eloquence (that is, of ideological support) contributes to the bringing in of force.

[41] See various writings of Aníbal Pinto, for example his *Tres ensayos sobre Chile y América Latina* (Buenos Aires: Solar, 1971), pp. 67ff.

components of the dynamic economic sector (land, cattle, sheep) were owned by nationals. Moreover, in Venezuela, where the exploitation of petroleum resources was in foreign hands, the demand that arose, perhaps because of the temper of the times after World War II, was less for redistribution than for the state itself to take on or promote entrepreneurial functions that would complement or rival those of the foreigners. It is therefore necessary to look for additional criteria if the timing of reform tendencies in relation to entrepreneurial activities is to be understood.

In an attempt to appraise why there may be prolonged ideological support for the entrepreneurial function in a society, Gramsci's influential notion of hegemony comes to mind.[42] Gramsci affirmed that, up to the point when an effective counter-ideology takes over, the ideology of the ruling class permeates and shapes the world view of all other classes and groups of society, even that of the most exploited – herein, rather than in naked force, resides the essence of stable social and political arrangements. When the capitalists rule, hegemony would presumably be reflected by the fact that all classes of society support capitalist growth, even though that growth may favor some classes, groups, and regions far more than others. But why should this happen? For Gramsci, hegemony was an insight of great importance for revolutionary politics. But he rather tends to treat it as an axiom and, unlike Machiavelli with regard to the state, he does not tell us much about the processes through which hegemony is established, maintained, or lost.[43]

An attempt to look, from one particular vantage point, into some of these processes, is made in Chapter 3 on "The Changing Tolerance for Income Inequality in the Course of Economic Development." I argue there that, during a first phase of rapid economic development, even those who are left behind will feel encouraged and will tend to support the existing order for a while because of the hope that their turn will surely come; and that this tolerance for inequality (the "tunnel effect") will last

---

[42] A review of Gramsci's widely scattered notes and observations on this topic is in Thomas R. Bates, "Gramsci and the Theory of Hegemony," *Journal of the History of Ideas*, 36 (1975): 351–66; see also Perry Anderson, "The Antinomies of Antonio Gramsci," *New Left Review* Number 100 (November 1976 to January 1977): 5–80.

[43] To give an account of "how [states] are acquired, how they are maintained, and how they are lost" is Machiavelli's intent in the *Prince* as defined by himself in a famous letter to Francesco Vettori of December 10, 1513.

longest when those who are left behind are able to empathize with those who are moving ahead socially and economically. Thus tolerance will be comparatively short-lived and appearance of the reform function accordingly prompt in societies where economic progress is restricted to one particular group that is perceived by the rest as distinct and closed. This argument can account for the early appearance of the reform function in *both* Chile and Uruguay, since the group of large landowners in Uruguay who prospered during the period of export-led growth were just as alien to the emerging urban middle class as the foreign mine owners in Chile.

I also argued that a shared historical experience – such as war, revolution or the achievement of important reforms – can act as a strong homogenizing influence on society so that, after such events, the stage is set for highly uneven development and prolonged tolerance thereof, even and perhaps particularly in countries where the reduction or elimination of inequalities was one of the principal aims of revolution or reform. With equality proclaimed as the essence of nationality, and with social barriers and cleavages supposedly overcome, the return of inequality will either be long unrecognized or, once recognized, will be tolerated for a long time. Mexico after Cárdenas is a case in point: under the cover of the accomplishments of the revolution, development proceeded here in a sharply uneven way, with political stability remaining unimpaired until the student uprising of 1968.

One point I did not make in Chapter 3 is that tolerance for inequality may well be stronger when growth is rapid than when it is slow. This may seem a surprising statement: normally, the more rapid growth is, the greater are the inequalities that arise in its wake. But with rapid growth, economic change and the concomitant physical transformation of the country and its cities are more apparent, so that the expectation or possibility of improvement is persuasively communicated to various groups and individuals. It is perfectly conceivable that this communication effect of rapid growth can outweigh its unequalizing effect with the paradoxical result that the country where inequality has widened *more* is actually *less* subject to reform pressures. It would be interesting to look at the recent history of Brazil and Argentina in the light of this proposition.

The early or late appearance of pressures toward reform in relation to entrepreneurial forces is a topic of considerable intrinsic interest. It is tempting to establish a relation between it and the breakdown of pluralist regimes along the following lines: if reform appears "too early," it will paralyze the entrepreneurial forces ("kill the goose that lays the golden eggs") and this will lead to stagnation, discontent – and an attempt to secure the process of accumulation and growth by means of an authoritarian regime. If reform appears "too late," the pressures for it, long held back, will explode with violence – and in its wake the identical political configuration is to be expected unless a successful revolution (presumably with its own authoritarian stamp) has been able to take over. But this result should give us pause: since no country is likely to achieve just the right timing, it looks as though there is hardly any escape from authoritarianism in the course of capitalist development. Clearly additional factors must be considered.

The obvious candidates are the identities of the *carriers* of the two functions. As was said at the outset of this section, both functions, entrepreneurial and reform, are essential for the successful achievement of development under capitalist auspices, even from the point of view of the longer-run interests of this process itself. But, at the same time, the reformers are unlikely ever to appear as "little helpers" of the entrepreneurial groups. When they enter the stage, they may well be full of invective against the latter, who will return the compliment. The breakdown of pluralist forms may then be related to the degree and nature of this hostility between the protagonists of the two functions.

This approach was suggested to me by what is almost received doctrine about Colombian politics: that political stability and maintenance of limited pluralism in that country has depended on some elements of the country's durable elite ("oligarchy") being able to take on the role of reformers while others pushed on with their entrepreneurial activities. Considerable hostility was often generated in the process between the two groups and there were some serious "accidents" – the *violencia* in the late 1940s and 1950s and the Rojas Pinilla dictatorship (1953–7). Yet, the resilience of pluralist forms during the critical 1930s or during the current authoritarian wave is remarkable and may have something to do with the ability of the elite to assure some minimal performance of both functions by splitting into two groups. Communication between the two groups was often strained, but was never quite cut off, in part because of personal relationships and in part because, after a while, it became obvious that the reformers, whatever their phraseology, were by no means revolutionaries, but were acting in the best interests of their brethren.

In Venezuela the two functions are carried out in a very different way, but the outcome has been similar, for the past twenty years at least. Here it is the state and its bureaucracy, rather than a "private" ruling group dominating both the economy and the state, that carries out both functions. Because of the petroleum-based wealth of the state, major impulses toward the founding of new economic activities originated with it and so did efforts to improve social services such as health and education, attempts at greater regional balance and agrarian reform, and similar reform ventures. There was little probability here that the activity of one part of the bureaucracy would paralyze that of the other. A modus vivendi with the private sector was comparatively easy to establish since the state was so obviously an important partner in virtually any major economic activity.

So much for the two major surviving pluralist regimes in Latin America. What of the others?

There is an old, and still useful, distinction between reform "from below" and "from above." The prototype of "reform from above" has long been the institution by Bismarck in the 1880s of various social security schemes in Germany. Probably as a result of this paradigmatic historical experience the idea has become firmly established that reform from above has the effect of stabilizing the political order, at least in the short run, and of preventing the social and political turmoil that would ensue if the reforms were achieved through the determined actions of workers or other claimant groups.

This notion needs to be thoroughly revised in the light of the experience of Latin America.[44] Because of the weakness of trade

---

[44] Actually, all that needs to be done is to show that in Latin America reform from above does not bring stability even in the short run; in the long run it did not do so in Germany either, as has been brought out by a number of studies connecting the advent of National Socialism with Bismarck's domestic policies.

unions and similar mass organizations, reform from above (often combined with mobilization from above) has been the rule rather than the exception here, but in many cases the result has been instability and eventually political disintegration followed by authoritarianism. One reason may be that the reform-minded social groups that capture the state on occasion are totally out of sympathy with the traditional elites, domestic and foreign, who are manning the entrepreneurial function and are in turn determined not to yield anything if they can help it. The reforms attempted under these conditions are therefore not conceived by the reform elites in the spirit of making the system work better, nor are they accepted by the entrepreneurial elites in the spirit of "giving up something in order not to lose everything." Moreover, not being hammered out in a direct confrontation between opposite classes (as would be the case with "reform from below"), the reforms imposed from above often turn out to be unrealistic, easy to emasculate, and sometimes not particularly helpful to their intended beneficiaries. The result can be the worst of both worlds: the enervation of the entrepreneurs, combined with an absence of real advances for the disadvantaged groups on behalf of whom reforms are introduced.

Viewing the development process in Latin America as the sequential unfolding of the entrepreneurial and reform functions appears to have its uses. The changing ideological support for the two functions, their timing in relation to one another, and the group identity of the reformers in relation to that of the entrepreneurs – all of these topics have yielded some understanding of the interaction between economic development and politics, although we are obviously far from any unified theory. One claim that can be made for the approach that has been sketched here is that it brings together "structural" and "ideological" factors in a way that has been missing from the attempts at explanation that have been considered earlier in this essay.

The conceptual framework that is suggested here can also be used to make contact with some of the earlier propositions of this essay. For example, it may well be that it is the impasse or *desencuentro* – an extraordinarily apt term coined in Argentina – between the entrepreneurial and the reform elites that acts as an irresistible invitation to the intellectuals to come forward with their own proposals and solutions. That impasse, then, may be responsible for the intellectual ferment of recent decades which was the topic of Section II.

From our new vantage point, it is also possible to achieve a better understanding of the introduction to this paper, where a good deal was made of policies that overestimate the "elasticity" of the economy. It now appears that to the extent that those policies are pursued by reformers, they may not be rooted in misperceptions, but could proceed from basic incompatibilities in outlook and values with other elites. In this manner, these policies become less wanton and more intelligible.

Envoi

This chapter has become something of a critical survey of possible approaches to an understanding of the turn to authoritarianism in Latin America. In addition to purely economic interpretations, others that stress ideology, politics, culture, and even personality have been presented. And in the end, a more general framework has been sketched that incorporates economic, political, social, and ideological forces. I believe that each of the attempts at explanation has something to contribute to the understanding of the disagreeable phenomenon that is being studied.

Two types of critiques can be leveled at the manner in which I have proceeded: first, that I have nibbled at my topic from too many sides, that I have been excessively eclectic; second, that by supplying so large a number of explanations I have made authoritarianism in Latin America appear as totally inevitable and perhaps even justified.

The first criticism does not really bother me: I would rather be eclectic than reductionist, and it is hard to say where the golden mean lies between these two alleged vices. But the second criticism is a serious matter. Fortunately it is wrong, because of a fundamental theorem about the social world which can be formulated as follows: As soon as a social phenomenon has been fully explained by a variety of converging approaches and is therefore understood in its majestic inevitability and perhaps even permanence, it vanishes. The existence of this basic law first dawned on me thirty years ago when, at a conference on France, all the reasons for French industrial and economic retardation were cogently set forth and substantiated, at the precise moment when that country was setting out on its remarkable postwar economic modernization and recovery.[45] Numerous other examples of the theorem in operation could be given. Why things should work this way is left to readers to figure out; just in case they find the proof of my theorem troublesome, they can take heart from the fact that Hegel expressed the same thought less paradoxically and more beautifully when he wrote "the owl of Minerva spreads its wings only with the falling of dusk."

It follows that the more thoroughly and multifariously we can account for the establishment of authoritarian regimes in Latin America, the sooner we will be done with them.

[45] For the proceedings of the conference, see Edward M. Earle, ed., *Modern France* (Princeton: Princeton University Press, 1951).

Around
Journeys Toward Progress

Introductory note

In the late forties or early fifties, a group of French industrialists and productivity specialists visited numerous plants and corporate headquarters in the United States. The resulting report carried the title "Comment font-ils?" (How do they do it?), "they" being obviously those remarkable "Américains." At that time, with American power and influence at its peak, many United States institutions were scrutinized, not only by foreigners anxious to pick up some fast "know-how," but also by Americans who were both surprised at their own success in the world and anxious to understand its reason, justification, and prospects for permanence. In this climate it is hardly surprising that the analysis of public policy and of the policymaking process should have become an important concern of American political scientists. The ensuing studies underlined the distance between the theoretical models and actual practice, but generally found that the latter, however weird, worked quite well, if for reasons heretofore poorly understood. Unfortunately, as soon as this reassuring research result had been proclaimed in the early or mid-sixties, the American style of policymaking stopped operating in its accustomed satisfactory manner.

In *Journeys Toward Progress: Studies of Economic Policy-Making in Latin America* (1963), I undertook to delineate, on the basis of three detailed case studies, a characteristic Latin American style of policymaking that contrasted in important ways with the United States style. In spite of a number of reservations, I tried to show that this style, too, could occasionally ameliorate pressing public policy problems. My purpose was twofold: to demonstrate to North Americans that their style is not uniquely effective and to convince Latin Americans that by scrutinizing their

139

own experience they can attain some confidence in their own problem-solving capability.

The three essays included in this section are direct descendants of *Journeys*. Chapter 6, "Policymaking and Policy Analysis in Latin America–A Return Journey," was actually commissioned as a summary review of the approaches and results of that book. Because of the intervening political changes in Latin America–the article was written in 1974 when Chile had just lost its democratic institutions, long thought to be the most solid in Latin America–the tone of this essay is much more somber than that of the book. The emphasis is now more on actual failure *(fracaso)* of policies than on what I called in the book the "failure complex" or *fracasomania*, that is, the habit of interpreting as utter failure policy experiences that actually contain elements of both failure and success. The very tendency toward systematic fracasomania is, of course, an important ingredient of the subsequent real fracasos, as I had already mentioned in the book.

Another important difference between the essay and the book is that by 1974 the contrast between Latin American and North American policymaking styles had lost much of its sharpness; in fact, a number of areas of convergence are noted in the essay.

That the United States and other advanced industrial countries may actually have something to learn from close observations of Latin American policy experiences and from their interpretations is a principal point of Chapter 8, "The Social and Political Matrix of Inflation: Elaborations on the Latin American Experience." To a considerable extent, this essay is based on the chapter in *Journeys Toward Progress* where I chronicled the story of the Chilean inflation and its attempted cures since the middle of the nineteenth century. The essay expands on points that were tentatively put forward there as sociopolitical generalizations. A special effort is made to go beyond the so-called sociological interpretation of inflation, which sees inflation as an expression and consequence of heightened intergroup conflict. This view, long held in countries like Chile, has gained considerable currency in the advanced industrial countries, but needs to be given more concrete meaning to be at all useful; it also needs to be qualified, as inflation can in some situations serve to reduce conflict–therein lies in fact one of its major attractions.

Finally a word about Chapter 7, "On Hegel, Imperialism, and Structural Stagnation." While doing research for *The Passions and the Interests* I found, to my considerable surprise, that the essentials of the economic theory of imperialism, usually associated with the names of J. A. Hobson and Rosa Luxemburg, are anticipated in Hegel's *Philosophy of Right*. The paper that resulted belongs nevertheless in the present group of essays, primarily because of its second section, in which I attempt to demonstrate the structural similarity between the economic theory of imperialism and certain theories about the evolution of "peripheral capitalism" that enjoyed a considerable vogue in Latin America in the sixties and early seventies. Here it is not so much fracasomania that is criticized as the related tendency, on the part of some analysts, to imprison reality into overly rigid schemes allowing typically for only "either-or" and usually extreme outcomes. Again, this essay was written not long after the military coup in Chile and, like Chapter 6 and also Section II of Chapter 5, probes the intellectual attitudes and ideologically based misperceptions that bear some of the responsibility for the disastrous course of political events in that country and elsewhere in much of Latin America during the past two decades.

6

Policymaking and policy analysis in Latin America – a return journey

Latin American economic, social, and political development prospects have become much more uncertain than they seemed a decade or two ago. Even though, at that time, most observers with a sense of elementary prudence did not venture outright predictions, they were fairly confident that the Latin American nations faced some clear-cut alternatives: in one direction lay the road toward greater social justice which would, in turn, lead to economic advance and a more stable and participatory political system (disagreement prevailed on whether revolution was required to open up this road); and there was a second road which led to another combined, but now all-round dismal product: economic stagnation, political decay, and worsened social inequities.

The events of the last decade have shattered this naive Manichean view. It took its most self-conscious stand in the early sixties with the ideology of the Alliance for Progress, and perhaps its last one in the mid-sixties with the theory of structural stagnation; common to both was the idea that without social progress (to be achieved through various reforms and redistribution of income and wealth), the countries of Latin America were condemned to economic stagnation. While the Alliance for Progress was built on the premise that "All Good Things Go Together,"[1] the theory of structural stagnation attempted to prove that all bad things go together and was thus the mirror image of the former. Both these ideological structures could not but suc-

Originally written for a Social Science Research Council Conference on Public Policy in Latin America, held in Buenos Aires in August 1974, and published in *Policy Sciences* 6 (1975): 385–402. © Elsevier Scientific Publishing Company, Amsterdam. Reprinted by permission.

[1] See Robert Packenham, *Liberal America and the Third World* (Princeton: Princeton University Press, 1973), pp. 123–9.

cumb after the telling blow they received from the reality that unfolded in the late sixties. A glance at developments in Brazil from 1968 on left no doubt about what should have been obvious anyway: economic growth, social progress, and "liberty" – or, more simply, the respect for human rights – do not necessarily advance jointly. In particular, it appeared that some varieties of economic growth are fully compatible with social and political retrogression.

The sense of shock produced by this experience could not fail to have its effect on the intellectual climate: one senses today a new willingness to explore, almost from scratch, the mechanisms of interactions between economy, society, and the state. This is at least how I choose to interpret the current interest in detailed studies of the determinants and consequences of public policies.

To undertake such studies obviously implies a "felt need" to make new discoveries about these interactions. Such discoveries could be about the mechanisms of change or about the mechanisms of resistance to change; they could be about successes in dealing with emerging problems, about failures, or about various intermediate cases. Admittedly, when I wrote *Journeys Toward Progress: Studies of Economic Policy-Making in Latin America*[2] some twelve years ago, I was interested in showing how progressive change can unexpectedly be smuggled into societies long dominated by traditional social forces and how some collective learning is acquired, in spite of many affirmations to the contrary, when a stubborn policy problem is encountered and tackled over a long period. But these biases are not consubstantial with the sort of effort on which I had set out and I shall attempt here to separate my method from my message, for the former may be of service even to those who disagree with the latter. In the first part of this paper, I therefore propose to reformulate some of the basic methodological and conceptual tools and approaches to be found in *Journeys*; in the second part I shall return to my biases and shall reexamine their validity. In both parts, in fact, new reflections will take up the major portion of the argument.

[2] New York, Twentieth Century Fund, 1963. A new paperback edition with a new preface was issued by W. W. Norton in 1973. Page numbers in the text refer to *Journeys* (page numbers in the Twentieth Century Fund and the Norton editions are identical).

It so happens that this somewhat egocentric approach results in a logical subdivision of our subject matter. The principal methodological contributions of *Journeys* are to be found in various typologies I established for the purposes of understanding *differences* in policy behavior. These differences depend, in part at least, on the structural characteristics of the various issues which concern policymakers, and my typologies attempted to pick out the more significant among these characteristics. In my biases, on the other hand, I underlined certain features of the policymaking processes in Latin America that seemed to me to be *common* to all of them.

Any comparative study of policy experiences will face the double task of calling attention to significant differences and of bringing out any similarities, obvious and nonobvious. This paper, then, shall offer in turn some conceptual handles for these two tasks.

I. Focusing on differences

An observation on research strategy

One of the major decisions I had to make at an early stage in my work on *Journeys* was whether I should analyze policymaking around the same problem, such as land reform in different countries, or whether I should select different problems in different countries. The former course was clearly that of prudence, for a minimal degree of comparability would be assured in an investigation of how different countries cope with identical or at least roughly similar problems. One difficulty with that course was that the same problem would normally not have the same salience in several countries and this fact would in turn reduce comparability. More important, to choose different problems in different countries was simply more varied and interesting; it also held out the promise of reaching conclusions at a higher level of generality – I would be able to conjecture about Latin American ways of handling policy problems in general rather than only about Latin American ways of dealing with, say, inflation.

I chose the second course and am still glad I did. I do not wish to imply that everyone should do so and even less that a collective research project should. The advantage of a single researcher carrying on such a far-flung enterprise is that he can constantly keep all comparable elements of the various policy experiences in a single central brain. The solitary researcher will notice an emerging similarity in the middle of his work and can pursue it in detail as soon as he perceives it. A contrasting mode is team or group research, in which different persons are normally in charge of different country studies, and the chances of encountering such similarities are poorer. Either they will be programmed in advance of research and writing through common guidelines that never quite fit, or they can only be established ex post, when the individual studies are already completed, in the course of writing the comparative chapters of the study.

But this is by way of a digression intended for those who are contemplating further comparative research on policymaking. The essential point to be made here relates to an unexpected benefit that accrued from the very heterogeneity of the problems I selected for study: it became easier to perceive those structural characteristics of each *individual* problem that helped in understanding policymaking with regard to that problem. For example, the following characteristic properties of the inflation problem (studied in Chile) stood out in contrast to those of regional underdevelopment (studied in Brazil) and maldistribution of land (studied in Colombia), (pp. 162–3):

(1) In contrast to the periodic droughts afflicting the Northeast of Brazil, inflation is clearly a man-made calamity and lends itself therefore peculiarly to recriminations among groups, to suspicions that one group is gaining at another's expense – in short, to political conflict.

(2) Inflation, in contrast to maldistribution of land, sends out regular signals, is measurable from month to month, and is therefore apt to get special attention from the policymakers as soon as it passes some tolerance threshold.

(3) Unlike regional underdevelopment, inflation is formally rather similar from country to country. It also deals with the arcane and technical subject of money. Therefore, dominant doctrine and international experts play particularly important roles in attempts at solution. But, in view of the previous point, both experts and doctrines are apt to play highly political roles, in spite of their technical garb.

(4) Inflation, unlike the two other problems, is easily "over-solved" – it can suddenly give way to deflation, perhaps an even greater evil than inflation. Fear of deflation may therefore inhibit policymakers dealing with inflation whereas policymaking on regional underdevelopment or on maldistribution of land can ordinarily proceed for a considerable distance without the danger of going too far.

Discovery of such structural characteristics is an important part of the analyst's task; through them it is possible to understand and perhaps predict alternative paths of decisionmaking. The trouble is that each new problem will exhibit some characteristics of its own that turn out to be critical for the behavior of policy-makers so that it would be futile and even dangerous to pretend having prepared a finite and definitive checklist of such character-istics that would claim to take care of this aspect of policy studies for future researchers. With this caveat, I shall nevertheless pro-ceed to compile and comment on my favorite list.[3]

Pressing and chosen policy problems

Which, among the many potential and conceivable policy issues, are those on which policymakers act? An obvious first distinc-tion, and one of some importance, is between issues that are forced on the policymakers through pressure from injured or interested outside parties and issues that they have "picked out of thin air" (pp. 254–335). This distinction between "pressing" and more or less autonomously "chosen" policies (my favorite example of the latter is the building of Brasília by Kubitschek)

[3] The attempt I made in *Journeys* to discover structural characteristics of policy problems that condition different ways of dealing with them within a given political system has much in common with Theodore J. Lowi's dictum "policies determine politics" and his distinction – designed to prove that dictum – between "distributive," "regulative," and "redistributive" policies. While I find this distinction and Lowi's use of it to explain different patterns of policymaking in the United States extremely illuminating, I do not believe it possible to establish once and for all a finite number of distinctions or list of characteristics that will adequately account for all important differences in policymak-ing behavior in relation to every conceivable issue. I am making a similar point with regard to the various linkages characteristic of staples in Chapter 4, p. 85. Lowi's fundamental article is "American Business, Public Policies, Case-Studies, and Political Theory," *World Politics*, 16 (4) (July 1964): 677–715; he subsequently elaborates and applies his scheme in "Decision Making vs. Policy Making: Toward an Antidote for Technocracy," *Public Administration Review*, 30 (3) (May–June 1970): 314–25, and "Four Systems of Policy, Politics and Choice" *Public Administration Review*, 32 (4) (July–Au-gust 1972): 298–310.

permits right away some prediction about the path problem-solving will take: in the case of a pressing problem that causes acute discomfort to some vocal group, policy actions will immediately be evaluated in terms of its success in relieving discomfort whereas no such immediate feedback occurs in the other situation.

Secondly, the extent to which a country's authorities are able to "choose" problems rather than merely respond to "pressing" ones says something of importance about the activity of pressure groups, and the relative autonomy of policymakers. This is an area, therefore, where policy studies can be quite revealing, in an empirical way, about the relationship between state and society and about the relative autonomy of the state.[4]

The point goes deeper and highlights one important possible bias of policy studies. In what was once the dominant view of political science, the state is endowed with a will of its own, such as the urge to expand its power in relation to other states or the desire to maximize the welfare of all or of a ruling section of its citizens. The state has an *interest*, a *raison d'état*, which it pursues single-mindedly. But if one focuses on "pressing" problems, as policy studies usually do (and as I largely did in *Journeys*), the state loses its august character of a sovereign pursuing its own objectives and initiating policies to this end; rather, it is seen as coping, as best it can, with a variety of emergencies, as constantly plugging holes, and stopping a wheel from creaking by applying a bit of grease in a hurry. Note that this conception of the *coping state* goes farther than the interest-group or even the bureaucratic-politics approaches; these are still concerned with improving our understanding of the state's actions, rather than with affirming that most of the time the state does not act, but reacts. The distinction between the view that sees the state as coping and the older concept according to which the state determines and pursues its interests has much in common with Herbert Simon's well-known distinction between the maximizing and the "satisficing" firm;[5]

---

[4] The question of the relative autonomy of the state remains a much debated issue in Marxist political theory. See, for example, Ralph Miliband, "Poulantzas and the Capitalist State," *New Left Review* (November/December 1973): 83–93.

[5] "A Behavioral Model of Rational Choice," *Quarterly Journal of Economics*, 69 (1952): 98–118.

in fact, "coping" would have been preferable to Simon's un-beautiful neologism.

Both views contain some truth, and the idea of the coping state is a useful counterweight to the more conventional notion of the state as initiating demiurge. But it certainly can be carried too far if the analyst loses sight of the fact that coping takes place within constraints arising out of the maintenance needs of the basic social and political structure. These constraints are least visible when existing social and political structures and institutions are wholly unchallenged. An interesting paradox follows: it is precisely when, in this manner, the state is at its strongest that its managers will have and give the impression that they are just coping, that is, forever handling the matters that somehow require immediate attention without pursuing any grand design. In other words, the more firmly established the power of the state, the more its managers feel without power to affect the course of events as they just keep busy "putting out fires." Perhaps it is by virtue of this paradox that the phrase "muddling through" came to characterize British policymaking in the nineteenth century when Great Britain was at the peak of its power, while the concept was given a theoretical underpinning in the United States in the 1950s when it was that country's turn to hold a position of unparalleled power in the world.[6]

On the contrary, when control weakens and the existing social and political structures are under serious attack, then the state, challenged to adapt the old order to new circumstances or to build a new order, is more likely to engage in a spate of autonomous policymaking. Such action is then likely to lead to a host of new problems with which the authorities will have to cope so that in a period of state-initiated structural change, both aspects of policymaking are apt to come to the fore.

The distinction between pressing and chosen problems can be developed in other directions. For example, various dynamic

---

[6] See C. E. Lindblom, "The Science of 'Muddling Through,' " *Public Administration Review*, 19 (1959): 79–88. Lindblom has commented to me that, in retrospect, he regrets the title of this widely known paper as it does not accurately reflect the nature of the method of decisionmaking he really advocated and has called "disjointed incrementalism." This method, so he argues, can be used effectively for achieving rapid and substantial change. I agree, but must also point out that the considerable impact of Lindblom's ideas owes much to their having been construed or misconstrued at the time as a theoretical foundation for a policy of muddling through.

paths might be explored. The pressing problems of one period can become the chosen problems of the next or vice versa. It is conceivable that solutions for a problem become available only when it no longer possesses real urgency, but that, because of the existence, real or imagined, of a solution, it is now tackled anew as a "chosen" problem. An example is perhaps the way Colombia's Lleras Restrepo took up the issue of agrarian reform in 1960 when there was little of the peasant unrest and land invasions that had marked earlier periods (p. 157). Alternatively, a chosen problem can turn into a pressing one if tinkering with the problem has the usually unintended effect of mobilizing those who stand to benefit from the proposed or advertised solution. This is the "sorcerer's apprentice" dynamic: timid or perfunctory reform moves lead to demands for far more vigorous policies than had been contemplated by the authorities who had initiated action without any visible outside pressures. This dynamic is not unknown on the Latin American political and socioeconomic scene, but it has received less attention than its familiar counterpart: we can all cite the sad story of some reform move that looked hopeful and vigorous at the outset but that was subsequently aborted or coopted.

A further observation on "pressing" problems: in *Journeys* and in this paper so far, pressures originate entirely outside the government. They arise as reactions of citizens and groups of citizens to drought, land hunger, and inflation. But a large portion of the pressures to act that are experienced by governments day-in, day-out is generated from within rather than from without. Appointments for jobs that mean choices between competing candidates have to be made, conflicts between government agencies and between groups composing the ruling coalition of forces have to be adjudicated, demands for public spending on all kinds of government-generated projects have to be dealt with. The relation between outside and inside pressures is complex and worth exploring. On the one hand, outside pressures are translated into and exacerbate inside pressures as when inflation leads to conflicting advice about the best way to restore price stability. On the other hand, when outside pressures decline as a result of, say, the establishment of an authoritarian regime that prohibits meetings and other channels through which citizens can voice their protest, it is possible and perhaps likely that conflict and intrigue within the government increase sufficiently to keep the aggregate pressures experienced by the top decisionmakers entirely undiminished. The result is the strange but frequently observed spectacle of an authoritarian government that has its hands full coping with the pressures arising from within its own ranks.

Privileged and neglected policy problems

Another not unrelated way of approaching this subject is to focus on the manner through which policy problems gain access to the policymaker. We are now talking primarily about "pressing" problems, and about degrees of pressure. In this respect, I have distinguished between *privileged* and *neglected* problems (pp. 229–34). I defined as "privileged" those problems whose victims have adequate access to the policymaker so that the latter are obliged to pay attention, for the sake of political stability in general and of their own political survival in particular. "Neglected" problems, on the other hand, do not enjoy this direct access, but they can be brought to the attention of policymakers in various indirect ways. One possible way of gaining access is to forge a link between the neglected and the privileged problem through the demonstration that the former lies at the root of the latter. For example, the problem of land distribution in Latin America, long a neglected problem in the above sense, gained considerably in access to the policymaker and in persuasiveness when it was connected, by the structuralist theorizers, to the problem of inflation which was eminently a privileged problem. The forging of such causal links is the job of intellectuals and of ideology, which is crucial in countries where channels of access for large groups of population are weak or blocked.

Neglected problems are likely to be tackled in a manner very different from the privileged ones. As long as the force behind them is by definition not overwhelming, policymaking on them will often be tentative, desultory and absent-minded. There is, however, the possibility that, however half-hearted, this sort of policymaking will lead to mobilization of those groups (e.g., the peasants, the poor, the aged) in whose favor it is being undertaken so that, as a result of tinkering, the problem turns into a privileged one, with direct access of the problem victims to the policymakers. In this view, the role of intellectuals and ideology is a temporary and transitional one; they extend a helping hand to the problem until such time as it can stand on its own feet.

In *Journeys* I expressed the opinion that the forging of ideological links through which neglected problems could "ride the coattails" of privileged problems is a characteristic feature of policymaking in less developed countries, precisely because of widespread lack of mobilization and access on the part of large groups of people. However, a look at United States and European politics during the last decade convinces one that access in these so-called advanced societies is not nearly as universal as was once thought. In the first place, of course, access is unequally distributed, in accordance with the uneven ability of different groups to achieve organization and influence.[7] Secondly, the advanced industrial societies have evolved ways of reconstituting and even *importing* groups that lack access as formerly deprived groups gain access. Finally, some of the problems characteristic of advanced societies, such as pollution and discontent about work conditions, are more diffuse and less obviously intolerable than earlier problems of misery and oppression, so that a considerable effort of intellectual focusing and clarification is needed for these problems to enter the consciousness of the victims.

A further qualification is needed. The distinction between privileged and neglected problems may be unnecessarily rigid and dichotomous. How privileged a problem is depends on answers to such questions as: how numerous and how concentrated are the problem victims, how important is the issue to them, and how much influence do they have? One reason for which policymaking on inflation is more continuously in evidence than policymaking on regional underdevelopment or on maldistribution of land is that inflation is felt by a majority rather than by a minority, that unhappiness over it cuts across class and regional lines, and that it lends itself to mass protest right in the capital city. A great deal depends therefore on visibility, and visibility changes over time, as a result, for example, of technological change. Better transportation and communication have made many previously invisible problems visible, as happened in the case of the droughts of Northeast Brazil: from the thirties

---

[7] See, for example, Grant McConnell, *Private Power and American Democracy* (New York: Knopf, 1966).

on, the drought victims no longer had to accept death by starvation in the parched countryside, but could board buses and trucks to drive to the cities where they proceeded to loot the food stores. Thus the ideological route that has been outlined is not the only one through which a hitherto neglected problem can gain recognition by the policymaker.

Motivation versus understanding in the taking-up of policy problems

In the previous section I noted a convergence of behavior of the less and the more developed countries. A similar convergence will be found to characterize the third distinction concerning policy problems that was made in *Journeys*. Mindful of Marx's famous dictum that "mankind always takes up only such problems as it can solve" and of Lindblom's elaboration to the effect that "perception of a problem or definition of a goal often follows and is stimulated by the identification of a possible policy" (p. 237), I suggested that understanding of a problem and motivation to attack it are two necessary inputs into policymaking and problem-solving, but that the timing of these two ingredients could be significantly out of phase: understanding can pace motivation (as is assumed by Marx and Lindblom), but in other situations motivation to solve a problem may arise in advance of adequate understanding. The latter situation, I argued, is characteristic of Latin American countries to the extent that they import "solutions" from the outside in the form of the most up-to-date central banking legislation, economic planning agencies, or common market schemes. This typically "dependent" behavior results, of course, in frustration precisely because these institutions are often established without the necessary minimal understanding of the problems they are set up to resolve. It seemed to follow that the incidence of this type of policymaking would be much less frequent in the more autonomous countries, that is, those less influenced by foreign models in the way they decide which problems to attack, how to attack them, and which ones to leave alone pending a gain in understanding.

Already in *Journeys*, however, I pointed to the possibility that the very success in problem-solving that is likely to result from initially following the Marx-Lindblom route "could breed . . . overconfidence in the solvability of all problems" and hence lead straight into the opposite style (p. 238). As I was writing in the heady days of the Kennedy era, it did not take great powers of prophecy to make this statement. The motivation-outruns-understanding style became in fact dominant in the sixties in the United States and unhappy experience with it has then led to the oft-heard complaint: "If we can put a man on the moon, why can't we solve the problems of the ghetto?"[8] Policymaking on poverty, pollution, cancer, and lately energy ("self-sufficiency in 1980") have all exhibited this style so that policymaking in the United States has now adopted the Latin American style of rushing in with impulsive pseudo-solutions.

Obviously irritated by the policymaking style lately so much in evidence in the United States, Anthony Downs has recently written some perceptive pages about what he calls the "issue-attention cycle" in American politics.[9] He distinguishes between the following phases of the cycle:

1. The "pre-problem stage" during which the problem exists all right, but not much public attention is paid to it.
2. Then comes "alarmed discovery and euphoric enthusiasm." The problem is considered a priori fully solvable "if only we devote sufficient effort to it."
3. In the next phase, it is realized that solving the problem may be costly and goes against the immediate interests of large and influential groups of people.
4. As a result of this realization, there is then a gradual decline of intense public interest, which is helped by the providential appearance of another problem that will occupy the limelight.
5. Finally, there is the "post-problem stage" which differs from the pre-problem stage in that a number of efforts and agencies that have been set up to "solve" the problem in Phase Two continue to exist and may actually make some quiet progress. Moreover, according to Downs, once the problem had passed through the cycle, it will continue to receive a modicum of public attention.

[8] Richard R. Nelson, "Intellectualizing about the Moon–Ghetto Metaphor: A Study of the Current Malaise of Rational Analysis of Social Problems," *Policy Sciences*, 5 (4) (Dec. 1974): 375–414.

[9] Up and Down with Ecology – the 'Issue-Attention Cycle,' " *The Public Interest*, 28 (Summer 1972): 38–50.

Downs then proceeds to analyze policymaking on pollution and other ecological problems with the help of this conceptual scheme. He does so quite successfully for the obvious reason that his scheme was directly inspired by experience with those particular issues. Nevertheless, it may be of interest to think about the applicability of the scheme to other policies. It seems to me to be particularly relevant to that class of policies for which motivation to solve a problem has pushed far ahead of understanding, but even then the Downs scheme can serve at best as a paradigm: in many situations of this type the actual sequence of policymaking may well exhibit a different pattern.

II. Focusing on similarities

The principal value of the distinctions that have been drawn in the preceding sections is that they permit some inferences and predictions about differential characteristics of policymaking and problem-solving. If the paths and sequences of policymaking exhibit similarities, within a country or from one country to another, this will often be so because one is looking at problems with the same basic characteristics – for example, they could all be "pressing" problems with motivation outrunning understanding. Nevertheless, one may well entertain the hypothesis that, over and above the characteristics that derive from the *intrinsic* nature of each policy issue that is being tackled, policy behavior in Latin America reflects some more general and common *environmental* factors, such as culture, history, and the stage of social and economic development. A search for such common characteristics is peculiarly conjectural and it is no accident that it is connected with what I called my biases earlier in this essay. I can plead, however, that the generalizations about the policy-making process I came up with in *Journeys* arose inductively from the close study of the three policymaking sequences rather than from the attempt to deduce the characteristics of Latin American policymaking from history or culture. In fact, I generally called attention to empirically encountered common traits without attempting any explanation. But without explanation or, at least, interpretation[10] such findings retain a fortuitous char-

---

[10] For this distinction see Clifford Geertz, *The Interpretation of Cultures* (New York: Basic Books, 1973), Chapter 1.

acter and do not carry conviction. To relate them to general features of Latin American societies will be one task of this part of the essay.

Fracasomania and real disasters

One of the principal patterns that emerged as a common feature of my three stories was the insistence on the part of each new set of policymakers to decry as utter failure everything that had been done before; consequently the impression was created that one had to start from scratch over and over again. I coined the term "fracasomania" or "failure complex" for this trait. I now return to this theme with a few comments, most of which are not to be found in *Journeys*, but are the result of further reflection and observation.

In the first place, it is of course possible, as in the old story about the inferiority complex (in which the psychiatrist tells the patient "do not worry about having a *complex,* you *are* inferior"), that policymaking actually *is* a string of failures. As has just been noted, policymaking that is prompted more by motivation than by understanding is particularly failure-prone. But in a good number of cases, I came to the conclusion that the claims of total failure, made with monotonous regularity soon after each new policy move, were considerably exaggerated. I then looked for the possibly hidden rationality of this "fracasomania," for the functions that it may possibly serve. One argument ran as follows: the alleged failure of past policymaking induces the expectation of renewed failure and this expectation – for example, that a land reform will not be vigorously enforced – may make it easier to adopt reform legislation than if there were not a general conviction that such legislation will remain only on paper (pp. 244–5 for this and other such observations).

Nevertheless, I did point out that fracasomania seemed to me in many respects an unfortunate trait: "It means to shut oneself off from newly emerging cues and insights as well as from the increased confidence in one's capabilities which should otherwise arise" (p. 245). Subsequently, I became more concerned over a closely related but more general phenomenon, namely, the pervasive "obstacles to the *perception* of change," and found that "when there are special difficulties in perceiving ongoing change, many opportunities for accelerating that change and for taking advantage of newly arising opportunities for change will surely be missed."[11] In that article I tried to account in various ways for these special difficulties, but I have since come upon some more general explanations that permit me to relate the phenomenon to Latin America's relative backwardness and to its dependence.

As a result of prolonged relative backwardness, a general expectation is that one's country will continue to perform poorly. Hence, any evidence that the country may possibly be doing better or may be emerging from its backwardness in one way or another is going to be dissonant with previous cognitions and is therefore likely to be suppressed; on the contrary, evidence that nothing at all has changed will be picked up, underlined, and even greeted, for it does not necessitate any change in preexisting cognitions to which one has become comfortably adjusted. The difficulty in perceiving change and any partial forward movement is thus related to the findings of social psychologists who have experimentally shown that persons with a low self-concept feel some discomfort when they suddenly perform well.[12]

The experience of prolonged backwardness, as just described, has much in common with that of prolonged powerlessness. Take situations in which politicians who have spent the largest part of their lives in the opposition suddenly and unexpectedly gain power: all too often their actions seem almost calculated to make them forfeit that power in the shortest possible time. The reason may once again be that they have become used to their earlier role, wish to return to it, and are therefore acting out an unconscious defeat wish.

The insistence on failure of past efforts and the conviction of each new policymaker that he is starting from scratch can also be understood as a result of protracted intellectual *dependence*. Both intellectuals and policymakers have long tended to look abroad for remedies and solutions instead of scrutinizing carefully their country's experiences and the travail that has gone into various proposals and experiments. The usual gap between the old and

---

[11] *Bias for Hope*, p. 337.

[12] Elliot Aronson, "Dissonance Theory: Progress and Problems," in R. P. Abelson et al., eds., *Theories of Cognitive Consistency: A Source Book* (Chicago: Rand McNally, 1968), p. 24.

young generations becomes a gulf when the educated young elite feels, as a result of foreign study and contacts, that they do not need to bother with what their elder compatriots' experience and reflection have to offer. To justify this action, they must, of course, deny that any accomplishment at all can be credited to the older generation. The difficulty of establishing a cumulative intellectual tradition under conditions of cultural dependence is thus closely related to the fact that policymaking exhibits so little cumulative learning.

A third reason for the proclamation of failure and for the wilful nonperception of change is almost too obvious to deserve notice. It is standard opposition politics to decry and deny any success on the part of one's adversary and it is standard revolutionary politics to propagate a "sense of being in a desperate predicament"[13] among the masses. My point is that this normal phenomenon of partisan politics is strongly reinforced by the presence of the other reasons for fracasomania. The proclamation of failure is a terrain on which those who are comfortably adjusted to protracted backwardness and dependence can unite with those who advocate total change. Indeed, one wonders sometimes whether they are two distinct groups.

Lack of learning is by no means the most serious consequence of fracasomania and of the inability or refusal to perceive change. In a government intent upon transforming a country's socio-economic structure, these traits can lead to complete mishandling of the political situation, from ignoring and needlessly antagonizing groups that could be won over to underestimating the strength of others that cannot. It is precisely such mishandling that marked the careers of the Goulart and Allende regimes. In the case of the latter, the inability to identify and win over, or at least neutralize, potentially progressive groups was reinforced by the influence of certain theories that specifically proclaimed the inexistence of any such groups and the impossibility of any economic advance or progressive change under conditions of "dependent capitalism." And the inability to gauge correctly the strength and determination of the opposition is also caused by the refusal to perceive that things can indeed change: for the basic belief behind the refusal to heed the most obvious storm

---

[13] Robert C. Tucker, "The Theory of Charismatic Leadership," *Daedalus* 97 (3) (Summer 1968): 75.

signals is always the refrain *"aquí no pasa nada"* – in other words, the deeply held and, in the event, fatal conviction that this is still a backward and sluggish society where nothing ever happens or changes.

This is obviously not the place to pursue these speculations. But the fact that I was led right into them from seemingly innocuous and abstract reasoning about the characteristics of policymaking sequences shows how studies in the field can serve to illuminate not just how tax or education policy is made – an important enough endeavor in itself, of course – but can contribute something to the understanding of the most important, baffling, and tragic events in recent Latin American history.

On "surprising" policy decisions

One of the topics that interested me most in *Journeys* was what I called "reform-mongering" and, in a subsequent book, the "smuggling in of change."[14] As a result of my studies, I became convinced that the conventional dichotomy of the early sixties, "violent revolution vs. peaceful reform" did poorly at catching the reality of social change in many Latin American countries. Instead of coming out with my own fully articulated theory of sociopolitical transformation, I brought together a number of significant episodes in the course of which decisions were taken that the preexisting climate of opinion or the prevailing sociopolitical structure made a priori rather unlikely. To understand the episodes I asked such questions as:

What was the role or contribution of crisis in leading up to such decisions? (pp. 260–4)

What was the role of violence? (pp. 256–60)

When new problems or crises arose, did they bring additional pressures to solve the older problem or did they divert attention and energy from it? (pp. 264–7)

As a result, I proposed a number of fairly low-level generalizations about the conditions which permit these "surprising" or "out-of-character" policy decisions to be taken. What is really at stake here once again is the question of the relative autonomy of the state. While I may have been excessively intent on making

[14] In *Development Projects Observed* (Washington, D.C.: Brookings Institution, 1967).

discoveries of the "out-of-character" sort, I was thereby reacting against most previous analysts who seemed to be determined never to be surprised by anything.

I still maintain that the "capacity to be surprised," considered by Raymond Poincaré to be the essence of scientific genius, needs to be cultivated by the policy analyst as well. This capacity may be actively suppressed by the analyst's desire not to upset the comfortable intellectual schema with which he has equipped himself. But even in the absence of such ideological rigidity, policy decisions that should really occasion surprise are often found to be "obvious" or "easy" *because that is how they look in retrospect.* For example, the absence of resistance to a decision on the part of interested parties which might have been expected to oppose it, is often taken as proof that the decision was easy to take. Thus, I have heard it said that it was easy for Peru's military government to expropriate large coastal sugar plantation owners in 1969 or that it was "easy" for the U.S. State Department in the early sixties to secure the agreement of the large U.S. food-processing corporations to the conclusion of the International Coffee Agreement.[15] The crucial difference here is between what *is* easy and what *proves* easy. In both situations, it *proved* easy to take decisions or to set upon a course that looked quite complex, risky, and daunting at the outset. At the moment and in the circumstances in which they were taken, these policies met with little resistance, but this would not have been the case at some earlier point of time. In other words, the social forces and groups that were expected to offer resistance, *turned out to be paper tigers, but for a long time they had been real tigers.*

To perceive and then act on this mutation (of one species of tigers into another) is an essential attribute of political leadership; to take notice and be appreciative when such leadership is forthcoming in the course of a policymaking sequence is the least one must ask of the policy analyst. We have recently witnessed some disastrous instances of just the inverse kind of policymaking: attacks on interests and social forces in the apparent belief that they were paper tigers, when in actual fact they turned out to be real tigers.

[15] For a good analysis, see Stephen Krasner, "Business-Government Relations: The Case of the International Coffee Agreement," *International Organization* 27 (Fall 1973): 495–516.

On indirect and unanticipated effects of public policies

It must nevertheless be admitted that Latin American analysts have developed a remarkably fine nose for a certain category of "surprises": I am now talking about such unanticipated consequences and side effects of new laws or reforms as might thwart or vitiate their original intent. The underlining of such negative side effects is, of course, part and parcel of fracasomania. It is therefore well for the analyst to be on his guard against possible exaggerations of these effects. For example, I strongly disputed the widespread notion that Colombia's progressive Land Law of 1936 (Law 200) had primarily had the effect of dispossessing tenant farmers and of converting crop lands to cattle pasture. In the first place, so I argued, there was very little real evidence of any widespread expulsion of tenant farmers. Secondly, and more important, exclusive focusing on this unforeseen and unfortunate side effect of the law has hidden from view its genuine achievement–the legalization of the breakup of certain large estates and plantations which had been invaded or taken over by squatters and tenants over many years of rural unrest (pp. 107–13).

Today we hear once again claims that land reforms that have taken place over the last decade are spawning some unfortunate side effects. This time the claim is that the beneficiaries of the reform are a minority of the peasantry and that other rural groups, the landless labourers in particular, may possibly be less well off than before the reform. The fact that the reform broke the power of an "oligarchy" which for decades had been held to be at the source of economic and political oppression in these societies is already forgotten.[16]

Interestingly enough, those who in Latin America stress the negative side effects of well-meaning reforms tend to be found among the more radical and revolutionary intellectuals who feel that "partial" reforms are bound to be ineffective. In the United States and Europe, to the contrary, those with the sharpest eye for such side effects are generally conservatives who have long

[16] A more contemporary example than Colombia's Land Law of 1936 is Latin America's postwar industrialization experience. Originally hailed as the only way out, industrialization has been found to spawn so many unfortunate side effects, from penetration of foreign capital to a reprieve and boost for lopsided income distribution, that it is widely regarded as yet another Latin American fracaso. For a discussion of some of these things, see *Bias for Hope*, Chapter 3 and this volume, Chapters 1 and 5.

argued that government interference with the market is futile at best, and usually perverse. In the last few years, in fact, a "new Conservatism" has emerged in the United States that stresses "The Limits of Social Policy" and the "Counter-intuitive Nature of Social Systems" and which warns against any such "simple-minded" attack on social problems as building houses when there is a housing shortage or providing welfare payments to people without means of support.[17] This literature argues not just that new problems emerge when old problems get solved, but that because of some "positive feedback loop" the old problem actually gets worse as a result of these well-meaning but hopelessly unsophisticated attempts at a cure.

A related line of attack on social and political reform emphasizes that the beneficiaries of reform measures are frequently different from those for whom the measures were originally (or ostensibly) taken and intended. Agencies set up to regulate corporations operating in monopoly-prone sectors end up being captured by these corporations and making their monopoly profits more secure; low-cost housing projects, as other social programs intended for the poor and as expenditures on public goods in general, end up benefiting primarily the middle class.[18] This criticism is actually a close analogue to that made in Latin America of land reforms which was mentioned before.

The third and perhaps best known line of attack on man-made change in the United States concentrates on the indirect effects and "externalities" of technological advance. Here we are in the vast realm of environmental pollution and degradation. However, the groups who warn, with this experience in mind, against the further uncontrolled proliferation of technology overlap only in part with those who would caution against social and political engineering. The irony here is that a great deal of brand new social engineering would be necessary to keep technical progress from "running riot."

These various new insights and resulting concerns have gener-

---

[17] See Nathan Glazer's influential article "The Limits of Social Policy," *Commentary*, 1971, and Jay W. Forrester, "Counter-intuitive Nature of Social Systems," *Technology Review*, 73 (January 1971). As is well known, Forrester's ideas and methods formed the basis for the *Limits to Growth* report by Donella M. Meadows et al. (New York: Universe Books, 1972).

[18] For a good survey of the literature in this area, see S. M. Miller and Martin Rein, "Can Income Redistribution Work?" *Social Policy* (May/June, 1975).

ated a diffuse mood of distrust toward the activity that was so highly regarded and advertised a mere decade ago as "problem-solving" and "decisionmaking." As a result of this converging United States–Latin American mood, of this stress on the ominous consequences and side effects of social action and public policy, the policy analyst's task is today, in part at least, to redress the balance and to examine carefully for any given policy whether it has really "done more harm than good" or "created more problems than it has solved." In leaning somewhat against the prevailing wind, the analyst may discover some hitherto unnoticed *positive* side effects[19] or he may find that the negative side effects are not beyond correction through some new policymaking, so that one deals with a converging rather than a continually expanding series of problems. This may, for example, be the case for some of the much advertised defects of Latin American industrialization, such as excessive participation of foreign capital, failure to export, and to develop an indigenous technology.

Nevertheless, the detection of unanticipated effects of public policy will always remain one of the principal purposes of policy studies. Public discussion will often focus on some of the most glaring of these effects, but many others will remain to be discovered. Those that stand in the forefront of the discussion are typically either "good" or "bad," but it is important to realize that a number of important side effects cannot be easily classified in this fashion. As I pointed out elsewhere, an irrigation project may have the unanticipated consequence of provoking a conflict over limited water resources between established plantation owners and new settlers, but it may be anything but obvious whether such a conflict will make a positive or negative contribution to the country's development and history.[20]

In addition, there are a number of side effects which, though perhaps more easily classified as either good or bad or as either costs or benefits, will hardly ever be subjects of public discussion

---

[19] For example, Simon Kuznets has called attention to the positive effects of new technology, once it is widely applied, on the further progress of science: "The extensive application of a major invention, its diffusion in mass production, is bound to add further detail and information about the underlying forces, processes, and materials not contained in the scientific discovery or even in the invention before its spread in mass use. . . . This additional knowledge may, in turn, provide a base for new advances in basic science, often in unexpected directions and ways." *Economic Growth of Nations* (Cambridge, Mass.: Harvard University Press, 1971), p. 330.

[20] *Development Projects Observed*, pp. 186–7.

because they are highly speculative and, for that reason, do not make good debating points. Three years ago, I conducted a brief preliminary inquiry into the experience with national economic planning under the Presidency of Carlos Lleras Restrepo (1966–70) in Colombia. Conversations with a number of key participants and observers brought out the following points:

1. There can be no doubt that for the first time in its tempestuous history[21] the Planning Office functioned properly: it played an important role in advising on basic economic policy and even more in contributing to public investment decisions, through the application of cost-benefit analyses;

2. Similarly, there is no doubt that the delegation of decision-making to a body of "cold" experts had a sizable political cost for President Lleras, the magnitude of which he probably did not perceive correctly. The fact that he recently lost the nomination for a second term on the Liberal ticket may in fact be related to enmities he incurred by curtailing traditional pork-barrel spending;

3. The orderly procedures for decisionmaking on investment projects that were established and the competent way in which they were analyzed in the Planning Office made Colombia a very attractive country for the international lending agencies. As a result, the Government found itself flush with foreign finance and pressures for needed fiscal reforms eased considerably;

4. In general, these orderly procedures in which the Government took such pride may have made it impossible to attack some of the more basic tasks which the Colombian economy faced, and to which Lleras Restrepo was in principle committed, such as urban reform or vigorous prosecution of the land reform. Making progress in these conflict-ridden areas would have required a readiness to maneuver and to surprise which was not easily compatible with the orderly decisionmaking in which the principal policymakers were revelling.

The last three propositions spell out some political and policy costs of economic planning in the Colombian environment. At this stage, they are, of course, the merest conjectures. But the possibility that the successes and the failures of the Lleras Administration are connected in these ways seems worth exploring.

---

[21] It would be interesting to inquire why most Planning Offices, set up to impart more stability and long-term perspective to economic policymaking, have themselves been among the most unstable of government agencies. See also Chapter 5, p. 120.

This sort of connection is much more obvious in the case of Mexico where the policy of "development with stability" (*desarrollo estabilizador*) of the sixties, while highly successful in its own terms, resulted in greater income inequalities, larger foreign indebtedness, and a strengthened veto power of the domestic financial community over national policy.[22]

There is, of course, some danger that this sort of analysis leads right back into the swamp of fracasomania, but I would hope not. The point of the exercise is not to prove that planning in Colombia or economic growth with monetary stability in Mexico were just two more miserable failures even though they had been touted as big successes. Nor is it to admonish policymakers that they have to solve all problems – planning *and* structural reforms, monetary stability *and* income redistribution – at the same time or be damned for falling down on one of the tests an analyst sets up in retrospect. The purpose of unraveling the indirect and roundabout consequences of a given policy is rather to understand how certain policies, in spite of their apparent success, may run into decreasing returns, how from a "spur" they may turn or have already turned into a "fetter," to use Marxian terminology. In this way policy studies could serve to sensitize opinion to needed changes and turnarounds in policymaking. And even without this practical use, they would tell us something about changing biases, blindspots, and lapses in foresight that have been typical, from time to time, of different political actors and systems.

Concluding lament

With the last two sentences I have touched upon the twin purpose of policy studies: (1) to learn more about the nature of policymaking and that means, in the last analysis, about the nature of state, society, and politics; and (2) to contribute to improvements ("reform") in policymaking in the specific area that is being studied. Clearly both motivations, the theoretical and the practical, are likely and ought to be present in the minds

---

[22] See, for example, the articles by Miguel S. Wionczek, Francisco Javier Alejo, and Jorge Eduardo Navarrete in M. S. Wionczek et al., *Crecimiento o desarrollo económico?* Secretaria de Educación Pública, 1971. Also Carlos Bazdresch, "La política económica" in *Plural*, No. 22 (July 1973).

of researchers in the field, but the balance between the two will vary considerably with different social and political settings. Whenever reform is perceived to be within easy reach, the practical "reformist" component will come to the fore. When, on the other hand, reform proposals are beyond the political realities of the moment, policymaking studies will tend to dwell on the nature of the state and society that rules out these partial improvements. It is of course anything but easy to diagnose the conditions under which reform is feasible and *Journeys* was in large part meant to correct what seemed to me to be misperceptions of these conditions on the part of both conventional reformers and orthodox revolutionaries.

But a correct appraisal of the feasibility of reform is no longer enough. In a number of Latin American situations the policy analyst will want to ask an additional question: supposing partial reform is possible, what would be its effect on the further dynamics of state and society? To explain this point I must go back to the introductory paragraphs of this essay where the notion that "all good things go together" was held up to some ridicule. The practically minded policy analyst operates normally on a weaker, yet related assumption: he likes to think that, at a minimum, a possible improvement in policymaking he has discovered as a result of his research will leave the area of his specialized concern better off and the rest of the world unchanged so that the world as a whole would find itself in a somewhat improved state. But what if even this modest assurance is no longer to be had? What if improved policymaking in, say, public health or education, is likely to result in more widespread violations of human rights? What if, in sum, we inhabit not a Faustian, but a Quixote-Buñuel-type world where he who wills the good forever creates evil?

One possible reaction to so parlous a state of affairs is for the policy analyst to retreat from any attempt to put the results of his research to any immediate practical use and to concentrate entirely on the theoretical aspects and findings of his work. But such a self-denying ordinance is excessive, unnatural, and, therefore, unlikely to be effective. Another course seems therefore indicated: the analyst should add to his labors a concern about the possibly perverse consequences in other areas of public policy of an advance that might be achieved in his own.

Considerations of this sort are formally similar to the canvassing for negative side effects that is today part and parcel of any policy study. The explorations we have hinted at here are of course far more speculative. Formerly they could legitimately be neglected. Unhappily, they are today essential, both for practical policy advice and for the understanding of the singularly "cold monster" that the State has become in a large number of Latin American countries.

7

On Hegel, imperialism, and structural stagnation[1]

The present paper has a double purpose. First, I shall attempt to show that Hegel, in 1821, formulated an economic theory of imperialism that was not taken up by Marx and that is very similar to ideas propounded some eighty or ninety years later – without any reference to Hegel – by J.A. Hobson and Rosa Luxemburg. Secondly, I shall briefly outline the structural similarity between those theories of imperialism and certain contemporary analyses of Latin American economic development prospects.

I

Hegel had an economic theory of imperialism when Marx did not. This is the stranger as Hegel's thoughts on this matter are laid down in the very *Philosophy of Right* (1821) which the young Marx recopied and annotated at great length.[1]

Originally written as a contribution to a volume of essays in honor of Felipe Pazos, published in Spanish in *Política económica en centro y periferia: Ensayos en homenaje a Felipe Pazos*, edited by Carlos F. Diaz Alejandro et al. (Mexico: Fondo de Cultura Económica, 1976), pp. 51–60, and in English in *Journal of Development Economics* 3 (March 1976): 1–8. Reprinted by permission of North-Holland Publishing Company.

[1] Marx's *Critique of Hegel's Philosophy of Right* was written in 1843, but was first published in 1927 and is now available in English (*Critique of Hegel's Philosophy of Right*, edited by Joseph O'Malley, Cambridge: Cambridge University Press, 1970). The *Critique* is a running commentary on paragraphs 261–313 of Hegel's work, that is, on the section of the *Philosophy of Right* which deals with the State. The passages I shall quote are in the preceding section on "Civil Society." Marx certainly had read that very important section and projected a commentary on it as well: see pp. liv, footnote 1, and 81–82 of the English edition. That, in general, Hegel's social and economic thought as expressed in that section had considerable influence on Marx is shown in J. Barion, *Hegel und die marxistische Staatslehre* (Bonn: Bouvier, 1963), pp. 100–102. Marx's *Critique* is not to be confused with his celebrated and much shorter "Contribution to the critique of Hegel's philosophy of right – Introduction," which he published in the *Deutsch-französische Jahrbücher* in 1844 and which is a standard item in Marx anthologies.

Before commenting further I must submit the evidence. It is to be found in two short paragraphs – 245 and 246 – in the section of the *Philosophy of Right* in which Hegel explains the development of modern "civil society." In the immediately preceding paragraphs Hegel deals with the expansion of population and of industry "within that society itself," that is, in a closed-economy model as we would say. This process leads to the "amassing of wealth," on the one hand, and, on the other, "to the subdivision and restriction of particular jobs and therewith to the dependence and misery of the class tied to that work." Furthermore, according to paragraph 244, the distribution of income and wealth is rendered even more uneven as "a large mass of people falls below a certain subsistence level," and becomes a "rabble" (Pöbel). The full text of paragraphs 245 and 246 follows:

245. When the masses begin to decline into poverty, (a) the burden of maintaining them at their ordinary standard of living might be directly laid on the wealthier classes, or they might receive the means of livelihood directly from other public sources of wealth (e.g. from the endowments of rich hospitals, monasteries, and other foundations). In either case, however, the needy would receive subsistence directly, not by means of their work, and this would violate the principle of civil society and the feeling of individual independence and self-respect in its individual members. (b) As an alternative, they might be given subsistence indirectly through being given work, i.e. the opportunity to work. In this event the volume of production would be increased, but the evil consists precisely in an excess of production and in the lack of a proportionate number of consumers who are themselves also producers, and thus it is simply intensified by both of the methods (a) and (b) by which it is sought to alleviate it. It hence becomes apparent that despite an excess of wealth civil society is not rich enough, i.e. its own resources are insufficient to check excessive poverty and the creation of a penurious rabble.

246. This inner dialectic of civil society thus drives it – or at any rate drives a specific civil society – to push beyond its own limits and seek markets, and so its necessary means of subsistence, in other lands, which are either deficient in the goods it has overproduced, or else generally backward in industry.[2]

In paragraph 245 Hegel completes his treatment of the closed-economy model by asserting that, under conditions of an increasingly uneven distribution of income, it will be impossible to sell all that is being produced. Neither direct assistance to the poor

[2] Hegel's *Philosophy of Right,* translated with notes by T. M. Knox (Oxford: Clarendon Press, 1942), pp. 150–1. See the comments on these paragraphs in Eric Weil, *Hegel et l'état* (Paris: J. Vrin, 1950), pp. 97–100, and Shlomo Avineri, *Hegel's Theory of the Modern State* (Cambridge: Cambridge University Press, 1972), pp. 152–4.

nor their productive employment can cure the resulting situation of overproduction or underconsumption. Hence, so concludes Hegel in the much shorter following paragraph, civil society – or "this certain civil society," a phrase which points to England – must break out of its confines and conquer new markets. In paragraph 248 he speaks further of the "colonizing activity – sporadic or systematic – to which the mature civil society is driven."

The analytics of this passage are obviously unimpressive. Hegel presents us with a chain of unproven assertions and deductions. What is remarkable is the presence of the principal elements on which some of the more important later theories of imperialism were based:

1. the increasing maldistribution of income;
2. as a result, the temporary or permanent shortfall of consumption in relation to production;
3. as a result again, the search for new outside markets on the part of the advanced capitalist country among countries that have not yet been "opened up" by capitalist enterprise.

The Hegelian passage is nearly perfect as a statement of the theory, if not as its justification.

There are a number of puzzles here. First of all, how did Hegel come to express these "premature" thoughts? Secondly, why did Marx fail to pick them up? And, finally, why has Hegel not been widely acknowledged as a precursor of Hobson and Luxemburg?

There is no easy answer to the first question, nor to any such inquiry into intellectual creativity. In the Berlin of the immediate post-Congress-of-Vienna period, Hegel hardly had the opportunity to observe the social impact of industrialization at first hand. But he was acquainted with the works of Adam Smith, Say, and Ricardo, as he himself indicates in the *Philosophy of Right* (para. 189), and knew not only about England's industrial upsurge, but probably also about the post-Napoleonic depressions of 1815 and 1818–19, which were among the first serious events of the kind.

Actually the first economics work that impugned Say's Law and proposed the notion of generalized overproduction, Sismondi's *Nouveaux principes de l'économie politique*, was published in 1819 and Malthus' *Principles of Political Economy* came one year later. But Hegel could hardly have become acquainted with these works in time, and the "excess of production" or paragraph 245 looks very much like an independent thought that Hegel deduced from the polarization of "civil society" between poor and rich, an important theme of the previous paragraphs. Even more remarkable is Hegel's leap from the malady of generalized overproduction in a closed economy to the remedy in the form of mercantile and colonial expansion: neither Sismondi nor Malthus was to come up with such a conclusion and Hegel wrote just *before* the first wave of British overseas lending to the newly independent countries of South America, in the 1820s. In both cases, Hegel's conclusions are therefore particularly striking guesses based on the imaginative use of his dialectic method.

The most intriguing question is the next one: Why did Marx fail to pay attention to this particular portion of Hegel's *Philosophy of Right?* For it is well known that Marx did not have any theory of imperialism. Marx and Engels emphasized the expansive vigor of capitalism and incorporated a forceful statement along such lines in *The Communist Manifesto.* But the idea that capitalism *had* to open up markets in nonindustrial countries in order to escape from domestic stagnation or crisis is simply not to be found in their works, even though Marx had only contempt for Say's Law.[3] At the end of the first volume of *Capital,* Marx anticipates the downfall of capitalism as a result of increasing concentration of capital, on the one hand, and of complete proletarianization of the noncapitalist strata of society, on the other. The chapter on colonization which is tacked on to this conclusion[4] deals primarily with the economic consequences which flow in regions of new European settlements, such as North America and Australia, from the availability of free land. Marx shows that this situation delays full-fledged capitalist development *in these countries,* but does not draw the conclusion that their existence could delay the downfall of capitalism *in Europe.*

The emergence of economic theories of imperialism from 1900 on and, implicitly, the absence of such a theory from the original

[3] For a discussion of this point, see E. N. Winslow, *The Pattern of Imperialism* (New York: Columbia University Press, 1948), pp. 116–21.

[4] The purpose of this arrangement was probably to avoid ending the book on too revolutionary a note, that is, to elude the censors. See comment by Maximilien Rubel in his edition of Marx, *Oeuvres* (Paris, Pléiade, NRF, 1965), Vol. I, p. 541.

Marxian system have always been plausibly explained by two considerations: in the first place, Marxists required an economic explanation for the explosion, from the later nineteenth century on, of expansionist policies on the part of all major advanced capitalist countries; secondly, an explanation was needed also for the failure of the confidently expected socialist revolution to occur during the Great Depression of the seventies and eighties and for the resumption of vigorous capitalist expansion in the nineties. But now that we know of Hegel's early insight, it is no longer so obvious that Marx had absolutely no way of hitting on the idea that the presence of vast noncapitalist regions and the possibility of their incorporation presented European capitalism of the nineteenth century with a safety valve and an opportunity for greater longevity than Marx was willing to grant it. Using Freudian terms, one may, in fact, advance the hypothesis that Marx *repressed* this thought (and the Hegelian passage which he knew) because of his will to believe in the immediate prospects of the proletarian revolution. The hypothesis is strengthened by the *late* emergence of the economic theory of imperialism under revolutionary Marxist auspices, some forty years after the inception of the new phase of imperialist expansion and more than a decade after the publication of Hobson's work on imperialism at the beginning of the century. In this manner, the thought that the revolution was retarded by the market and investment opportunities opened up by imperialism made its appearance only at the point when it could be reasonably argued that the retardation had virtually run its course, *so that revolution was imminent once again!* Luxemburg almost says as much when she writes, toward the end of her book:

Measured against the huge mass of already accumulated capital of the old capitalist countries, a mass which needs markets for its surplus product and investment opportunities for its surplus value, measured further against the speed with which regions of pre-capitalist cultures are today cast into the capitalist mold, in other words: measured against the already attained high degree of development of productive forces of capital, the area of expansion that is still available to capital represents a small remainder. Imperialism is both a historic method of prolonging the existence of capitalism and the surest way of setting an objective terminal point to its existence along the shortest possible route.[5]

[5] Rosa Luxemburg, *Die Akkumulation des Kapitals,* reproduction of 1913 edition (Frankfurt: Neue Kritik, 1966), pp. 423–4.

This passage is obviously influenced by Hegel's dialectic, but it makes one also think of his famous metaphor on the characteristic tardiness of theoretical understanding of reality: "the owl of Minerva spreads its wings only with the falling of the dusk."

Now briefly to the last *and* least question which I promised I would try to answer: Why has Hegel not been acknowledged, by the Marxists in particular, as the rightful originator of the economic theory of imperialism? The simplest explanation of this neglect is implicit in what has already been said. Since it was so well known that Marx had been a profound student of Hegel, it was inconceivable that Hegel might have come forward with an economic analysis that was not to be found also, even though in duly altered form, in Marx. If an economic idea was not in Marx, then a fortiori it could not be in Hegel. Secondly, the *Philosophy of Right* has had a strange fate: it came to be thought of as a conservative work in which the mature Hegel, now a state professor, glorified the Prussian state as the ultimate "rational" creation of world history. Marxists therefore tended to shun the "old" and rather studied the young Hegel. In fact, the two paragraphs which have been discussed here do not stand alone by any means: in a brilliant reinterpretation, Weil has shown, some twenty-five years ago, that the *Philosophy of Right* may well be the work of Hegel that is most fundamentally critical of state and society.[6]

II

The foregoing is primarily of antiquarian interest. But perhaps not exclusively. The sharpness of the Hegelian formulation lays bare the structure of a certain type of theory which is still very much with us. In fact, there is considerable similarity between the principal economic theories of imperialism and some contemporary reasoning about the development prospects of Latin American and other semi-industrialized countries.

According to Hegel, the problem of overproduction, faced by civil society, cannot be solved by simple transfer payments to the poor nor by creation of work for them; hence the only way

[6] Nevertheless, the spectrum of opinion about Hegel's political position, affinities, and influence in general remains extremely wide; see Walter A. Kaufmann, ed., *Hegel's Political Philosophy* (New York: Atherton Press, 1970). On Weil, see fn. 2, this chapter.

out is export and expansion. Hobson's way of attacking the problem was almost identical. He explained the imperialist drive by overproduction, and the latter by a chronic tendency to over-saving on the part of the rich, given the current distribution of income. But he was less categorical than Hegel in ruling out any domestic remedy. As a social reformer, he made an eloquent plea for the redirection of Britain's resources and energies and looked toward Trade Unionism and State Socialism (by which he meant taxation of the rich for social ends) for bringing it about.[7] Luxemburg went back to the much more rigid Hegelian model: once she had concluded, on the basis of her study of the Marx-ian schemes of reproduction of capital, that excess surplus value was an inherent characteristic of capitalist production and that its "realization" required a widening of the area of capitalist penetration, she could not conceive of any alternative to imperi-alism but "catastrophe" and revolution – phenomena that would take place during the final phase of imperialistic expansion.

After Keynes, any theory purporting to show that, short of revolution, there was no way out of a situation of undercon-sumption and oversaving was bound to have a hard time. But these "no-way-out" or "only-one-way-out" theories must corre-spond to an important psychic need, for they soon reemerged in a new guise. Keynesian economics had merely shown that there was a variety of policy instruments which could be used, simply or in manifold "mixes," to maintain aggregate effective demand at a level that insures full employment. But it did not make any such statement with respect to the maintenance of a specific rate of economic growth. Thus it remained possible to argue that a country which does not wish to experience a decline in its growth rate faced, once again, some very stark alternatives. The-ories of this sort have precisely been characteristic of the way in which Latin America's development prospects have frequently been analyzed, by among others the United Nations Economic Commission for Latin America.[8] It was argued that after the first "easy" stages of import-substituting industrialization (ISI) a con-tinuation of economic growth faces considerable problems be-cause of the difficulties of production for export and because the

[7] J. A. Hobson, *Imperialism: A Study* (New York: James Pott, 1902), pp. 93–9.
[8] *The Economic Development of Latin America in the Post-War Period* (New York: United Nations, 1964).

very uneven income distribution makes for slow growth in domestic demand for mass consumer goods. I have no intention to examine here the analytic content of these theories of "structural stagnation"; but their structure is strikingly similar to that of the theories of imperialism which have just been examined. Let us take, for example, the two reformist theories, Hobson's on imperialism, and ECLA's on post-"easy"-ISI Latin America. Both theories envisage the following three outcomes:

1. a decline in the rate of growth and stagnation in the case of Latin America, or depression in the case of the advanced industrial countries of Hobson's time;
2. an expansion of exports (accompanied by export of capital in Hobson's model); and
3. a redistribution of income in favor of the poor, favored by both theories as a solution.

The only difference between the two theories lies in the probabilities which are assigned to the first two outcomes. To compare the structures of these and similar theories a tabular form using some shorthand notation may be useful. In the following table we write: E for the expected (dismal or objectionable) outcome; H for the hopeful alternative solution which one exhorts the people and the policymakers to strive for; and D for another outcome that is dismissed as unthinkable, unattainable or so intolerable that it will not be allowed to persist for any length of time.

It would not be difficult to make similar comparisons of current thinking on development prospects and policies with Hegel's or Luxemburg's schemes. The analyses and policy recommendations of orthodox economists who criticize the various distortions import-substituting industrialization brings with it, without seeing the need for redistribution or other structural change, can also be fitted into the scheme. This has been done in the last column of the table. According to the orthodox analysts, the post-"easy"-ISI country faces stagnation unless it reduces effective protection levels and discontinues a variety of other irrational economic policies. Once these various recommended policies are adopted, both traditional and new exports will increase and the country's economy can resume its forward movement.

As is brought out by the schematic arrangement of the table,

Prospective outcomes	Prospects for industrial countries, circa 1900, according to Hobson's theory of imperialism	Prospects for developing countries in the post-"easy"-ISI phase, according to:	
		Theory of structural stagnation	Orthodox analysis
Export expansion	E	D	H
Stagnation or depression	D	E	E
Income redistribution	H	H	D

the theory of structural stagnation has a nexus both with the theory of imperialism and with orthodox analysis: while it agrees with the theory of imperialism on income distribution as the only remedy, it joins orthodox analysis in an unnatural alliance that is bent on indicting import-substituting industrialization and all its works.[9]

The arrangement further shows how each theory, by dismissing or ignoring one of the possible courses events may take, selects its own blindspot. Changes in income distribution which are normally premised on a substantial social and political transformation are not within the horizon of those who hold that the existing system can be made to work quite satisfactorily if only a few irrational policies are abandoned. On the other hand, reformers and revolutionaries such as the partisans of the theories of structural stagnation and imperialism tend to develop a symmetrical blindspot: in their eagerness for structural change they often fail to appreciate the ability of the "tottering system" to remedy its worst weaknesses or simply to hang on. As was suggested before this eagerness may have had something to do with Marx's neglect of Hegel's insights. The same blindspot affected the theory of structural stagnation with the result that it had to be hastily abandoned after a brief lifespan in the mid-sixties because Brazil, that paradigm for the "exhaustion" of import-substitution early in the decade, suddenly resumed rapid growth *without* prior redistribution of income in the egalitarian direction – in fact with the opposite kind of redistribution.

Around the time when Lenin criticized European communists

[9] For more on this alliance, see Chapter 1, Section IV.

for their "infantile diseases" he issued a warning against the sort of theorizing that is at issue here and that so often misleads those who are eager for change:

Revolutionaries sometimes try to prove that there is absolutely no way out of a crisis [for the ruling class]. This is a mistake. There is no such thing as an absolutely hopeless situation.[10]

As Lenin well knew, to underestimate the adaptability and resourcefulness of one's adversary can have consequences far more serious than the premature death of *theories*.

[10] "The International Situation and the Fundamental Tasks of the Communist International," *Report to the Second Congress of the Communist International*, July 19, 1920.

8

The social and political matrix of inflation: elaborations on the Latin American experience

Introduction

It has long been obvious that the roots of inflation – whether in Western Europe, the United States, Latin America or elsewhere – lie deep in the social and political structure in general, and in social and political conflict and conflict management in particular. The disputes among Keynesians, monetarists, and other economists about the causes of inflation deal with the modeling of inflationary processes that unfold among the various spheres and sectors of economic activity and, consequently, with the improvement of economic policymaking. But it would be difficult to find an economist who would not agree that "underlying" social and political forces play a decisive role in causing both inflation and the success of failure of anti-inflationary policies.[1]

The reason why the economic theories of inflation nevertheless dominate the field is not that the participants in the discussion are deeply convinced that they have got hold of the crucial variables, but rather that they have developed intricate analytical structures which lend themselves to ever further elaboration, some empirical testing, and – most important – to the formulation of policy advice. In contrast, much of the writing on the (undoubted) social and political roots of inflation has remained satisfied with vague notions – "rising expectations," "faltering social cohesion," "governability crisis" – that are neither intellectu-

Originally prepared in 1978 for the Brookings Institution's Project on the Politics and Sociology of Global Inflation and to be published in a collective volume edited by Charles S. Maier and Leon N. Lindberg.
[1] Even Milton Friedman is reported to have distinguished between the "proximate" cause (excessive increase in money supply) and the "deeper" social causes, in a seminar. See Arthur Seldon, "Preface" in F. A. Hayek, *Full Employment at Any Price?* Occasional Paper, The Institute of Economic Affairs (London, 1975), p. 9.

ally articulate nor politically helpful. In the present paper I shall attempt to demonstrate that it is possible to go considerably beyond such obvious and almost tautological assertions about the sociopolitical context of inflation. For the purposes of this demonstration I shall extensively call upon the experience of Latin America and upon the analyses which are based on this experience. In the process I shall also show that some of the more unorthodox ideas about inflation that are now being proposed in the West as considerable novelties have long been current, if in somewhat different form, in Latin America. The purpose of such an exercise is not so much to claim some historic firsts for the analysts of Latin America's inflations, as to note interesting differences and modulations and to achieve a more general view of the matter.

I. Two sociopolitical explanations of inflation

The persistent and strong inflationary pressures that have characterized a large number of Latin American countries have given rise to two principal currents of interpretation. One is the well-known "structuralist" thesis that was articulated by a relatively cohesive group of economists during a well delimited period of time, the late fifties and the early sixties. The other is what might be called the "tug-of-war thesis" whose authorship is much more diffuse and spread out in time.[2] Elements of the tug-of-war thesis are frequently found even among the supporters of the structuralist argument. Nevertheless the logical structures of the two theses are different, although some convergences will be pointed out later.

1. *The structuralist thesis*

Because of its comparative compactness I shall start with the structuralist thesis. It emerged in the late fifties as an antagonist of "orthodox" thinking which insisted that inflation was

---

[2] The Spanish term often used in the literature and which I am attempting to render–or improve upon–here is *empate* which is normally translated as "tie," "stalemate" or "standoff"; but when it is used to describe the social situations underlying inflations, *empate* means less a final, evenly divided outcome of a social game (as implied at best by "tie" and "stalemate") than a continuing pulling and hauling by major social groups with no decisive victory being scored by any–hence "tug of war" seems a better term.

merely a matter of too much money. The economists who proposed it tended to underplay the important political dimensions of the thesis, in part perhaps to make it respectable among their confreres.

The structuralist approach concentrates on what happens on the *supply side* in an economy that grows or attempts to do so. The early formulations of the thesis criticized the excessive aggregation of traditional growth models. Their common starting point was the observation that in the course of economic growth in less developed countries certain supply bottlenecks inevitably appear in important sectors. Such sectoral bottlenecks could result simply from the tendency of growth in these countries to be accompanied by a wide variety of imbalances and disproportionalities in their productive structures; it may also be possible to specify one or two sectors, in particular agriculture for domestic food production and the "production of foreign exchange" through exports, as those in which supply is particularly likely to be inadequate in relation to the demands of a growing and industrializing economy.[3] As a result of these supply shortfalls, the affected items either will rise in price or will be rationed – the latter will be the case of foreign exchange when the exchange rate is not devalued. In either case the economy experiences a "supply shock,"[4] which, in the absence of downward flexibility of other prices, is bound to impart an inflationary stimulus to the economy.

It is immediately evident that the structuralist argument has a

---

[3] The earliest analysis of inflation along structuralist lines is by Juan Noyola Vasquez, "El desarrollo económico y la inflación en México y en otros países latinoamericanos," *Investigación Económica* (Mexico), Cuarto Trimestre 1956, pp. 602–48. The best known systematic exposition of the structuralist point of view is in Osvaldo Sunkel, "La inflación chilena – un enfoque heterodoxo," *El Trimestre Econonómico* (Mexico), October-December 1958. For further discussion and references, see Joseph Grunwald, "The Structuralist School on Price Stability and Development: The Chilean Case" in Albert O. Hirschman, ed., *Latin American Issues* (New York: Twentieth Century Fund, 1961), pp. 95–124, and Dudley Seers, "A Theory of Inflation and Growth in Underdeveloped Countries," *Oxford Economic Papers*, June 1962, pp. 173–95. An interpretation of inflation as resulting from supply imbalances that arise in the course of growth was developed independently by the present writer in *The Strategy of Economic Development* (New Haven: Yale University Press, 1958), Chapter 9. The structuralist-monetarist controversy was the principal subject of an international conference, held in Rio de Janeiro in 1963; the papers presented there were published in Werner Baer and Isaac Kerstenetzky, eds., *Inflation and Growth in Latin America* (Homewood, Ill.: Irwin, 1964).

[4] This is of course the currently used term; see, for example, Franco Modigliani, "The Monetarist Controversy or, Should We Forsake Stabilization Policies?" *American Economic Review* 67 (March 1977): 14.

great deal in common with the one that holds—naively yet correctly—that the 1973 rise in petroleum prices, coming on top of
the boom in food and raw materials prices, made a powerful
contribution to the intensification of inflation in the Western
countries during the following years. It took this searing experience to make the structuralist position, which up to then had
dwelt in the "academic underworld" of the economics of development, respectable in the advanced industrial countries. But
the matter was never put that way: those who now spoke of a
"new" kind of inflation appeared to be unaware of the Latin
American pedigree of their theses.[5] Other ideas that have a great
deal in common with the structuralist thesis have recently come
to the fore in the United States. A certain structure of wages and
wage differentials is felt as "natural" or "fair" at any one time,
so it has been argued; as a result, when some wages rise, there
will be considerable pressure to restore the relative position of
other wage earners,[6] with a consequent general increase in inflationary pressures.

It is an underlying assumption of all these writings that any
important change in relative prices or wages is inflationary, because the maintenance of price stability under these conditions
would require a compensatory drop in some prices or wages—
something the monetary managers are unlikely to enforce. Of
course inflation would never occur or accelerate if these managers
always rose to the occasion. But it seems quite unlikely that the
policymakers' determination to undertake anti-inflationary action
is always identical, no matter what its cost may be in terms of
unemployment, widespread bankruptcies, social turmoil and the

---

[5] A particularly striking example is the well-known short article by James Tobin, "There
are Three Types of Inflation: We Have Two," *New York Times*, September 6, 1974,
which identifies one of these three types as being due to "shortages and price increases in important commodities" and then says that it is ill-advised to apply the
classical remedies of "tight monetary policy and fiscal austerity" to this variety. This
was of course exactly the point of the structuralist critique.

[6] This point, which has recently been argued by Michael Piore and others, has long been
familiar in Latin American countries with groups of privileged and powerful workers
(Chilean miners, Venezuelan petroleum workers). For an early similar argument, with
respect to price profiles, see Charles Schultze, *Recent Inflation in the United States* in
Employment Growth and Price Levels, Hearings before the Joint Economic Committee,
86th Congress, 1st session, 25–28 May 1959.

[7] I argued along these lines in *Strategy*, pp. 160, 164. The argument has recently been
formalized in Robert J. Gordon, "The Demand for and Supply of Inflation," *Journal of
Law and Economics* 18 (December 1975): 807–36.

like.[7] Policy makers simply do not have either lexicographical preferences or suicidal instincts of that sort.

Except for this point about the sensitivities of the policymakers, the question could well be asked whether the structuralists have not come forward with simply another *economic* analysis of inflation. To some extent that is undoubtedly true, but as has just begun to appear, social and political implications grow almost naturally out of the structuralist position. For many of the structuralists the cause of inflation is not some, perhaps accidental, lapse of attention or virtue on the part of the monetary authorities or a misguided concentration on the "wrong" variables such as the rate of interest in lieu of the quantity of money, but some fundamental defect of the social and economic structure which presumably can only be remedied through political action. For example, if the culprit is stagnation or slow growth of food production that is in turn due to an antiquated land tenure system, then effective anti-inflationary action requires a change in that system; that is, a change in basic property and power relations. Or, if the origin of inflation lies in the power of OPEC to raise the price of oil, then the best hope for avoiding a repetition of the experience is in fostering the ability of the oil-consuming countries to apply countervailing economic or political power.

The political "vocation" of much of structuralist theorizing becomes more obvious still when the basic reasoning involved is carried one step further. Instead of invoking a *sectoral* lag in output as the original cause of inflation, a *generalized* decline in productivity might be assumed. Provided such a decline is unanticipated it will lead to a rise in prices, in line with the most elementary notions of monetary theory. This sort of *generalized structuralist explanation of inflation* is actually rampant today in the West: some attribute inflation to increasing lack of motivation on the part of the workers, others to sluggishness, amateurism or other forms of "X-inefficiency" on the part of the managers, others yet to excessive state intervention and regulation or to the parasitic growth of the service sector.[8] Whereas the Latin American economists who had first advanced the structuralist thesis

---

[8] See, for example, Amartya Sen, "Rational Fools: A Critique of the Behavioral Foundations of Economic Theory," *Philosophy and Public Affairs* 6 (Summer 1977): 334: "I am persuaded that Britain's present economic difficulties have a great deal to do with work motivation problems . . ."

were in general identified with the Left, it now appears that structuralist theorizing is a game at which all kinds of believers in the need for "fundamental" reform and change can and do play. The more persistent and intractable the inflation, the more likely are all of these parties to come forward with their favorite "deep" diagnosis and cure, as is shown by the earlier Latin American and subsequent Western European experiences [and, most recently, by the emergence of "supply-side economics" in the United States].

Among the more technical economists, structuralist reasoning has often been dismissed as ideological in nature. As has just been pointed out, there can be no doubt that ideologues of every stamp are going to be attracted to the structuralist camp. Since in many of its versions the structuralist thesis asserts that achievement of a certain social or political change is essential for success in the battle against inflation, it does not take a great deal of psychological insight to suspect that the thesis is, in part at least, being propounded ("invented") for the purpose of reaching that conclusion. Those who feel that inflation is due to certain fundamental flaws of the social and political structure are likely to be convinced at the outset that there are such flaws; once so convinced, they will be strongly tempted to link the abolition of a widely acknowledged evil, such as inflation, to the achievement of a program for sociopolitical change that has normally a much narrower appeal.

But the fact that this sort of ideological element is going to be present among the structuralists should not make their endeavor a priori suspect. After all, inflation might well be the symptom of one or several hidden social faults that had better be corrected; and these faults are more likely to be ferreted out by those who are naturally predisposed toward noticing and doing something about them, as a result of their political views and their position in society.

Attention must nevertheless be drawn to other possible and much less auspicious outcomes of the activity of the structuralists. In practice, their advice often amounts to substituting a sociopolitical problem, such as land tenure, excessive state intervention, and so on, for the economic problem of inflation. In order to be able to ameliorate problem A, so they argue, a solution must *first* be found to the more "fundamental" problem B.

Now there are two difficulties with this prescription. In the first place, what if B turns out to be even less manageable or solvable than A? In that case, the structuralists are in effect responsible for an escalation in the difficulty of the tasks that are being proposed to the body politic. Something of this sort appears to have happened in Latin America over the past thirty years.[9] Obviously this process can be counterproductive. Instead of contributing to the vaunted fundamental solution, the structuralist strategy could generate a spreading feeling of inability to cope. We have here a special case of the proposition that a certain type of self-analysis can actually worsen the trouble the patient is in, be it a person or a country.[10]

The second, more practical difficulty with the structuralist strategy of substituting problem B for problem A has been that problem A, inflation, often became so pressing that some relief *had* to be found for it right away regardless of whether the remedy at hand was alleged to deal only with the symptoms of the disease. But the Latin American structuralists were reluctant to forsake their doctrinal purity and condemned as "monetarist futility" the most elementary and obviously needed anti-inflationary measures in situations of hyperinflation. Because of this lack of flexibility, the structuralists rapidly lost influence and not much has been heard from them since the mid-sixties, so that, when the more solid among their ideas might have come into their own in the mid-seventies, they were all but forgotten.

2. The tug-of-war thesis

This thesis is well known today. As was recently pointed out, the explanation of inflation in terms of social conflict between groups, each aspiring to a greater share of the social product, has become the sociologist's platitudinous equivalent of the economist's monotonous stress on the undue expansion of the money supply.[11] In Latin America, in fact, the structuralist thesis

[9] See Chapter 5, this volume.

[10] This idea is implicit in J. H. Elliott, "Self-Perception and Decline in Early Seventeenth-Century Spain," *Past and Present* (February 1977): 41–61.

[11] "A functional view of inflation as a vent for distributional conflict does not tell us very much in itself – it is perhaps the political economy equivalent of the monetarist characterization of inflation as too much money." Fred Hirsch, "The Ideological Underlay of Inflation" in Fred Hirsch and John H. Goldthorpe, eds., *The Political Economy of Inflation* (London: Robertson, 1978).

was developed not only as an antidote to the orthodox approach, but as a counter to, or a relief from, the "sociological" thesis that sought a remedy to inflation in a greater degree of social harmony, to be achieved through "equality of sacrifices," a phrase much used in Chile during the fifties *before* the rise of structuralist thinking (in more contemporary terms, equality of sacrifices would of course be called "incomes policy" or a "new social contract").

As I put it in my study of the Chilean experience:

> It should be noted that the structuralist critique of the traditional "monetary discipline" is quite different from the one that views inflation as the consequence of the struggle of different social groups for ever-larger slices of the social product. Those who hold this "sociological" view concede that inflation would stop if the increase in monetary supply and income could be restrained; but they point out to the innocent foreign adviser that this is a far taller order than he realizes, that inflation results not merely from irresponsible profligacy, from some isolated failure of will power, but represents the difficult-to-change outcome of group attitudes and conflicts. *The structuralist, on the other hand, affirms that, to eliminate inflation, not only attitudes but basic economic relationships must be altered.*[12]

At this point, the distinction between the two views is perhaps no longer as neat as I made it out to be fifteen years ago. In the first place, as I have just shown, the *generalized* structuralist thesis makes inflation depend on aggregate production falling behind expectations and a major reason for such a development would presumably consist in some difficulty to cooperate that is experienced by the various productive agents. To the extent the structuralist thesis considers this difficulty as the basic cause of inflation, it rejoins the sociological explanation except that it adds an intermediate link to the causal chain – the shortfall in production. The sociological thesis sees, plausibly enough, inflation as the *direct* outcome of conflicting demands for higher income shares; for the structuralist it could be an indirect outcome of these or other conflicts.

Secondly, the sociological or tug-of-war thesis has begun to resemble the structuralist position also in its policy conclusions. It has become increasingly clear that terminating or abating the tug of war is more than a matter of "changing attitudes": mere exhortation to all parties to be reasonable has proven to be futile

[12] Albert O. Hirschman, *Journeys Toward Progress: Studies of Economic Policy-Making in Latin America* (New York: Twentieth Century Fund, 1963), p. 215 (emphasis in original).

and conviction has been spreading in the "sociological" camp that the institutional relations among various interest groups and between them and the state must undergo important changes.

Today the main remaining difference between the structuralist and sociological theories consists in the fact that the former, like the economic theories of inflation, makes some basic statements about causal relationships that can conceivably be tested, while the sociological theory, *perhaps just because it is intuitively so persuasive*, has not articulated a "fine" structure of distinctions, propositions, and hypotheses. It is my contention, hopefully to be borne out by the next sections of this paper, that, thanks in large part to Latin American contributions, elements of such a fine structure exist and that the theory is much richer than it is ordinarily given credit for.

II. The redistributive impact of inflation and the tug of war

1. Contributions of economic analysis

Since economists have a considerable advance over other social scientists in thinking about inflation, it is not surprising that they should have supplied the first building blocks for a more serviceable tug-of-war or social-conflict theory of inflation. They have done so by inquiring into the effects of inflation on income distribution, a topic that is almost as old as inflation itself.

At one time, it was taken for granted that inflation would make for greater income inequality. The argument emerged first in the analysis of the business cycle: the expansion of bank credit in the course of the boom places extra purchasing power at the disposal of business which uses it to increase investments beyond the level permitted by voluntary savings. This inflationary financing of the investment boom is equivalent to "forced savings," that is, to an expansion of investment at the expense of consumption (in an assumed full employment situation), with the curtailment of consumption being imposed upon the buying public through price rises.[13]

[13] Gottfried Haberler, *Prosperity and Depression* (Geneva: League of Nations, 1939), pp. 42–44, and F. A Hayek, "A Note on the Development of the Doctrine of Forced Saving," *Quarterly Journal of Economics* 47 (November 1932): 123–33.

This doctrine of forced savings was one of the first to take an interest in the distributional impact of inflation. But the idea that inflation is an engine making the rich richer – and is therefore probably designed to do so – appeared during the first decade of the century, although in a rather different form, in at least one country of the "periphery." Chile had been subject to recurring inflationary pressures since the eighteen seventies, and here a chorus of voices came to accuse the large, "well-heeled and well-mortgaged" landowners of being behind inflation which permitted them to repay their peso loans in depreciated paper money.[14] This thesis is in a sense the exact equivalent, for the countries of the periphery, of the forced-savings doctrine in the central, industrial countries. In both cases inflation is assumed to be a manipulation by and on behalf of the respective ruling groups: industrialists in the center, landowners and primary products exporters in the periphery.

There is of course another possible profiteer from inflation: the state that runs a deficit and finances it by issuing paper money or by borrowing from the Central Bank. During the heyday of the gold standard before World War I governments were under serious disciplines in this regard as their direct or indirect borrowings from the Central Bank were often subject to strict limits. The role of the state as potentially the prime "profiteer" from inflation became clear as these disciplines were lifted during World War I and its aftermath. The state can combine in its favor the two types of income shifts that have just been noted: it can extract "forced savings" for its own investment or other spending projects and it also gains in its capacity as a large-scale debtor and distributor of fixed incomes (pensions, etc.). While these gains depend largely on inflation being unanticipated, the state gains even when inflation is fully anticipated because of the need of firms and households to increase their cash balances: this need is supplied by the state which thereby obtains "free" command over real resources.[15]

---

[14] Propounded by a number of Chilean writers early in the century, the thesis was given wide circulation and the authority of "developed-country" economic thought by Frank W. Fetter in his monograph *Monetary Inflation in Chile* (Princeton: Princeton University Press, 1931). For a critical evaluation of what I called the "Fetter Doctrine" see *Journeys*, pp. 164–75.

[15] David Laidler and Michael Parkin, "Inflation: A Survey," *Economic Journal* 85 (December 1975): 791–3.

In many instances of state "profiteering" from inflation the state is of course only a "conduit": the power of the state is used for the purpose of shunting the resources acquired through inflationary finance in this or that direction. Here the possibility arises for previously neglected groups to become the beneficiaries: for example, the state can decide on new transfer payments, such as social security benefits, and in this manner groups that are unable to play the inflationary game unaided can be included. Eventually such groups can become full participants in the game, either by learning how to lean on the state or because they develop the capacity for independent action, as through successful demands for higher wages and salaries, or through a combination of these two modes. Lately, in fact, the early analyses of inflation as a mechanism necessarily leading to a more regressive distribution of income have given place to the conviction that inflation is invariably the outcome of attempts on the part of the lower-income groups – frequently aided by a reformist or "populist" state – to increase their share in the national product through higher wages, increased social security benefits and other transfer payments. The Argentine experience during the first Perón regime (1946–55) is well known as an early example of this sort of attempted redistribution via inflation.

How to reap an initial redistributive advantage from inflation is thus something that one social group after another has learned until all major groups of society are expert at it. This is indeed the very meaning of the tug-of-war metaphor. But once this multilateral learning process is more or less completed and the tug of war is therefore on in earnest, it is no longer sufficient to understand how any one group can gain an *initial* advantage or suffer an *initial* setback. In order to grasp the nature and dynamics of the tug of war one must inquire into the pattern of countermoves that is likely to be unleashed by the initial move.

To this topic economic analysis and particularly the monetarist school have contributed the idea that, no matter to which group the initial advantage has accrued, it is not likely to stick. This is of course an application of the equilibrium concept: inflation is viewed as a disturbance which cannot lastingly affect the distribution of income in society, this distribution being due to the play of "natural forces." In the early thirties and before, this thesis was asserted with respect to "forced savings" and to "profit inflation";[16] lately it has been put forward primarily to criticize the idea that unemployment can be reduced through expansionary monetary or fiscal policies at the limited cost of some increase in inflation. If this increase is unanticipated, so the modern monetarist thesis goes,[17] then various categories of income receivers will be disagreeably surprised and their reactions, in combination with official policies, will make either for ever more rapid inflation or for a return to the starting point, i.e. to the rate of unemployment that policymakers were originally intent on bringing down. The aim of this train of reasoning was to demonstrate that policies purporting to reduce unemployment through expansionary economic policy are self-defeating; for the purposes of this demonstration the monetarists were forced to think beyond the initial redistributive impact of inflation, and that meant a step forward in the understanding of the tug of war. Nevertheless their analyses of the sequential moves remain very general – probably for the reason that they were much less interested in the process than in the outcome – the return to the starting point – with its chastening morale for "interventionist" policymakers.

2. Intersectoral shifts: A Latin American emphasis

At this point, Latin American experience and analysis can be called upon to enrich the picture. First of all, the experience of Latin America has made for a more diversified group of actors than has generally been admitted to the scenarios of First World economists. The latter have written primarily in terms of the distribution of income between profits and wages, with the state

[16] See, for example, F. A. Hayek, *Prices and Production* (London: Routledge, 1931).

[17] I call it "modern monetarist" to distinguish it from the monetarist theory that used to be contrasted with the structuralist point of view and which simply insisted that in accounting for inflation it is not necessary to look beyond monetary phenomena.

The standard references for the modern monetarist thesis, with its emphasis on anticipated versus unanticipated inflation, are Edmund S. Phelps, "Phillips Curves, Expectations of Inflation and Optimal Unemployment over Time," *Economica* 34 (1967): 254–81 and Milton Friedman, "The Role of Monetary Policy," *American Economic Review* 58 (March 1968): 1–17. Here again, the long experience of inflation in Latin America has led observers to anticipate the essentials of a thesis that was later celebrated as an original and capital insight when it was formulated by "advanced-country" economists looking at their own economy. I am referring to the remarkable paper by W. Arthur Lewis, "Closing Remarks" (in W. Baer and I. Kerstenetzky, eds., *Inflation and Growth in Latin America*, pp. 21–33), where the expectation of inflation is given a key role in the mechanism of continuing inflation.

being a third potential beneficiary. Discussion of the modern Latin American inflations, that is, those that have taken place since World War II, had to go beyond this limited framework as it became obvious that inflation often favored one group of property holders or entrepreneurs at the expense of another. For example, when, as frequently happened, inflation is combined with a fixed exchange rate and hence necessarily with import controls (otherwise mounting imports would cause intolerable balance-of-payments deficits), exporters experience a decline in their real incomes whereas those who are entitled by the control authorities to import at the overvalued exchange rate make an equivalent gain. As Latin America's exports consisted, until the mid-sixties at least, largely of primary products whereas imports were heavily weighted with capital goods and intermediate inputs for the expanding industrial establishment, inflation, no matter how it got started, tended here systematically to favor the new industries at the expense of the primary producers.

That inflation in an open economy could have profound effects on the intersectoral income distribution no less than on the division of income between wages and profits has been noted first by Brazilian economists.[18] The reason is probably that in Brazil the shift, toward the import-substituting industries and away from coffee growers and other primary producers, was substantial and particularly protracted; effective countermoves on the part or on behalf of the coffee growers were slow in coming, one reason being that in the short run the supply of coffee does not respond much to price changes: the trees are in place and bear beans which it remains profitable to harvest even when prices drop substantially. Supply reactions are considerably stronger and faster in the case of annual crops and also of cattle, especially when a switch to other land uses is possible. The speed with which the initial redistributive impact of inflation is counteracted by a group that is being squeezed depends

[18] Alexandre Kafka, "The Theoretical Interpretation of Latin American Economic Development," in H. S. Ellis, ed., *Economic Development in Latin America* (New York: St. Martin's Press, 1961), p. 21; and Celso Furtado, "Industrialization and Inflation," *International Economic Papers* 12 (1967): 101–19. Subsequently, Mamalakis attempted to show that "sectoral clashes" provide the clue to the understanding of all of Latin American history and society. See Markos Mamalakis, "The Theory of the Sectoral Clashes" and "The Theory of Sectoral Clashes and Coalitions Revisited," *Latin American Research Review* 4 (Fall 1969): 9–46, and 6, (Fall 1971): 89–126.

of course on the political and economic leverage of that group; this leverage depends, at least in part, on the economic damage the group can inflict on the economy by withholding its contribution; and the ability to inflict damage and to withhold depends in turn on the physical and economic characteristics of the product line in which the group has specialized.[19]

While intersectoral income shifts provoked by inflation have occasionally played a constructive role in making extra resources available to some sector with a key role in development, they have at other times been quite erratic and needlessly disruptive. Recognition of this fact lies behind the indexation experiments, particularly in the case of countries with persistent two-digit inflations, such as Brazil. Indexation (that is, adjusting salaries, rents, interest payments, etc., in line with price changes, at regular, at least yearly intervals) has often been presented as part of the anti-inflationary package that was introduced in that country after the military took over in 1964. Actually, the device was anti-inflationary primarily to the extent that it was grossly incomplete as it did not interfere with the considerable compression of real wages that occurred in the first years of the military regime. The real function of indexation was to avoid some of the more damaging intersectoral repercussions of the substantial inflation that continued to take place after 1964 (it never fell below 15%). In this respect, indexation has been fairly effective: it safeguarded the real income of exporters (through frequent mini-devaluations of the exchange rate), the assets of creditors and savers (through indexing of interest rates on loans and savings deposits), and the revenues of the state (through indexing of back taxes). But the system was always a highly administered one; it could be and, as time went on, it was used to award special favors to economic activities newly considered essential, by exempting them from the indexing mechanism. For example, in 1975 it was decided that medium- and long-term loans to capital goods industries from the official development bank (BNDE) would carry a preferential rate of interest with a ceiling of 20%, which was considerably below the actual rate of inflation (which at that time rose back to 40–50% where it has stayed since). Just as the earlier combination of inflation and overvaluation of the currency, such officially arranged

[19] For further observations along these lines, see *Bias for Hope*, pp. 11–12, and Chapter 4, this volume.

loopholes in the system of indexation had once again the dual effect of shifting resources toward a favored sector and of doing so in an inflationary manner.[20]

A political point follows. Considerable puzzlement is often expressed over the fact that in a number of countries like Brazil where authoritarian regimes hold sway and where wages are rigidly controlled, inflation remains a considerable problem. One reason is precisely that the tug of war can take place not just between profits and wages, but, for example, between profits of one business group and profits of another. In authoritarian Brazil since 1964 the opening, on a large scale, of consumer credit facilities for the purchasers of durables made possible the sustained boom of the automobile and appliance industries in the second half of the sixties and early seventies, somewhat at the expense of both the traditional consumer goods industries and the industries producing basic inputs and capital goods; then, during the new, more difficult phase since 1974, machinery and intermediate goods industries are in turn being showered with incentives and credit facilities.[21] As in the case of the earlier shift of resources from primary producers to industrial entrepreneurs, such changes in priorities *within* the industrial sector are politically easier to accomplish through an inflationary, if selective, credit expansion than through noninflationary schemes such as the coupling of subsidies with taxes or of credit expansion in one direction with credit restriction in another.

I do not wish to intimate that the choice of an inflationary rather than noninflationary method of shunting resources to certain sectors was always a conscious decision of the policymakers. On the contrary, it is well known that the combination of inflation with overvaluation of the currency as a means of diverting income from the primary exporters to the import-

---

[20] For evaluations of the indexation experience, see Werner Baer and Paul Beckerman, "Indexing in Brazil," *World Development* 2 (October–December 1974): 35–47; Albert Fishlow, "Indexing Brazilian Style: Inflation Without Tears?" *Brookings Papers on Economic Activity* 1(1974): 261–82; and the papers on *Indexation, the Brazilian Experience* in *Explorations in Economic Research* (NBER) 4 (Winter 1977). The information about the officially arranged loopholes in the indexing system was made available in 1976 to the author during a trip to Brazil.

[21] José Serra, "Three Mistaken Theses Regarding the Connection between Industrialization and Authoritarian Regimes" in David Collier, ed., *The New Authoritarianism in Latin America* (Princeton: Princeton University Press, 1979), pp. 129–45.

substituting industrialists was stumbled on by the policymakers and grew out of arrangements that originally had very different purposes.[22] Nevertheless, if policymakers choose time and again to make resource reallocation decisions in such a way as to fuel the inflation even though other methods are available, this tells us something about the nature of the relations between the state and various groups of producers. I shall come back to this point.

3. Combining intersectoral and interclass shifts: political economy cycles in Argentina and New York City

The importance of intersectoral income shifts and conflicts in the course of Latin American inflations makes one suspect that not enough attention has been paid to these matters in the analysis of inflation in the advanced industrial countries.[23] Latin American inflations, on the other hand, have by no means been neutral with respect to the wage-profit balance. Everywhere wage and salary earners have been very much affected by the inflationary process. But since their role comes on top of the intersectoral conflicts there immediately arises the possibility of a three- or multi-cornered act, in lieu of the simple wage-profit scenario of traditional economic analysis. And along with this increase in the number of actors comes the possibility of shifting alliances providing a key to the changing dynamics of the inflation.

Interesting attempts have recently been made to account for the course of Argentina's inflation and recurrent stop-go cycles in this manner.[24] The three principal groups involved are here the cattle breeders and cereal growers of the Pampas, the industrial bourgeoisie, and the urban masses. The pivotal group is the industrial bourgeoisie: it tends to make common cause with the urban masses in a recession when both groups can agree on a

[22] See Celso Furtado, "Industrialization and Inflation."

[23] An interesting attempt to delineate types of coalitions that are associated with different types of inflation is made by Charles S. Maier in "The Politics of Inflation in the Twentieth Century" in John H. Goldthorpe and Fred Hirsch, eds., *The Political Economy of Inflation* (London: Robertson, 1978), pp. 37–72; but his analysis is still primarily in vertical class terms even though he allows for the distinct existence and separate interests of intermediate groups, such as white-collar workers.

[24] Adolfo Canitrot, "La experiencia populista de redistribución de ingresos," *Desarrollo Económico* 15 (October-December 1975): 331–51, and Guillermo O'Donnell, "Estado y alianzas en la Argentina, 1956–1976," *Desarrollo Económico* 16 (January–March 1977): 523–54. O'Donnell makes a further distinction between the small national bourgeoisie and the larger, more cosmopolitan- and multinational-oriented industrialists.

strongly expansionary economic policy and on holding down the price of Argentina's principal export product, meat, which also happens to be its principal wage good. But exports tend to decline under those circumstances and to do so fairly rapidly both because the workers, with their increasing incomes, literally eat up the country's exports and because the cattle breeders, unlike Brazil's coffee planters, can react to a price squeeze by liquidating their herds. As a result the industrialists soon experience supply difficulties for their imported inputs and capital goods. With meat prices, among others, starting to rise, the workers make demands for higher wages; soon the industrialists find their allies too demanding. At this point they join the agricultural elites and this new coalition can now agree on holding real wages down and on raising prices for agricultural output. Policies directed to this end, and to fight inflation in general, cause a recession which eventually leads to a new switch by the industrial bourgeoisie so that the play starts over again. The different phases of the play are marked by different kinds of political regimes: during the expansive, inflationary phase an uneasy coalition is maintained between populist forces and certain sectors of the business community; the military take over when these sectors become concerned about excessive inflation and ally themselves with the land- and cattle owners.

Whereas this tripartite model is still too synthetic to be totally convincing, it does shed new light on the social background to Argentina's inflation and stop-go cycles. It invites further refinement and comparison with similar experiences elsewhere.

One such experience is New York's fiscal crisis of the seventies.[25] Here the "populist" administration of Mayor Lindsay was able, in the mid-sixties, to put together a strange coalition of liberal reformers, largely from the upper middle class, black (and other minority) civil rights movements, and – large commercial banks who "were quite happy to endorse deficit financing because bond and note issues provided them with healthy commissions and good investment opportunities."[26] Arrayed against Lindsay were civil service unions and strong elements of the middle and lower middle class. Given the institutional frame-

[25] Martin Shefter, "New York City's Fiscal Crisis: The Politics of Inflation and Retrenchment," *The Public Interest* (Summer 1977): 98–127.
[26] *Ibid.*, p. 109.

work, the equivalent of inflation was here spiraling indebtedness:
Lindsay was politically too weak to raise taxes sufficiently or to
limit expansion of expenditures to his preferred projects.[27] But
like accelerating inflation, so does increasing indebtedness cause
worry to some partners of the ruling coalition. Eventually, under
the Beame Administration, the banks switched sides and support
from the upper middle class weakened; joining the middle and
lower middle class the banking and business interests now enforced a strict austerity regime whose principal victims were the
black and Hispanic communities. While the city was spared a
military coup, it did suffer a substantial loss of fiscal autonomy in
the wake of its near default.[28]

With their parallels – as well as differences – the Argentine and
New York stories are of much interest. By drawing on intersectoral cleavages, on class conflicts and on the dynamics of inflation itself, they succeed in explaining the various phases of the
inflationary policy cycle and the transition from one to another
as old alliances disintegrate and new ones are being formed. In
this manner, they manage to breathe a good deal of life into the
tug-of-war metaphor.[29]

III. The sociopolitical interpretation of
inflationary group behavior

In the course of the preceding pages some forms of inflationary
group behavior have already come into view; but they remain to
be better understood. Inflation often starts or intensifies, so it
seems, when a social group holds enough power or influence to
command additional wealth and income for itself (or to escape
participation in some loss that is suffered by the economy), *but
not enough* to do so in a permanent way through a definitive

---

[27] This phenomenon will be discussed further on as the "complementarity effect" of
public spending or investment.
[28] Shefter distinguishes between externally and internally imposed disciplines, "New
York City's Fiscal Crisis," pp. 99–101, 124.
[29] A more general appraoch to the understanding of multi-cornered inflationary man-
euvering proceeds from the simple observation that individuals and groups operate in
several markets: most are price takers in some markets, but have or can acquire price-
making powers in others. An attempt to trace through the consequences of this situation for the economic and political dynamics of inflation is made in Harvey Leibenstein, "The Inflation Process: A Microbehavioral Approach," *American Economic Review*
71 (May 1981).

transfer. Inflation is a means of effectuating a temporary transfer. Partial, complete, or even overcomplete cancellation of that transfer can take place, first of all, through subsequent turns in the inflationary spiral, specially when other groups use their retaliatory power and do some grabbing (or escaping) of their own. The temporarily gained advantage can also evaporate and turn into a setback in the course of a stabilization, retrenchment, and austerity program that may follow a bout of inflation.

Today inflation is ubiquitous, has gone on for a long time and therefore seems familiar and almost "normal." Nevertheless, the just noted characteristics mark it as a rather unusual social game. To appreciate this fact it suffices to take a comparative look at some of the better known social and political movements of the last hundred years or so. Here there was no expectation on the part of the actors that gains, once achieved, would have to be given up again in short order. Take the battles for universal suffrage, for women's vote, for the right of workers to strike or to join a union, for the 48- or 40-hour week or for paid vacations; or take, on the other hand, business demands for subsidies or tariff protection: it was a premise of all of these actions that the sought after gains would "stick" – and, in the large majority of cases, they did and proved irreversible, in spite of frequently very strong initial resistance. In fact, the mobilization of social energy needed to secure these gains would probably have been impossible if there had been any expectation that the gains would be reversible – on the contrary, the expectations at the outset were ordinarily for gains much *greater* than those that were eventually secured.

This historical reminder serves to demonstrate that inflation, familiar as it is, does hold a genuine puzzle: why would any social group choose an inflationary strategy of income augmentation, that is, a strategy that brings a strictly temporary improvement, but whose outcome is uncertain and may land it in a worse position? A simple reason is, first of all, that the group in question may be so naive as not to realize that other groups can retaliate. Secondly and more interestingly, the group may expect its initial gain to be reduced and perhaps even more than annihilated by subsequent inflation as well as by countermoves of others, but may nevertheless decide that it is necessary or worthwhile to engage in the action. I shall deal with these two situations in turn.

1. Naive inflationary behavior and populism

The first explanation is likely to apply primarily where serious inflation has not been experienced for some time. The belief that the economy is "elastic" enough to afford something to one group without taking away from others is periodically reborn, the more so as it is occasionally correct – that is, in Keynesian situations when there is both unemployment and unused capacity as a result of recession. "Populist" policies – that is, policies that give something to popular groups without directly taking away from others – can be relatively successful in such a situation, but their very success is apt to blind policymakers to the fact that it can only be of limited duration. The sequence from initial "elasticity" and smooth redistributive success to increasing problems and eventual disaster, in part because of overconfidence born from the initial success, was characteristic of Argentine economic policies under the first Perón regime and of Chilean policies under Allende.[30]

The naive incapacity to visualize the power of other groups to retaliate, through demands or actions of their own, against an initial inflationary foray affects not only social groups in relation to each other. It often happens *within* the public sector as the government sponsors one particular program without foreseeing that other agencies will react to that program by pushing through their own demands. A government that decides to undertake a major effort in one particular sector or region will frequently find that, as a result of these highly visible favors, demands from other sectors or regions become activated and have to be granted at least in part for the purpose of putting together the political coalition that will permit the original plan to go forward. I have noted this "complementarity effect of public investment" in Brazil while studying the history of official development moves in the country's underdeveloped Northeast: for example, when Kubitschek gave top priority to the building of Brasília, the new capital, he found that to secure the necessary political support for this venture he had to promise funds for wholly unrelated projects in the Northeast.[31] Every dollar that a government intends to spend on

[30] For an analysis of the Chilean experience under Allende, see José Serra, "Economic Policy and Structural Change in Chile, 1970–73," doctoral dissertation, Cornell University, 1976, Chapters 8 and 9.

[31] *Journeys*, pp. 36, 86.

a project of its own choice is thus likely to lead, via a *political* complementarity or multiplier, to some additional, originally *unintended* public spending. The size of the complementarity effect depends both on the enterprisingness of the government and on its ability to push through its own priorities without having to make too many promises or compromises in other directions – that is, on its political strength vis à vis claimants for public funds. A government that is both enterprising and politically weak is most likely to be overwhelmed by the unintended inflationary consequences of its development moves – not too surprising a conclusion and one that points, once again, in the direction of "populist" governments.

2. Gratification of pseudo-hostility and of pseudo-friendliness among social groups

Once inflation has become a fixture in the economic landscape, most groups will be aware that demands on their part for higher incomes will give rise to countermoves that will cancel much of those gains, with some probability even that one may end up in a worse position than the initial one. Under such (non-naive) circumstances, the continuation of inflationary group behavior becomes more difficult to explain.

Predominant opinion nevertheless denies that there is much of a problem here. This is because it is alleged that, once inflation is under way and rolling, an individual group with some power over prices or wages has no choice but to behave in such a way as to further contribute to the inflationary spiral. In fact, each group that does so can justifiably claim that it is just engaging in defensive moves "in view of what inflation is doing to us." Essentially this thesis accounts for inflationary behavior in terms of a prisoners' dilemma situation: in the absence of some sort of deus or social contract ex machina that could produce a cooperative solution, an ongoing inflation condemns all social groups to behave in the well-known noncooperative manner that perpetuates the inflation.

While this analysis obviously catches a part of reality, its total denial of responsibility or of freedom of action on the part of admittedly powerful social groups seems to me unconvincing. It takes protestations of innocence and of powerlessness on the part of these groups far too much at face value. To raise some doubt that the prisoners' dilemma model can explain adequately what happens in an inflation one might perhaps point out that the prisoner in solitary confinement of the model is an extraordinarily inapt metaphor for such inflationary actors as giant corporations, producers' associations, and powerful trade unions.

Assuming, therefore, that such groups are not just acting under duress, but engage, to some extent at least, in inflationary behavior because that is what they have decided to do even though they know all about inflation, the question remains: Why would they do it?

To begin with, the situation can be explored through a rational action model of individual or group behavior, along standard lines. Suppose a group attempts to estimate the impact of an inflationary action or demand on its eventual position. This involves estimating a probability distribution with a mean or expected value and a variance. For a group to engage in any action at all the expected value must be positive—otherwise it would not be worthwhile for it to shoulder the risk that is expressed through the variance. With any given positive expected value the willingness to engage in inflationary action will depend on the degree to which the group is risk-averse. It will also depend on the group's time preference and horizon. The bigger its preference for present over future income, the more will a group be prone to engage in inflationary actions. This is so because the group is assumed to be able to obtain immediately an increase in its income through its actions or demands, an increase that is then whittled down as a result of the inflationary consequences of that increase and of the countermoves of others. Inflationary group behavior that is aware of these repercussions thus requires that willingness to take risks be combined with a short time horizon, that is, with a strong preference for present over future income. Now this combination of attitudes is not easy to find among the social groups of the real world: low-income people are usually risk-averse, while perhaps having a short time horizon; middle- and upper-class people, on the other hand, may be willing to take risks but their time horizon tends to be long. It is therefore troublesome to account along "rational action" lines for non-naive inflationary group behavior, that is, after it has become clear to everyone concerned that such behavior will only result in temporary advantages and may carry a long-term penalty.

One interesting explanation was suggested some years ago by a Brazilian economist.[32] It is essentially an application of the Duesenberry axiom that people will always strain to get back to the highest income they have ever experienced.[33] It is one of the characteristics of inflation (without instantaneous indexation) that different groups experience their respective highest levels of income at different points in time. To simplify, if there are just two groups, the highest level for group A will coincide with the lowest level for group B, and vice versa. This seesaw relationship is inevitable: because of resource limitations it would be impossible for both A and B to reach their respective peak income at the same point in time; they can do so only alternatingly, each group reaching its peak at the expense of the other. Attempts to recapture the peaks on the part of either or both groups must lead therefore to continuing inflation.

Elaborating on this point it is also clear that only inflation permits each group to reach (in rotation) higher real income levels, even though temporarily, than it could achieve with a stable price-wage structure. Within limits people may actually prefer an income that fluctuates around an average to a stable income that would be equal to that average, provided they do not suffer intolerable hardship when their income cycle hits its low point. A reason for such preference could precisely be the achievement, be it but temporarily, of an otherwise unattainable income level, and perhaps the taste for hope-sustaining movement and variety in general.[34] To the extent that such group preferences exist, their satisfaction via inflation would constitute a latent benefit of inflation.

Speaking of such latent benefits, it is possible to suggest a more weighty explanation for inflationary group behavior and its persistence in a number of sociopolitical settings: such behavior could come to be engaged in less for its normally expected material results – additional real income – than because it is enjoyed

---

[32] Mario Henrique Simonsen, "Brazilian Inflation" in Committee for Economic Development, *Economic Development Issues: Latin America* (New York: Frederick A. Praeger, 1967), pp. 272–3.

[33] J. S. Duesenberry, *Income, Saving, and the Theory of Consumer Behavior* (Cambridge, Mass.: Harvard University Press, 1949), p. 89.

[34] See Tibor Scitovsky, *The Joyless Economy* (New York: Oxford University Press, 1976).

for its own sake, in a situation of high social tension and group antagonism. This means inverting the usual means-end relationship: the gratification of intergroup hostility that is obtained by the achievement of a highly inflationary price or wage rise can be the real benefit, to the point where it would not matter if inflation eroded, totally and in short order, the gains achieved. As I put it in my account of the Chilean inflation:

> . . . various groups maintain and prize an attitude and phraseology of unbending opposition and hostility: they coexist, but are most anxious to avoid *overt agreement* and compromise. . . . The Chilean situation appears to be weighted more heavily with the avoidance of agreement, with the maintenance of a militant stance on the part of all contending groups. In a sense this stance is the desired benefit and inflation is its cost.[35]

Yet, as I also pointed out, the acting out of social conflict that takes place through inflationary group behavior carries with it a certain amount of playacting. Each group knows that the others have the means to retaliate, no decisive victory is ever scored, and the division of the social product does effectively take place in the midst of what only *looks* like irreconcilable conflict over how it should be shared. The extent to which there is playacting can be made clear by comparison with other conflict situations. Ordinarily when there is lack of agreement over the division, say, of some treasure, booty, or spoils, the disputants either fight it out or come to an agreement *before* the actual division takes place. With inflation, the disputants somehow manage to have both fight and division at the same time. Looked at in this light, the fight loses some of its reality. Inflation appears now as a device that permits a society to have its cake and eat it, in the sense of having a great deal of social conflict while going about its business of generating and distributing the social product.

The matter can be put another way. In a society that is divided into groups that have roughly equal power to affect prices and wages, the distribution of income which prevails when inflation is "on" could quite conceivably be similar to that which is experienced when there is price stability. What, then, is the actual difference between these two situations? Not much, except that, with inflation, each group is able to engage in conflictive behavior and to demonstrate its power and its antagonism to other

[35] *Journeys*, pp. 208–9.

groups. From this point it is not far to the conclusion that such demonstration is an important function of inflation, and perhaps its real motive.

Inflation then is a remarkable invention that permits a society to exist in a situation that is intermediate between the extremes of social harmony and civil war. Hence the dual performance of inflation in the arena of politics. Depending on the circumstances, it can act either as a substitute for civil war or as a preface to much more serious social and political turmoil. It is well known of course that inflation has served as a school for social conflict: the social shadowboxing that is its earmark can turn readily enough into the real match. But at times, the deflecting of intergroup hostility into the making of inflationary demands has helped gain time for reducing tensions that, in the absence of the inflationary outlet, would have become right away much more explosive. As a commentator on the post-Franco inflation in Spain put it recently:

> To explain the current inflation by appealing to economic factors is . . . sterile. Inflation must be understood as an expression of the open or muted conflicts between various social classes and economic groups. . . . [T]he structure of the Spanish economy, as inherited from the past, fosters at present a propensity to social conflict which is not easily assimilated. . . . The intention to dominate the inflationary process by imposing a drastically restrictive monetary policy would mean . . . to transfer the underlying social conflict to other areas of political and social life where conflict would take a more radical form. The propensity to conflict receives after all a transitory relief through the inflation. This relief cannot be permanent because of the collateral problems which inflation generates, but in a moment of political transition and of change in the relative positions of the various social forces, inflation is the least harsh form which this struggle can take; it involves the most indirect confrontation available to each social group for the defense of its interests.[36]

This quote is of particular interest as inflation is widely believed to pave the way for the establishment of authoritarian and repressive regimes. While several instances of this sequence can of course be cited, especially when hyperinflation is involved,[37] inflation can apparently also ease the difficult transition from authoritarianism to polyarchy. Like emigration or the "open frontier," inflation can act as a safety valve for accumulated so-

---

[36] "Comentario sobre la situación económica al comenzar el segundo semestre," *Moneda y Crédito*, Madrid, June 1977, unsigned, p. 110.

[37] See also pp. 203–4, this volume.

cial and political tensions. But *unlike* these social mechanisms it is unreliable in this role and can change character in the middle of the play.

Moreover, the situation of intergroup conflict, with everyone insisting on a rigid, compromise-excluding posture, does not exhaust the sociopolitical environments in which inflation thrives. In fact, the opposite social configuration, one that is characterized by a great deal of friendliness among different groups and particularly between them and the state, provides an equally favorable breeding ground. Evidently inflation can be the outcome of a social process in which the state defers readily to all the successive demands that are made upon it by one group or one government department after another. Inflation has here the function of denying part of what the state, in its weakness and excessive friendliness, has granted. To the extent that the process is understood one might say that the state hands over to inflation the disagreeable job of saying no.

This additional interpretation explains why inflation has led a vigorous existence in several repressive, authoritarian states of Latin America that have eliminated independent trade union activity: this sort of state is precisely premised on professions of great friendliness with business groups which are often showered with incentives and credit facilities; moreover, such a state is far from immune to pressures emanating from its own subdivisions: with powerful and power-hungry generals heading the spending ministries, the allocation of public funds can be less subject to central control than under civilian governments.

One objection may be raised against this additional interpretation coming on top of the previous one: As in the case of the Frenchman who drinks wine with only two kinds of meals, namely (1) when the first dish is pâté, and (2) when it is not, so inflation seems to be fated to be the invariable result no matter whether hostility or friendliness pervade society and its groups. In defense of what has been said, it may however be pointed out that the attitudes which were shown to be conducive to inflation were not just *any* kind of hostility and friendliness. Rather, they had one specialized element in common, that is, a certain amount of playacting. That there is an element of playacting in the kind of intergroup hostility that leads to inflation has already been demonstrated and it is clear that the same holds for exaggerated or pseudo-friendliness – the inability to say no to any new group demand. Specially when a country has already become closely acquainted with inflation, easy acquiescence to inflationary demands rather reminds one of Charles Addams's "friendly" truckdriver on a curvy mountain road, who waves on the car that is trying to pass him when there is an oncoming truck in sight that will surely "get" the passing car. Friendliness is here not so friendly after all, just as successive rounds of highly inflationary wage and price increases that stem from intergroup hostility are largely sham battles and are intimately known as such to the participants. The two seemingly opposite types of inflationary behavior thus merge into one: the strenuous avoidance of cooperative encounter and agreement on the part of social groups.

IV. Some social and political effects of inflation

In the preceding pages an attempt has been made to show how inflation originates and evolves as a result of certain social and political realities: the attitudes of groups, their relations to each other, their power and propensity to initiate inflationary action and to retaliate against it. To contribute to an understanding of the distinctive sociopolitical environment in which inflation thrives is probably the most important task at the present time. But some attention should be paid to the other side of the picture, namely to the *effects* of inflation on social and political developments. Inflation is a social and political phenomenon no less for its outcome than for its causes. This is a vast topic, of course, and I shall limit myself to a few selected themes.

1. The political disasters of hyperinflation

One sequence from inflation to politics is well known and has indeed already been touched upon: the possibility that accelerating inflation contributes to political crisis and regime breakdown. This particular and particularly striking sequence has in fact monopolized our attention ever since Keynes erroneously reported Lenin to have said that there is no surer way to revolutionize a society than to "debauch its currency."[38] Even though ten years elapsed between the German hyperinflation of 1923 and the seizure of power by Hitler, it is often suggested that the two events are causally related. Looking at more recent regime break-downs or important political changes that were preceded by rapidly accelerating inflations, such as Brazil (1964), Ghana (1966), Indonesia (1966), Chile (1973), and Argentina (1975), it would be more correct to consider inflation as one symptom among many of the disintegration of faltering regimes than as the principal factor to be held responsible for their downfall. Nevertheless, in all these cases the enervating reality of hyperinflation certainly helped to signal regime crisis to a mass public.

When accelerating inflation is followed by sharp political change the new government will ordinarily proclaim and try to maintain a strong anti-inflationary stand. While success in actually bringing inflation under control has varied considerably, one of the principal effects of inflation, and particularly of hyperinflation, is to bring to power governments which have a commitment to control inflation and will be judged accordingly, at least for a while and until some other evil or problem such as unemployment or stagnation takes the center of the stage. In recent decades, strongly inflationary policies have been characteristic of populist regimes, and anti-inflationary programs have subsequently often been carried on under the aegis of right-wing, business-oriented governments. In the great majority of cases hyperinflation has not led to revolution, but to military intervention, repression, and attempted suppression of trade union activity.[39] In fact, the one country in Latin America that experienced an anticapitalist revolution, Cuba, enjoyed near-perfect monetary stability for many years prior to that event.

2. Some political uses of moderate inflation

As I said before, the spectacular and generally dismal macropolitics of hyperinflation have perhaps unduly occupied our atten-

[38] In *The Economic Consequences of the Peace Treaty*. For a detailed account and a convincing demonstration that Lenin never said anything of the sort, see Frank Whitson Fetter, "Lenin, Keynes and Inflation," *Economica* 44 (February 1977): 77–80.

[39] Thomas E. Skidmore, "The Politics of Economic Stabilization in Postwar Latin America" in James Malloy, ed., *Authoritarianism and Corporatism in Latin America* (Pittsburgh: University of Pittsburgh Press, 1976), pp. 149–90.

tion. Moderate inflationary experiences have been much more prevalent, yet the study of their political effects has been largely neglected. This may in part be due to the blinkers we have come to wear as a result of our preoccupation with hyperinflation: We *know* that inflation is bad and has disastrous consequences and therefore are unable to detect situations in which the effects of inflation tend not to be disastrous, and perhaps even, here and there, benign.

At this point it is useful to return briefly to the reasoning of the structuralists. It will be recalled that they saw inflation as the consequence of some deep-seated faults in a country's socioeconomic structure. They use the "evidence" of inflation for the purpose of calling attention to these faults and of enlarging public support for measures intended to deal with them. To the extent that this structuralist strategy would work, inflation could be credited with inducing action on a country's more hidden, but perhaps also more fundamental ills.

Now it must be said right away that inflation has hardly anywhere played that grandly constructive a role. But if it is reformulated in a more modest way, something like the sequence that has just been pointed out can be encountered here and there in the real world.

Many years ago I asserted that moderate inflation may be helpful to a government and particularly to a finance minister who is trying to resist political pressures toward more spending.[40] Inflation is a telling proof that spending is already taking place at an excessive rate. To have a moderate inflation is thus similar to the tactic French ministers of finance used to follow when they hid away in some hard-to-identify account any extra cash they happened to have on hand – they knew that otherwise it would be impossible not to have it spent. It used to be said that one of the principal purposes of having a development plan for public investments is for a government to be able to restrain extravagant sectional demands. A moderate inflation can have the same effect, probably more persuasively. The matter helps explain the strange incapacity to reduce inflation to zero of the authoritarian, stability-oriented governments that have come to power in various Latin American countries in the wake of hyperinflation. The

---

[40] In "Economic Policy in Underdeveloped Countries" (1957), reprinted as Chapter 12 in *A Bias for Hope*.

fact is that even in the new political environment there is need to keep up defenses against new highly inflationary projects and demands. And one such defense is afforded by some residual inflation.

The point can be extended. Inflation supplies not only evidence that spending must be controlled; when expenditures consistently outrun revenue the resulting inflation may have the effect of convincing public opinion and government that taxes must be raised to finance public investment. It is well known that in the advanced industrial countries income taxation, and big spurts in taxation generally, have become possible only under the impact of major emergency and crisis, mostly in wartime. In a number of developing countries inflation has acted as an equivalent of war in setting the stage for more forceful taxation. A recent example is the 1974 tax reform in Colombia whose centerpiece was the levying of a tax on the "presumed" income from all real assets. This concept, which had been proposed many times in the past to deal with the problem of idle land,[41] was this time adopted only as a result of a peculiar combination of circumstances: one of these was the fact that the newly elected López Michelsen administration faced a serious inflationary and balance-of-payments crisis. Occasionally, the sequence is inverted: the Echeverría Government in Mexico set out on a highly inflationary course *after* it had been frustrated, in 1971, in its project to carry out a long overdue fiscal reform. The government increased spending *as though* the reform had gone through. Perhaps it sought in this way to administer a lesson to the powerful business interests that had once again blocked the reform; unfortunately those who had to bear the cost of the lesson were not necessarily those for whom it was intended.

It begins to look as though the experience of inflation and the pressures that it brings could be put to certain positive uses. Beyond a threshold of tolerance, inflation certainly is the kind of pressing policy problem that increases the willingness of governments to take action, in spite of opposition from powerful interests, if there is firm expectation that the action will help restrain the inflation. In the two instances just cited, the connection between the inflationary process and the required action is particu-

[41] *Journeys*, pp. 117–21, 125–38.

larly transparent: with public expenditures outpacing revenues in the course of the early stages of a country's economic development, the resulting inflation points directly to decisions on the expenditure or revenue side that would be helpful. Even then, decisions such as tax reform are often extremely difficult to take, but the crisis atmosphere generated by inflation may make it possible to modify structures that are part and parcel of the "order of things" under normal circumstances.

The ability of protracted inflation to raise questions about existing social arrangements has lately been noted in advanced capitalist societies. In a number of them, inflation is leading trade unions to change what might be called the money-power mix of their demands. Realizing that the quest for higher wages and benefits can be futile because of inflation or pressed by official policies to adhere to noninflationary "guidelines," unions have requested more participation in management decisionmaking as well as in firm profits as a counterpart to wage restraint.[42] It seems increasingly likely that the inflationary experiences the advanced capitalist countries are going through will, in a number of them, lead to important modifications of the social and economic system under which they operate.

The social and political impact of inflation can thus range from the installation of authoritarian-repressive regimes that impose highly regressive income distributions to the adoption of tax reform and other measures in the direction of greater equality, participation, and democracy. "Like test-tube solutions that respond differently to the same reagent, these societies reveal their characters in divergent responses to the same stimulus."[43] An effective way to write the comparative social and political history of the last thirty years of the twentieth century may well be to focus on the distinctive reactions of various countries to identical pressures of worldwide inflation.

[42] For England, see Colin Crouch, "The Drive for Equality: Experience of Incomes Policy in Britain," and for Sweden, Andrew Martin, "Is Democratic Control of Capitalist Economies Possible?" both in Leon Lindberg et al., eds., *Stress and Contradiction in Modern Capitalism* (Lexington, Mass.: Lexington Books, 1975), pp. 225–7 and pp. 40ff., respectively. For the Netherlands, see "The Dutch Grope for a New Social Contract," *Business Week* (August 8, 1977), p. 46.

[43] Peter A. Gourevitch, "International Trade, Domestic Coalitions, and Liberty: Comparative Responses to the Crisis of 1873–1896," *Journal of Interdisciplinary History* 8 (Autumn 1977): 281.

Around
Exit, Voice, and Loyalty

Introductory note

It has become common to think of the seventies as a time of conservative backlash against the hyper-liberal and would-be revolutionary sixties. This is of course an oversimplification and, from the vantage point of intellectual history, a misrepresentation. A closer look at the changing intellectual landscape reveals that key pieces of neo-conservative thinking had already been put into place by 1970, particularly insofar as the contribution of economists is concerned. For example, the extension of market and individual choice mechanisms to new areas of social decision-making was first advocated by Milton Friedman, in particular for the public school system, in 1962. The "flight to the suburbs" was celebrated even earlier by Charles Tiebout through a model which showed how a social optimum could be achieved as perfectly mobile individuals "vote with their feet" for that combination of public services and environment best suited to each. The power and rationality of *individual* decentralized activity in various newly emerging or to-be-organized markets were thus stressed while, at the same time, in a novel application of individual cost-benefit calculus, Mancur Olson purported to demonstrate that the odds against successful *collective* action on the part of large numbers of people were far heavier than had been realized.

The events of the middle and late sixties failed, to be sure, to confirm this particular theory. Along with the abundant *practice* of collective action, that period witnessed a considerable interest in new theoretical approaches to a more participatory political system and society. These works either ignored the literature mentioned in the preceding paragraph or coexisted with it in a posture of unbridgeable ideological antagonism.

In this intellectual atmosphere I undertook in 1968 to write

211

Exit, Voice, and Loyalty. Perhaps it was because I appreciated the power of the market mechanism, but also believed in the irreplaceability and perfectibility of the democratic political process that I was able to develop a "problem-solving" approach which permitted a junction of the political (voice) and economic (exit) modes of action. The two were not viewed as mutually exclusive; while they were alternatives they could in some situations be combined for best results; moreover, the exit-voice polarity did not yield a systematic instinctive preference for one mechanism over the other, in contrast to more traditional, not unrelated dichotomies, such as Gesellschaft vs. Gemeinschaft, or universalism vs. particularism.

The ensuing possibility of establishing communication between two disciplines and two ideologies, all of them equally hidebound, hit some sort of sensitive nerve in the social science community. Reactions to my book were numerous and applications of the exit-voice dichotomy were tried out in many quarters, from early modern historians to public health specialists. Chapters 9 and 10 were written for two occasions during which the book was discussed by groups of political scientists and economists, respectively. As stated in the Preface, these essays are no mere postscripts: the theme I had come upon was richer than I had suspected and it simply proved impossible to exhaust it in one sitting. The points I make and the questions I raise in these two essays should be considered essential additions to the original volume.

Chapters 11 and 12 are more specialized applications of the exit-voice approach. Chapter 11, "Exit, Voice, and the State," deals in some detail with exits from the state in the form of secession, capital flight, and emigration, and with their effects on voice. Chapter 12, "Three Uses of Political Economy and Analyzing European Integration," discusses–among other political economy themes–the modifications that must be introduced when the members of the group that is subject to voice or exit are themselves states rather than individuals. The project of European integration had been the central focus of my work in Washington from 1946 to 1952 and I was therefore eager to explore whether concepts such as linkage effects and exit-voice which I had since developed in quite different contexts could shed some new light on the old problems.

9

Exit, voice, and loyalty:
further reflections and a survey
of recent contributions

My book *Exit, Voice, and Loyalty: Responses to Decline in Firms, Organizations, and States* was published in 1970.[1] Reactions to it and applications of its concepts have been fairly numerous and I have myself had quite a few afterthoughts. It will therefore be difficult to bring these matters together in a passably structured paper. In the following, I shall limit myself to four broad areas of inquiry which have been so arranged that my own further reflections figure rather prominently though by no means exclusively in the first two sections while the latter two are more heavily weighted with reports and comments on the research and contributions of others.

I. New economic arguments in favor of voice

As most economists who have made contributions to political science in recent decades, I have occasionally used economic models and modes of reasoning to dissect political phenomena. While such exercises in interdisciplinary imperialism can be genuinely enlightening, only a small part of my work has been of this particular kind. In fact, in much of *Exit, Voice, and Loyalty* I have been guilty, not of imperialist ambition or designs, but

Reprinted with permission from *Social Science Information* 13 (1974): 7–26. The paper was written for a conference on my book, held in 1973 at the Rockefeller Foundation's Villa Serbelloni in Bellagio, Italy, and organized by the International Social Science Council. I remain deeply grateful to the late Stein Rokkan, then President of the International Political Science Association, for his contributions as convener and moving spirit extraordinary of the conference.

[1] By Harvard University Press which published a slightly revised paperback edition in 1972.

rather of the opposite: namely, of the desire to convince economists of the importance and usefulness, for the analysis of economic phenomena, of an essentially political concept such as
voice. Perhaps it is in recognition of these somewhat treasonable
services on behalf of political science that political scientists
rather than economists have honored me by calling together a
seminar with my book as basic document for discussion.

In the large portion of my book which was an essay in persuasion on behalf of voice I argued that voice can and should
complement and occasionally supersede exit as a recuperation
mechanism when business firms, public services, and other organizations deteriorate. My approach was both positive and nor-
mative. I explained the conditions under which voice comes into
existence and can be expected to be powerful, but I also argued
that, in some situations, the proper balance of institutional incentives ought to be adjusted so as to strengthen voice in relation to exit. I now find that my advocacy of voice was not exaggerated, but, on the contrary, too timid. This is not surprising.
Since voice is an entirely new category for economists, our
thought processes are not properly attuned to it and it will take
some time to uncover all the situations in which the importance
of voice has been underrated. In this section I propose to discuss
three such situations.

1. When the cost of voice turns into a benefit[2]

In discussing customers' or members' choice between exit and
voice I naturally gave some attention to the cost of exit as compared to the cost of voice. This comparison tipped the scales
against voice, for I considered exit to be generally costless, except when loyalty is present, while resort to voice is typically
costly as buyers of a product or members of an organization
spend time, effort, and perhaps even money in the attempt to
exert influence on the firm or organization with whose products
or policies they are dissatisfied.[3]

This was good economic reasoning, appropriate to "normal-

---

[2] Some of the arguments of this section have been previously put forward in *Bias for Hope*, Introduction, pp. 4–7.

[3] See *Exit*, pp. 39–40. See also further on, pp. 222–3, for situations in which exit is costly for reasons other than loyalty.

cy." It took the explosion of protest activities after the Cambodia invasion and the Kent State shootings to remind me that, in certain situations, the use of voice can suddenly become a most sought after, fulfilling activity, in fact, the ultimate justification of human existence.

In other words, while normally felt as a chore and a cost which one tries to minimize or shirk, the activities connected with voice can on occasion become a highly desired end in itself. How is it possible to account for this strange mutation?

In addition to choosing and allocating their time and income between various consumer goods, individuals also decide how to apportion their activities between all private pursuits, on the one hand, and such contributions as they choose to make to the "public happiness" on the other. Decisions to make such contributions appear to be subject to a number of characteristic properties in comparison to private consumption decisions. For one thing, simple observation reveals that the preference for participation in public affairs over the "idiocy" of private life is much more unstable, and subject to much wider fluctuations, than the preference for, say, apples over pears or for present over future consumption. Events such as demonstrations, marches, riots, and revolutions are "participation explosions," that is, they result from a sudden enormous intensification of the preference for public actions for which there are no parallels, with the possible exception of the world of fashion, in the realm of private consumption choices.

The reason for this instability of the taste for participation in public affairs lies in the peculiar dual character of this activity. On the one hand, such participation is equivalent to expressing a demand for certain public policies, and since such public policies, once established, can be enjoyed or "consumed" by everyone in the community, the demand for public policies has the earmarks of the demand for public goods. It follows that actual participation on the part of those who favor a given policy is undermined by the well-known tendency to lie low and to hide or understate the true intensity of one's demand for a public good in the hope of getting a "free ride" through the exertion of others. This is a major reason for the much lamented "apathy" in relation to public issues. What looks like apathy is often not absence of interest in a public policy, but considerable interest combined with the expectation that someone else will exert himself on one's own behalf.

But there is another side to the story which has not been analyzed by the public goods theorists and which works in exactly the opposite direction. In the case of the acquisition of normal public goods – say, public parks or police protection – the usual distinction between the value of the services rendered by these amenities and their cost is sufficiently clear cut. But ambiguities arise when one transfers these categories to public policies. The cost of obtaining or pushing through these policies is the cost, in time spent, risk shouldered, and perhaps money expended in the course of their advocacy. In other words, striving for these policies through various acts of participation and voice is their cost, which, in accordance with the theory of public goods, tends to be shirked by the individual. However, it is in the nature of *the* "public good" or *the* "public happiness" that striving for it cannot be neatly separated from possessing it. This is so because striving for the public happiness will often be felt not so much as a cost, but as the closest available substitute for it. We all know that participation in a movement to bring about a desirable policy is (and, unfortunately, may be for a long time) the next best thing to having that policy.[4]

Uncertainty is an important element in this strange transformation of means into ends, and of costs into benefits. Success in the advocacy of a public policy is always uncertain: nobody knows the size of citizens' advocacy or protest that is needed to impose, change, or stop a given public policy. If a citizen feels strongly, he may therefore experience the need to negate the uncertainty about the desired outcome by the certainty of participation in the movement to bring about that outcome. In a more

---

[4] In *Bias for Hope*, p. 7, I have shown that the distinction between private and public goods goes back to Pascal who contrasted "particular things which can only be possessed by a single individual" with "the true good [which] must be such that all can possess it at the same time" (*Pensées*, 425, Brunschvicg edn.). Pascal refers here to God who is indeed the quintessential public good since His possession, unlike that of public parks, can never become "rival" or "exclusive." But Pascal's analysis went one step farther: God is also the archetype of that category of public goods in whose case striving cannot be separated from possessing and this important property of some public goods was again contrasted by Pascal with private goods: "The hope Christians have to possess an infinite good is mixed with actual enjoyment . . . for they are not like those who would hope for a kingdom of which they have nothing, being subjects; rather, they hope for holiness, for freedom from injustice, and they partake of it" (*Pensées*, 540).

rational vein, uncertainty may act at times as a discriminating monopolist as it extracts from each person with a "taste" for a certain policy the *full* amount he would be willing to pay to have that policy; this would happen if each individual becomes convinced that his contribution makes the difference between success and failure of the movement.

No matter what the precise explanation – one could simply take refuge in the definition of man as an animal with the ability and propensity to transform means into ends – the sudden, historically so decisive outbursts of popular energies must be explained by precisely this change in sign, by the turning of what is normally sensed as a cost that is to be shirked into a benefit, a rewarding experience, and a "happiness of pursuit" in which one simply must share.

The possibility of this mutation is fundamental for the understanding of political change: achieving change often requires such a mutation. It is also helpful in reconciling the conflicting views on political participation in a democracy which are perhaps best epitomized by Rousseau's *Contrat social,* on the one hand, and Benjamin Constant's *De la liberté des Anciens comparée à celle des Modernes,* on the other. The total participation considered as essential for the preservation of liberty by Rousseau and the strictly limited participation advocated by Constant can both characterize, *in turn,* the same polity, whose good health may actually be served by some alternation or oscillation between the Rousseau and the Constant model.

The moral of this excursion into political theory for the exit-voice alternative is clear: If active concern with the public happiness can on occasion be felt as a benefit and as an important contribution to the private happiness rather than as a subtraction from it and as a cost, then voice will have an occasional edge over exit in those situations that clearly impinge on the public happiness. This means that voice can be expected to play a role in relation to those goods and in particular to those dimensions of goods and services that have a strong public interest component. Thus, deterioration in the taste of a firm's food product will give rise to exit; but the presence of a health hazard will lead to voice. Similarly, in the case of automobiles, unattractive design will lead to exit, while safety problems will bring out voice. Wherever the public interest is involved, voice will not be felt as a cost but as a benefit by some people at some time, and, in this way, one of the primary handicaps of voice in relation to exit will be reduced and, on occasion, eliminated.

A recent illustration of these matters is the changing role of the shareholder in the corporation. As I had mentioned in my book, exit had long reigned supreme in this area, in obedience to the Wall Street rule "if you don't like the management, you should sell your stock" and in spite of remonstrances against this practice on the part of some financial writers (see *Exit*, p. 46). In connection with the ordinary, private-regarding, return-maximizing activities of investors there has been no overwhelming change in this respect even though, according to some indications, institutional investors, such as trust departments of banks, have tended to vote against management proposals somewhat more frequently.[5] But a considerable shift occurred when institutional investors took an interest in, and became concerned over, corporate policies and practices in such matters of public concern as pollution or racial discrimination. In these situations, the concerned investors generally decided not to exit by selling their stock, but to use what influence they could marshal in order to modify corporate policies.

The institutional investors that were most active or, perhaps, reactive in this field were the large private universities. They had to respond to campaigns, such as "Campaign G.M." in 1970 and again in 1971, which had been launched by citizens' groups outside of the universities, but soon received support from important student and faculty groups. Committees were appointed and new policies developed. As a result, universities generally decided to take a more activist role in shareholder meetings and, in general, in relation to the management of corporations in which they are important stockholders. At the same time, a consensus developed on rejecting exit (i.e., sale) as the only or even as the proper response to discontent in matters where the public interest was at stake, as can be seen from a very cautious committee report issue at Harvard University.[6] The most emphatic and elaborate statement on the problem appears in a book, *The*

[5] M. A. Eisenberg, "The Legal Roles of Shareholders and Management in Modern Corporate Decision-Making," *California: Law Review* 57 (1969): 50–2.
[6] *Report of the Committee on University Relations with Corporate Enterprise*, January 1971 (Mimeo).

Ethical Investor by John G. Simon et al. that grew out of the discussion of these issues at Yale University.[7] Here exit is advocated only as a last resort after voice has failed:

"We have expressed dissatisfaction with attempts to cleanse a portfolio through the sale of morally or socially objectionable holdings. Such efforts . . . tend to involve one in illusions about moral purity . . . we advocate such action when other attempts to correct or avert a servious wrong have failed."[8]

The corporation thus stands as an example of a private organization in which the relation between management and stockholders was dominated by exit until such time as some activities of the corporation were shown to affect the public interest; and as soon as stockholders had complaints on the ground of these activities, the use of voice seemed the more natural choice. It is of course possible that the use of voice, once well established in connection with public-interest issues, will contaminate the private, hitherto exit-dominated areas, and will come to play a greater role in stockholder-management relations in general, for better or worse.

2. Ignorance of consumers and producers

A second, not completely unrelated way of identifying goods, services, and organizations that are or should be voice- rather than exit-intensive was suggested to me through recent papers of Richard Nelson and Michael Krashinsky[9] and Kenneth Arrow.[10] In discussing institutional alternatives for the delivery of day-care services, Nelson and Krashinsky make a distinction between goods in which "the consumer can be assumed to be an expert in knowing what he likes, *e.g.* sweet juicy oranges" and such services as day care for small children whose quality is difficult to fathom for the parents. Besides, clear quality standards for day care are simply not available. Arrow addresses himself somewhat similarly to situations in which there is a disproportion of knowl-

[7] New Haven, Conn.: Yale University Press, 1972.
[8] *Ethical Investor*, p. 53. That voice is in fact more effective than exit in changing corporate policies that are objectionable to some of its stockholders on public-interest grounds is shown in B. G. Malkiel and R. E. Quandt, "Moral Issues in Investment Policy," *Harvard Business Review* (March–April): 37–47.
[9] "Public Control and Economic Organization of Day Care for Young Children," *Public Policy* 22 (Winter 1974): 53–76.
[10] "Social Responsibility and Economic Efficiency," *Public Policy* 21 (Summer 1973): 303–18.

edge between seller and buyer – as in the case of medical services or in that of complex technological products such as drugs and automobiles – and he underlines the importance of ethical codes (about disclosure of information, for example) which sellers ought to observe in such situations as a restraint on socially undesirable profit-maximization. Both Nelson-Krashinky and Arrow are concerned with institutional implications of market situations in which the buyer lacks knowledge about product quality or is far inferior in this respect to the seller. As in the case of exploitation of the consumer by a monopolist, some form of public intervention or self-policing on the part of the producers or sellers seems to be the answer to these situations inasmuch as the consumers are assumed to be in an inferior and impotent position in which neither exit nor voice on their part is likely to perform as an adequate safeguard of their interests.

The case of day care goes beyond these important, but still traditional concerns about "market failure." As Nelson-Krashinsky almost intimate at one point, we have here a situation in which ignorance about quality, about what one is really after, is by no means limited to the buyer or consumer or member. Day care is typical of a whole class of services for which, for a number of reasons, a strong demand arises at some point; some people are willing to pay for it or feel that it should be offered as a public service and some other people step forward claiming to be able to accommodate the new demand or are willing to do so to the best of their ability. The reality of the situation is that demand for a service has arisen *in advance of real knowledge of how to satisfy it;* society then delegates some of its members to search for the best method of filling the new demand and of supplying the newly arisen need; and the institutional question is here not one of protecting the consumer, but of educating the producer, of providing him with as much information as possible about his performance. In such situations, the contribution of voice can clearly be of the greatest importance, simply because the information it supplies is rich and detailed as compared to the bareness and blankness of silent exit. Moreover, exit may fail to supply even the bare information about the existence of discontent, if dissatisfied consumers switch back and forth between various equally unsatisfactory suppliers so that each individual supplier gains new customers as fast as he loses them. This phenomenon has been described in my book under the heading "Competition as collusive behavior."

Producers' ignorance, or a substantial degree of such ignorance, about ways and means of satisfying certain demands is probably more widespread than is generally realized. It characterizes a large portion of sectors that show a high rate of growth in modern economies, namely education, health, and leisure activities. When the delivery of health services can proceed along standard lines within well-charted territory as, say, in the case of minor dentistry, consumer dissatisfaction with one dentist is likely to take the form of exit. But the individual who has some as yet poorly articulated complaint with respect to his general physical or mental health is probably well advised not to abandon his family doctor or psychiatrist at the slightest disappointment, but to help them grope on his behalf and to collaborate intensively with them through active use of voice.

To repeat, the second new criterion for discriminating between exit-prone and voice-prone situations can be defined as ignorance and uncertainty, shared by consumers and producers, about the manner of procuring a desired good or service and, in fact, about their precise nature. It is clear that there is a strong affinity between this criterion and the first one which centered on the presence of a "public happiness" component. Generalized ignorance and uncertainty about what one is after exist typically when motivation to solve a problem is outrunning understanding,[11] and this situation arises in turn when there are pressing *public* demands to "do something" about a poorly understood problem. In such situations, then, the use of voice rather than exit is to be expected and recommended on both counts.

The ignorance criterion is also helpful in accounting for swings from the predominance of exit to that of voice in relation to the *same* goods or services. Ignorance and uncertainty with respect to the desired nature of a good or service are not always conquered once and for all. For a number of such goods and services, doubts are periodically *reborn* in the light of new experience. In fact, in many cases doubts about the desirability of the product in its present form arise for the first time after a more or less prolonged period of unquestioning acceptance. Recent examples are auto-

[11] This topic is discussed in my *Journeys Toward Progress*, pp. 235–8.

mobiles, DDT, and some drugs. Products which are subject to cycles of acceptance and questioning are typically such complex and ignorance-intensive services as psychiatric help and higher education. It is then quite proper that exit should be the principal reaction of dissatisfied students when no fundamental questions are widely asked about the value and current methods of the university, while voice will predominate during periods of generalized loss of confidence in the traditional system.

3. *Vertical integration and marriage as institutionalized voice*

I now come to a third criterion which throws light on the difference between exit-prone and voice-prone situations and which had been neglected in my book. It is somewhat symmetrical to the first criterion which dealt with situations in which voice becomes less costly than it would be under "normal" circumstances, or is even sensed as a benefit by the customer-member. Just as I failed to question adequately whether voice is costly under all circumstances, so I took the costlessness of exit too much for granted. I did allow for the existence of a cost of exit to the extent that loyalty was present; but exit can imply considerable cost in purely economic market situations even in the absence of loyalty. Such costs are least in evidence in the case of consumer purchases on which I had principally focused; but they come to the fore in interindustry transactions when a firm buys a specialized input from one among a limited number of potential suppliers. In such situations, the firm will often spend considerable time and money in apprenticing the supplier and these costs would have to be incurred over again if the firm were to switch to another supplier because, for some reason, it becomes dissatisfied with the current relationship. The same applies to the supplier firm to the extent that it has shouldered some of the costs of apprenticeship – they would be largely lost to it if it had to look for a new customer. This situation will therefore cause voice to become relatively more attractive than exit for both firms in case of friction, but it also is one of the basic motivations for vertical integration of firms as Oliver Williamson has pointed out.[12] Integration can indeed be con-

---

[12] "The Vertical Integration of Production: Market Failure Considerations," *American Economic Review* 61 (May 1971): 112–23 and "Markets and Hierarchies: some Elementary Considerations," *American Economic Review* 63 (May 1973): 316–25.

sidered as an arrangement, not for suppressing voice through hierarchy, but rather for institutionalizing and routinizing it; it is voice from one unit to another within a unified organization with a common goal, supplemented by an established mechanism for adjudicating any unresolvable disputes that may arise between the various producing units. The logic that makes for this sort of institutionalized voice has asserted itself also in the Soviet Union where "direct ties" between input-using and input-producing firms, and between producers and retail outlets, have made their appearance. This is regarded by one observer as a "major innovation without overwhelming support from the highest places."[13]

It is not easy to think of analogues for this phenomenon outside of the economy. But marriage could perhaps be interpreted as a similar institutional arrangement: when a man and a woman have reached an advanced degree of mutual understanding and adjustment, the costs of exit from this relationship are high – one has to start from scratch with the next partner. An attempt will therefore be made to take care of remaining and recurring frictions through voice, and marriage can be considered, just like the merger of two firms, as a way of routinizing this voice – with unresolvable disputes being referred to the psychotherapist in lieu of the Executive Vice-President. There are probably other situations in which the decision to enter a formal organization is not prompted so much by fundamental agreement on values and goals or by the desire to eliminate conflict, but, on the contrary, by the need to bring necessarily recurrent conflict more frankly and more routinely into the open without risking, each time, the survival of the relationship. It is precisely because voice hides here behind the facade of organization, hierarchy, and harmonious unity that I failed to become aware of these situations.

II. Exit and voice: the view from the top

In 1970 a reader of *Exit, Voice, and Loyalty* remarked to me that the book was written almost entirely "from below," that is, from the point of view of customers or members as victims of deteriorating quality, and that he would have liked to see the topic of

[13] Martin C. Spechler, *The Economics of Product Quality in Soviet Industry*. Unpublished dissertation, Department of Economics, Harvard University, 1971.

exit versus voice treated from the point of view of top management of various organizations. No wonder he expressed such a preference, for this was right after the Cambodia events and the poor fellow had just been appointed president of one of our more turbulent colleges! I could of course point out to him that throughout the book and especially in my concluding chapter I had made an attempt to look at those institutional combinations of exit and voice that might be optimal from the point of view of the survival and strength of the organization. But I admit that I had not addressed myself directly and systematically to the possible manipulation of exit and voice as "management tools," to use the language of our business schools. I shall try to do a little better now, although only in connection with one particular organization: the State.

Fortunately, Stein Rokkan has since made a considerable contribution in this area through his paper for this seminar.[14] As I wrote him after he sent it to me, I was first rather stunned to see the sweep of European political development since the Middle Ages reinterpreted through my concepts, but while I am still a bit puzzled about the marriage he arranged in the process between Talcott Parsons and myself, I do find the historical scheme he traces in the second part of his paper remarkably illuminating.

Let me briefly paraphrase this portion of Rokkan's argument in order to bring it into contact with the general notion of exit and voice as "management tools." Every state – and indeed every organization – requires for its establishment and existence some limitations or *ceilings* on the extent of exit or of voice or of both. In other words, there are levels of exit (disintegration) and voice (disruption) beyond which it is impossible for an organization to exist as an organization. At the same time, an organization needs *minimal* or *floor* levels of exit and voice in order to receive the necessary feedback about its performance. Every organization thus navigates between the Scylla of disintegration-disruption and the Charybdis of deterioration due to lack of feedback. A territorial organization such as a national state must by its very nature suppress exit in the form of secession (though

---

[14] "Dimensions of State Formation and Nation-Building: A Possible Paradigm for Research on Variations within Europe" in C. Tilly, ed., *The Formation of National States in Western Europe* (Princeton: Princeton University Press, 1975), pp. 562–600. [This paper was available to me in draft form at the time of writing.]

not necessarily the emigration of individual citizens); hence, feedback is here bound to take primarily the form of voice. But, as Rokkan shows, in the center of Europe the suppression of territorial exit – and the assertion of the right to control the movement of men and commodities across borders – required so great a concentration of effort and authority that the attempt to achieve manageably low levels of exit led also to the crushing of voice, which was reduced in the process to levels far below those required for long-run stability and health. The countries of the European periphery (and a few others) found it easier to control their borders and therefore "managed to keep a better balance between exit controls and voice channeling during the crucial phases of state-building."[15]

Rokkan is probably right in asserting that, particularly during some initial phase of organization, attempts to restrict exit and to choke off voice tend to go hand in hand and to feed on each other. I had looked primarily at selective manipulations of one of these two levers and had suggested that they would be engaged in by management, not in order to receive feedback about its performance, but on the contrary to encourage that particular reaction mode that is least unsettling to it and least dangerous to its perpetuation in power (*Exit*, p. 124).

Rokkan's paper provides a stimulus for going over this terrain with greater care and perhaps somewhat greater charity toward the political managers. For one thing, just as the process of state-building required restricting both exit and voice, so liberalization and widening of participation may not be possible, or may be extraordinarily difficult to handle, unless exit and voice controls can be eased jointly. The reason is simple: the forces of criticism and dissent that have been dammed up by stringent voice and exit controls may be so powerful, especially during a period of economic transformation, that, if they are released into one channel (usually voice) only, they will exceed tolerable levels or, at any rate, such levels as are thought to be tolerable by the rulers. Illustrations from recent and current history come to mind immediately. The history of Europe in the nineteenth century would probably have been either far more turbulent or far more repressive and the trend toward representative govern-

[15] *Ibid.*, p. 589.

ment much more halting, had it not been possible for millions of people to emigrate toward the United States and elsewhere.

This proposition represents an application to Europe of the "labor safety valve" theory which was originally put forward in the United States to explain, by the availability of the "frontier," the lack of militancy of the American working class during the nineteenth century in comparison to its European counterpart. While the theory has been strongly controverted for the United States, a European safety valve theory might well be proposed: for all the class-consciousness of the European workers, it is well known that their revolutionary accomplishments did not quite come up to the expectations of, say, Marx and Engels and one reason may be the availability of overseas emigration. Some empirical backing for such a European safety valve theory has recently come to my attention: according to a study of emigration from rural Italy for the decade preceding World War I, the socialist vote and labor militancy was high in those Italian provinces that showed low rates of emigration, and vice versa.[16] The author argues quite convincingly that the differential response to rural poverty – labor militancy in central Italy and in Apulia and emigration in the rest of the South – can be explained by differences in land tenure and other aspects of agricultural organization. But, at the same time, his data suggest strongly that the availability of mass migration reduced the total amount of social conflict with which the Italian State might otherwise have had to cope.[17]

It is interesting to look at contemporary non-European politics in the light of this European experience. Today the safety valve, or outlet for excess voice which emigration represents, is largely nonexistent, except for the Mediterranean countries in relation to Western Europe. This may well be a factor rendering more difficult the introduction and maintenance of a measure of voice in the newly independent and industrializing countries of the twentieth century.[18] Similarly, the difficulties of liberalization in the countries of Eastern Europe (including the USSR) are intensi-

---

[16] J. S. MacDonald, "Agricultural Organization, Migration and Labour Militancy in Rural Italy," *Economic History Review*, second series 16 (1963–1964): 61–75.

[17] See also Chapter 11, Section III.

[18] In line with this reasoning, the poor countries might well be advised to demand the opening up of immigration into the rich countries on political as well as on purely economic grounds.

fied by the insistence of their political managers on maintaining strict exit controls.

The manipulation of exit and voice controls on the part of "management" can be constrained in yet another way. In my book, I considered lack of feedback as the principal cost an organization incurs as a result of suppressing voice and exit. But, at the level of the state, a very important immediate cost, in contrast to lack of feedback and information which is primarily a cost in the longer run, can be the need for repression. Many countries find it entirely impossible (that is, unacceptably expensive) to control their frontiers and some rulers may not be willing to go beyond a certain degree of repression in limiting or choking off voice, possibly for humane reasons, but also because they know by now that unlimited repression brings rule by the secret police. The immediate cost of repressing exit and voice – admittedly, in the case of some sadistic rulers, some of this cost also turns into a benefit – is then an important element in explaining the behavior of states in relation to the limitation of exit and voice. I believe, for example, that the puzzling and unique permissiveness of the Cuban socialist regime with respect to emigration can be interpreted in this fashion: Fidel Castro was determined to establish an authoritarian political order with a strictly limited amount of voice, but at the same time he did *not* want Cuba to become a state with an all-powerful secret police and, given the size of the internal opposition, he preferred to let as many disaffected Cubans as possible depart rather than having to subject them to permanent police surveillance and worse.

The interaction of these three variables – suppression of exit, suppression of voice, and repression – can also be observed in other settings. One might even propose a theorem: a state can control only two out of these three variables. In Cuba, Fidel Castro chose to suppress voice and to limit the amount of repression: so he had to put up with an unexpectedly large loss of skilled manpower as hundreds of thousands of Cubans chose to emigrate. In Stalin's Russia, complete suppression of exit and voice yielded repression of a size and kind that surely had not been fully intended at the outset, while in post-Stalinist Russia, the decision to set limits to repression, combined with the continued strict controls on exit, has led to the voicing of considerably more dissent than the authorities had planned for.

I do not wish to make too much of this theorem. Its merit is to create a richer field of forces than the usual two-way alternative between participation and repression. The trouble with the theorem is that the freedom to exit will not always act as a brake on voice: Fidel Castro may have been particularly lucky in that so many Cubans thought of Miami as a potentially satisfactory second home. As we know from Ronald Dore, in countries such as Japan the permission to exit is likely to be as feeble a restraint on voice as the permission to commit suicide.

III. Exit and voice in political parties and politics

Political parties in polyarchies are among the rare organizations in which both voice and exit have well recognized, important roles to play. They should be therefore privileged topics for the testing and refinement of the hypotheses I developed in my book.

Before reviewing the work of others in this area, I cannot resist pointing out that the critique of the Hotelling-Downs model which I put forward in Chapter 6 of my book was confirmed by the decision of the Democratic National Convention to nominate George McGovern for president in 1972. Once again, as eight years earlier in the case of Barry Goldwater's nomination by the Republicans, it has been shown that those members who are farthest from the center can wield considerable power in the party even though, according to Hotelling-Downs, they have "nowhere to go" and should therefore be powerless while the party was expected to cater to the middle vote which can wield the power of exit. My point was of course that power grows not only out of the ability to exit, but also out of voice and that voice will be wielded with special energy and dedication by those who have nowhere to exit to.

One proposition I put forward about party politics dealt with the probable amount of internal democracy within parties as opposed to bureaucratic or machine control. I suggested that in a two-party system articulation of opinion on the part of party members and therefore a degree of internal democracy are more likely to be forthcoming than in multi-party systems because in the former ideological distance between parties can be assumed to be greater and loyalty stronger so that dissatisfied members will ordinarily voice rather than exit, the opposite being true for multi-party systems. This was of course a very general deduction from an admittedly primitive political model: in it there is just one spectrum of opinion (left to right) and the ideological distance from extreme left to extreme right is everywhere the same. Clearly the world isn't that simple, as Val Lorwin soon pointed out to me in correspondence. In particular, so he stressed, there are democracies such as Belgium and the Netherlands, whose religious and cultural cleavages have made for a multiparty system in which parties may occupy some position along the left-right continuum but are also, and sometimes principally, identified with a religious or language group. In this situation, a country can obviously have more than two parties and yet the distance between any two of them need not be any shorter, and may in fact be larger, than in a country with a two-party system, but without overriding cleavages. It is therefore quite in line with exit-voice theory when Lorwin writes in an article on the smaller European democracies (Belgium, Netherlands, Austria, Switzerland): "The pluralism due to segmentation (= cleavage) has, on the whole, made for more, rather than for less, participation in voluntary organization."[19]

The foregoing does not mean, of course, that cleavages, and what the Dutch call *verzuiling*, that is, the organization of parties, interest groups, etc., along strictly confessional or language lines, are guarantees of democracy. While *verzuiling* may strengthen feeling of identification and participation *within* parties and other organizations, it is only too obvious that the cleavages which give rise to *verzuiling*, also tear countries and communities apart: Nigeria, Pakistan and Northern Ireland are among the more recent examples. Looking at the range of these outcomes an economist cannot suppress the mechanical and perfectly unhelpful thought that there may be some optimal degree of *verzuiling* which would assure internal democracy and participation within organizations while permitting peaceful and democratic coexistence of the various segmented groups in the wider society.

My model of political parties was excessively simple and general from a number of other points of view. For example, I did not distinguish between the voters, the party members, and the

---

[19] "Segmented Pluralism: Ideological Cleavages and Political Cohesion in the Smaller European Democracies," *Comparative Politics* 3 (January 1971): 157.

party leaders. Clearly the propensity to voice rather than exit can be expected to increase along this dimension. It follows that in the more traditional European-type parties, where members are supposed to be permanently active and represent a sizable fraction of the total vote, one can expect voice to be more in evidence than in "electoral" or "catchall" parties of the American type. To the extent that "catchall" parties predominate in two-party systems, this structural factor may then detract from the propensity toward voice that parties in a two-party system were expected to exhibit, according to my analysis, in comparison with multi-party systems.

An important further complication is dealt with in an article on party organization and strategy.[20] In my scheme, dissatisfaction with one's party arises exclusively on ideological grounds as the party pursues policies that are not to the liking of some of the membership. Another potent reason for dissatisfaction is quite simply the failure of a party to grow and to score at election time. In this view, a party must supply its voters with the satisfaction to be on the winning side and its active members with the more tangible benefits of a widening supply of party jobs and, eventually, of public offices. If members are dissatisfied with the party's performance in these respects, their possible reactions are once again exit or voice, and the authors show that, contrary to what one might expect, exit is not necessarily the dominant reaction of those who are primarily success- and office-oriented.

In any event, the voice or exit pattern of those who are primarily ideology-oriented is likely to be quite different from those who are primarily success- and office-oriented–it is easy to imagine party moves that will anger the former while delighting the latter and vice versa. It may, however, be a mistake to make too much of this distinction. Every "political animal" is part ideologue and part reward-oriented, and is therefore willing to accept a certain amount of opportunism on the part of the party for the sake of its power and success at the polls.

Similar mixtures of motivations lie behind resignations from public office, a subject to which I addressed myself toward the

[20] E. S. Wellhofer and T. M. Hennessy, "Models of Political Party Organization and Strategy: Some New Analytic Approaches to Oligarchy" in Ivor Crewe, ed., *Elites in Western Democracy* (London: Croom Helm, 1974), pp. 279–316.

end of my book. I showed that exit from the United States Government had fallen into excessive disuse and speculated about possible psychological and institutional reasons. The record of the last few years has, on the whole, confirmed my analysis, although there have been a few interesting exits. An important research project in this area is now in progress: Professors Thomas Franck of New York University and Edward Weisband of the State University of New York at Stony Brook have compiled and are analyzing all resignations from the Cabinet and from certain other top administrative positions that have occurred since 1900 in the United States and Great Britain.[21] A principal question they are interested in is whether resignations were accompanied by reasoned declarations of dissent or were silent, in deference to some loyalty code or simply on opportunistic grounds, and whether resignation behavior of one or the other kind had noticeably different effects on reentry into public office. It is my hope that the study will lead to a better understanding of how the present scarcity of exit behavior in the United States has come about.

IV. Exit and voice in the urban context and in the organization of public services

In the field of urban studies, the exit-voice dichotomy was obviously one of those ideas whose time had come. Without having seen my book, Oliver P. Williams writes in *Metropolitan Political Analysis:* "There are essentially two options for those who wish to employ a location strategy to change their access within the urban complex. They can move or they can change the characteristics of the place they presently occupy."[22]

To appreciate the change this approach means in comparison to earlier analyses, it is useful to recall the well-known paper by C. M. Tiebout, which had celebrated mobility as making possible an efficient allocation of public services to the consumer-citizens in a metropolitan area.[23] Each municipality was viewed as a firm offering a differentiated set of services to customers with differ-

---

[21] Their research was published in 1975 under the title *Resignation and Protest* (New York: Grossman).

[22] New York: Free Press of Glencoe, 1971, p. 29.

[23] "A Pure Theory of Local Expenditure," *Journal of Political Economy* 64 (October 1956): 416–24.

ent preferences; and, in the model, the only way in which a customer could express his preferences was by moving – there was no room in it for voting or for other political action tending to make his *own* community more to his liking. Together with the advocacy of competition in education by Milton Friedman, which is mentioned in my book, this article can stand as the perfect expression of the economist's bias against voice and in favor of exit.

In the fifties it was perhaps forgivable to search for the hidden rationality of the drive to the suburbs. In the sixties, of course, the overt irrationalities of the phenomenon exploded. The merit of exit-voice theory is to call attention to hitherto neglected, alternative courses of action. Very much in this spirit, Williams calls the current preference for exit "mobility as a substitute for formal politics" (p. 110) and raises critical questions about the institutional framework that has led to this abdication.

A striking case of convergence with my work is an article of J. M. Orbell and T. Uno.[24] In 1966, they had conducted a sample survey in Columbus, Ohio, to elicit information on the kind of neighborhood problems residents were concerned about and on how these residents were planning to react to whatever problems they perceived. It turned out that people's intentions could be arranged into two categories: either they planned to move or they intended to ameliorate the problems they experienced through political action. Subsequently, Orbell and Uno learned about my book, came to correspond with me, and decided to use my terminology in presenting and analyzing their data. In the process they were able to test a number of my hypotheses. One of those confidently expected findings which it is nevertheless nice to see empirically confirmed was that "blacks are more likely to voice in response to problems than are whites of similar status who live in similar urban areas" (p. 484). The reason for this greater propensity to voice on the part of blacks is of course their lower mobility because of de facto segregation of housing in numerous urban and suburban areas.

On the whole, the study confirms what we know about proneness of whites to exit rather than to voice from urban areas as a response to neighborhood problems; but Orbell and Uno un-

---

[24] "A Theory of Neighbourhood Problem Solving: Political Action vs. Residential Mobility," *American Political Science Review* 66 (June 1972): 471–89.

covered interesting differential behavior patterns not only for whites and blacks, but also for higher-status and lower-status whites, with the latter particularly prone to exit while higher-status whites are also often inclined to take political action. Once people reach the suburbs, the pattern changes of course radically and the first reaction to newly arising neighborhood problems in the suburbs is voice rather than exit. This leads Orbell and Uno to an interesting analysis of "exit-fatigue," the reality of which anyone who has recently moved can readily confirm.

The concept of exit-fatigue invites a brief digression about the general topic of exit-voice sequences. One might ask: does exit (and subsequent entry elsewhere) lead to more exit in faster and faster succession? Or do exit and voice typically alternate? Obviously such questions cannot be given a uniform answer but they serve to lead us to diverse situations and to the identification of contrasting sequences and critical variables. For example, when highly structured and hierarchical organizations lose their hold on some members, as the Catholic Church did during the Reformation, or Communist Parties in the West during various twists of the party line, then such first exits tend to be followed by many others as is shown by the proneness to splintering among both Protestant sects and groups belonging to the ex-Communist Left. On the other hand, there are cases where exit-fatigue after a first exit leads to the determination to be "loyal," or to use voice within the new community, as in the case of those who have moved to the suburbs or who have emigrated to a new country (see *Exit*, pp. 112–14). Finally there must be many sequences about which it is difficult to have a strong intuitive a priori feeling: for example, is a person who remarries after one divorce more or less likely to divorce than when he or she married for the first time? I am told that the second time around one tends to try harder to make the marriage work; on the other hand, those who divorce once contain a good proportion of men and women who really cannot abide married life, but insist on trying again and again.[25]

To return to the city. Both Williams and Orbell-Uno lament the victory of exit over voice, that is, of mobility over politics which is responsible for the deterioration of the American city

---

[25] For some data for the United States, see R. R. Bell, *Marriage and Family Interaction* (Homewood, Ill.: Dorsey Press, 1967), pp. 509ff.

over recent decades, and both end up speculating about remedial policies. One of the more interesting findings of Orbell-Uno
is that many people seem to be considering both exit and voice
in response to neighborhood problems so that the actual exit
decision may often win out only by a narrow margin. Hence
small improvements in the attractiveness and efficiency of voice
could make a great deal of difference and the further deterioration of the central city is not an irresistible wave of the future
after all. It could be arrested and reversed by improvements in
the political process, supplemented perhaps by economic measures that would tax exit and subsidize nonexit. As to the political process in the urban context, both the movement toward
decentralization and "community control," and the proposals
for metropolitan integration are relevant to the strengthening of
voice, but these huge topics obviously fall outside the scope of
the present paper, as does the closely related issue of ghetto
improvement versus ghetto-dispersal.

The exit-voice framework has also been found useful in connection with the search for optimal ways of organizing urban public
services. In this field, Dennis Young proposed in 1971, once again
without prior knowledge of my book, a systematic survey of three
possible ways of improving efficiency: one was systematic performance evaluation, the second decentralization which can be considered a form of intensifying voice, and the third competition-
exit.[26] In a subsequent paper he uses the exit-voice framework
explicitly in order to look at a wide range of public services, from
taxis, garbage collection, cable television, fire protection and police, to school systems, day care for children, medical care and
criminal correction.[27] A systematic examination of organizational
alternatives yields some surprising conclusions: for example, the
introduction of a measure of competition is recommended for
garbage collection,[28] whereas decentralization and other ways of
strengthening voice are advocated for police departments. A particularly interesting combination of exit and voice is proposed for
the organization of day care for children, on the basis of the

[26] "Institutional Change and the Delivery of Urban Public Services," *Policy Sciences* 2
(1971): 425–38.
[27] "Exit and Voice in the Organization of Public Services," *Social Science Information* 13
(June 1974): 49–65.
[28] This is consistent with the notion that competition is at its best when the consumer
knows exactly what sort of good and service he is after (see this chapter, p. 219).

already noted contribution of Nelson and Krashinsky, and even more ingenious proposals for introducing some measure of both exit and voice are made with respect to criminal correction and prison reform.

Finally, the exit-voice framework appears to be particularly applicable to certain debates around the British National Health Service. The partisans of the NHS have taken a stand against extending some of its benefits (cheaper medicines and laboratory tests) to those who would avail themselves of private rather than public medicine for the precise reason why I advocated "locking in" of the dissatisfied customer in certain situations. The defenders of the NHS, well aware of its possible failings, feel that NHS needs precisely the potential exiters—educated, vocal middle-class people—as critics *within* the service; hence exit should not be made too easy or cheap for them. A detailed review of the issue and of the debates around it is presented in a doctoral dissertation in economics at the University of Pennsylvania.[29] The author has also extensively reformulated some of my own analysis of exit and voice so as to make it more amenable to mathematical treatment. While I naturally welcome this effort, I have nevertheless somewhat mixed feelings about it. If successful, it may well spawn a large and increasingly complex mathematical literature with the result that it will become ever harder for me to read the papers that will be written on exit and voice, let alone to comment on them in the easy-going fashion which I have been able to use this time around.

[29] Hugh B. Davies, *Exit, Voice and the British National Health Service.* Unpublished dissertation, Department of Economics, University of Pennsylvania, 1975.

10

Exit and voice: some further distinctions

In the venerable folklore of traditional economics political action in the economic sphere has typically been considered as noxious interference with the totally beneficent market mechanism. The equally venerable opposing point of view castigates the Invisible Hand as the Blind Forces of the Market – note the clever replacement of Adam Smith's metaphor by one that uses a closely related image – and instead advocates planning by a political authority that, in turn, is assumed to be totally beneficent. A principal intent of my work on exit and voice, considerably bolstered by all

Originally published, in a shortened version, in *American Economic Review, Papers and Proceedings* 66 (May 1976): 386–9, and reprinted by permission. During its 1975 annual meeting, the American Economic Association held a session with the title "Political Economy: Some Uses of the Exit-Voice Approach." Papers given at the session were Richard B. Freeman, "Individual Mobility and Union Voice in the Labor Market," Oliver E. Williamson, "The Economics of Internal Organization: Exit and Voice in Relation to Markets and Hierarchies," and Dennis R. Young, "Consolidation or Diversity: Choices in the Structure of Urban Governance," all published in the same issue of *American Economic Review*, pp. 361–8, 369–77, and 378–85. I was asked to comment on these papers, and used the occasion for a general review of some major issues that had surfaced in various discussions around *Exit, Voice, and Loyalty*.

Freeman's paper has been followed by a considerable amount of further work, done jointly by Freeman and James L. Medoff, in which the reinterpretation of unions as collective voice is developed into a full-fledged theory. The new Freeman-Medoff view of unions yields a richer, more realistic understanding of their role and function in the economy than either the neoclassical or the (closely related) Marxist positions, which consider unions as purely monopolistic devices or as instruments in the class struggle, respectively. The authors present considerable empirical materials regarding the effects of unionization on turnover, productivity, etc., which tend to confirm their interpretation. This work is probably the most fruitful development to date of the exit-voice dichotomy. See Freeman and Medoff, "The Two Faces of Unionism," *Public Interest*, no. 57 (Fall 1979): 69–93, and *What Do Unions Do?* (New York: Basic Books, forthcoming).

three papers presented at this session, was to show that there is a wide range of economic processes for the efficient unfolding of which both individual, economic action (via exit) and participatory, political action (via voice) have important constructive roles to play. The novelty of the theory for the economist – apt to infuriate or to disconcert both market and planning enthusiasts – consists in its stress on voice not as a substitute for the market nor as a restraint on it in a few well-defined situations, but as another generally available mechanism that, like the market, has its strengths and weaknesses, its successes and failures. There is also a stress on the possibility of unstable equilibria between exit and voice as one drives out the other and on the lack of once-and-for-all solutions through optimal mixes of exit and voice. In other words, the new approach does not satisfy our craving for equilibrium, harmony, and final repose. If it has met, nevertheless, with the beginning of a response from economists, this is probably because of the new or renewed emphasis on such phenomena as ignorance and the cost of information, transaction costs, bounded rationality, X-efficiency, and even altruism. The possibility of "market failure" is today no longer limited – as was taught not long ago by received doctrine – to the presence of externalities, and I welcome Dennis Young's proposal to redefine this concept broadly in terms of situations where exit does not do a good job of stirring up management and of restoring efficiency. In this perspective the availability of another mechanism – voice – should not be viewed as a threatening rival, but as a welcome resource whose potential contribution to a containment of our multiple troubles deserves to be closely studied. For example, while looking at the provision of medical services precisely in this manner, Carl Stevens has recently proposed to complement consumer sovereignty – that is, exit – by *consumer participation* and to limit professional producer sovereignty by *lay management constraints.*[1] These terms are useful modulations of the perhaps excessively compact "voice."

My comments, including some further thoughts, will be in four parts.

---

[1] Carl M. Stevens, "Voice in Medical-Care Markets: 'Consumer Participation,' " *Social Science Information* 13 (1974): 33–48.

1. Voice conveys more information than exit

In all three papers, when voice scores over exit this is primarily because it is information-rich whereas exit conveys little beyond the fact of restlessness or restiveness on the part of the consumer, customer, employee, or whoever else one has an economic relation with. Take Freeman's paper on labor and the employment relationship: Here dissatisfaction arises from a mixture of motives that includes unhappiness about a whole array of working conditions no less than the desire for higher wages and benefits. Unions are more efficient in communicating information about this complex mixture of complaints than the personnel turnover rate. To make this point even stronger I would add that the *content of discontent* is apt to change over time: Exit always takes the same form no matter what the complaint; but voice can articulate newly arising demands–often, to be sure, with a considerable lag as the union leadership takes its own time to understand and adopt the new "outlandish" grievances of its members.

According to Williamson, markets are not working properly whenever the parties are involved in a relationship which it is difficult to specify fully in writing because of uncertainty and complexity or which lends itself peculiarly to the display of bargaining behavior. In these cases the substitution of hierarchy for market relationships between the parties is indicated. In my language hierarchy can be considered as a special variety of institutionalized voice and here is therefore another case where voice wins out over exit because of the fullness and frankness of information which it carries.

Finally, Dennis Young uses the same criterion in favoring a large admixture of voice for the organization of certain public services. He mentions primarily situations in which exit is costly and disruptive to the consumers of the services, as in the case of day-care centers or nursing homes. In my view, these are also frequently situations in which the producers themselves are still groping for satisfactory ways of doing a job which they have taken on because there was a demand for it.[2] In such increasingly important cases of *producer ignorance*, information-rich voice on

---

[2] See Chapter 9, pp. 219–22, above.

the part of consumers, or of Young's "proxy consumers," is far more helpful than the blankness of exit.

2. Voice is more apt than exit to become an end in itself – consequences for participation in elections

That voice conveys more information than exit is one facet of the polarity which is highly important for economic applications, and which I had neglected in my book. Another on which I have already commented in a subsequent paper[3] is the fact that voice, to the extent that it is political action or action in the public interest, is liable to escape from the fetters of the benefit-cost calculus and can therefore suddenly gain an unexpected edge over silent, self-regarding exit. A point in Dennis Young's paper provides an opportunity for further comment on this matter which is, to my mind, fundamental for a genuine "political economy."

Young notes one dilemma in the design of local government: the larger the territorial unit encompassed by municipal government, or by a subdivision of that government such as a school district, the less feasible will it be for the individual citizen to practice exit and the more important is it therefore for voice to function actively and intelligently; yet voice is presumably more apt to become mobilized when the area to which it extends is none too large. Decentralization of public schools and of public services has been advocated precisely for the purpose of facilitating and activating citizen participation.

It may be questioned, however, whether the propensity to voice is likely to increase *indefinitely* as the territorial unit within which voice is raised shrinks in size. Voice can become an end in itself, and its exercise can become confused with the attainment of its objective. As soon as that happens its *cost* (in time spent, for example) can measure instead the *satisfaction* or *benefit* received from its exercise or "consumption." For this mutation of cost into benefit to occur it is necessary that the exercise of voice be felt as something beyond the many activities that are primarily self-regarding. Though originally prompted by personal concerns, voice becomes an enjoyable, exhilarating experience when it is also action in the public interest, sometimes just because it is

---

[3] Reprinted as Chapter 9, in this volume.

felt as a release from the unremitting pursuit of purely self-regarding activity. But voice stands to lose this public-interest dimension if the area within and on behalf of which it is raised shrinks unduly; it then becomes essentially self-regarding like exit and at that point its cost will once again be rigidly computed. Here is perhaps a simple explanation of the frequently higher voter turnout in national as compared to local elections, which is puzzling from the point of view of a self-interest model of political participation. In local elections, the public-interest dimension is less obvious and the cost of voting tends to be computed and related to its conceivable benefits; national elections, on the other hand, partake of the character of public celebrations and even of the traditional "feast of fools": the lowly citizen is transformed into the sovereign–though only for one day as Rousseau lamented–and he enjoys himself thoroughly in the process.

This argument, then, raises doubt about the value of indefinite territorial subdivision as a means of increasing citizen participation; it should be placed alongside and serve to qualify the much more usual view that the larger a political unit the greater will be the individual citizen's feeling of powerlessness and alienation.

3. Voice is more exposed than exit to retaliation and to being bought off

What has just been said explains much about the economist's preference for exit: voice is a far more complex, less predictable mechanism. Let me illustrate this proposition further. In my book I stressed the similarities between the ways in which exit and voice operate, and overlooked, or failed to stress sufficiently, certain characteristic differences. Two complementary observations have been made in this respect about hazards that are particularly relevant to the modus operandi of voice. They both arise out of the basic fact that he who voices remains within the organization, maintains a relationship with it. Hence the organization and its management can do things to him and in particular can treat him, because he voices, differently from the way in which it treats the other members.

In the first place, it can treat him *worse*, punish him for daring to voice. There may be *retaliation* and *reprisals* against someone who criticizes an organization, but remains within its reach. For that reason, it has been argued that the availability of a fast getaway (exit) is a precondition for a good volume of voice.[4] I agree that the availability of exit is useful in thwarting retaliation, but would also point out that a number of social mechanisms have been evolved to make voice retaliation-proof even in the absence of exit. Perhaps the best known such mechanism is the secret vote. Another is the Ombudsman institution which makes it possible for individuals in a bureaucratic organization to complain outside of hierarchical channels. Freeman's remarks on the history of trade unionism further illustrate this search for protection against retaliation which is an integral part of the development of voice. Nevertheless, in evaluating the comparative costs of voice and exit I should have given some attention not only to the expenditure of time and money, but to the risk of retaliation which is usually greater in the case of voice.

The other hazard that exists for voice far more than for exit is the exact opposite of retaliation: instead of being penalized he who voices is singled out for *special favors*. By giving the complainant preferential treatment the delinquent organization seeks to still his voice and to buy him off: in this manner, it may once again avoid having to improve the general quality of its performance. I had briefly mentioned this managerial strategy in connection with the "goldplated service" some companies extend to their more important customers.[5] Its importance has since been stressed by Schaffer and Lamb for situations in which a good or service is distributed to applicants by an administrative agency according to nonmarket criteria.[6]

This strategy of countering voice is employed not only for the purpose of appeasing important individual customers; it can be particularly useful to management in dealing with voice that takes collective form, as in the case of trade unions, consumer organizations and the like. Special treatment and favors extended to the leaders of such organizations could have results that range all the way from a slight reduction in militancy to outright corruption. This is one of the major risks to which the

[4] A. H. Birch, "Economic Models in Political Science: The Case of 'Exit, Voice, and Loyalty,' " *British Journal of Political Science* 5 (1974): 69–82.

[5] *Exit*, p. 60.

[6] Bernard B. Schaffer and Geoff B. Lamb, "Exit, Voice and Access," *Social Science Information* 13 (1974): 73–90.

effectiveness of collective organized voice is exposed. As might be expected, the rank and file can protect itself against it either through voice or through exit; but I am not going to engage here in this sort of infinite regress. Rather, I wish to end my remarks by briefly analyzing yet another related situation in which the functioning of voice is exposed to special problems not likely to be encountered by exit.

4. Voice, more than exit, can become a tool that only serves the activists

It was a general underlying assumption of my book that both forms of activism, voice and exit, would, if successful, achieve a benefit (a positive externality) for the nonactivists. This assumption would hold whenever a firm turns out a product (or the government a policy) the tastes for which are so constrained that any improvement in quality or performance undertaken by management in response to exit and voice is sensed as a positive event by everyone, activists as well as nonactivists. What happens when this constraint is relaxed? Suppose that different consumer-members have different ideas about what sort of improvements are needed and further that the ideas and tastes of the activists differ systematically from those of the nonactivists. To the extent that it is successful, the voice of the activists will then cause the quality of the product or policy to vary in such a fashion that benefits are bestowed primarily or exclusively on them.[7] The reason is simple: voice is information-rich and is able to give precise instructions to management. Note that those who voice will here receive special benefits without any conscious buying-off activity on the part of the organization.

This constellation has implications that differ considerably from my previous model. I had argued that, when exit is available and loyalty weak, deterioration would make for rapid desertion of the potentially most influential carriers of voice and would thereby cause further deterioration of organizations that are so constituted as to respond more to voice than to exit. I still hold that this model corresponds to one set of important situations in the real world. But to the extent that the just noted

[7] See Sidney Verba and Norman H. Nie, *Participation in America: Political Democracy and Social Equality* (New York: Harper & Row, 1972), Part III.

conditions prevail, the outlines of another set with almost opposite characteristics appear. It can happen that an institution originally or nominally set up to service a wide group comes to cater predominantly, in Michels-type fashion, to the wishes and tastes of an articulate minority or oligarchy within that group. If exit is available at all under these circumstances, it could then become the weapon that will typically be wielded by the "silent majority." In this perspective, the articulate few would develop a preference for voice whereas the comparative advantage of the underarticulate mass would lie in exit; exit might in fact be the only means of defense of the voiceless not so much against deterioration as against voice-induced quality changes that are not in their own interest.

Actually examples of this reversal of roles of exit and voice are not easy to find. While it is commonplace for voice to function as an instrument of the privileged and for the privileged, exit has not often been used to provide an avenue of self-defense for the voiceless. An important case in which exit did approximate this function was during the nineteenth and early twentieth centuries in connection with mass emigration from Europe to the New World. But, on the whole, the masses have had to assert themselves the hard way through passive resistance, revolts, and other attempts at voice. It simply is not often the case that the advantage of the privileged with respect to voice is offset by a similar advantage the underprivileged might have with respect to exit – the world, alas, is not arranged either so neatly or so equitably. To the contrary, because of a number of technological and institutional innovations, the privileged have in recent times compounded their traditional superiority in voice with a remarkable prowess in exit – witness the flight to the suburbs, capital flight, the multinational corporation and the brain drain. A substantial portion of my book was meant to advert to these developments and to their disruptive social consequences. Consequently, I was looking for ways of making voice more and exit less attractive, with the thought that retaining the articulate, yet exit-prone within the organization would often serve to promote the general interest. I may well not have given sufficient attention to the possibility that by using voice the articulate might just be feathering their own nest. I still believe, nevertheless, that, once in a while, they will do a bit better than that, if only because they cannot help it, that is, because my original assumption – the benefits achieved by the activists will also be available and useful to the nonactivists – does in fact apply.

Conclusion

I have now spelled out four characteristics of voice that differentiate it from exit:

1. Voice is rich and modulated: Voice conveys more information than exit.
2. Voice is exuberant: Voice is more apt than exit to become an activity that is enjoyed for its own sake, that has its own reward, especially when it is felt as action in the public interest.
3. Voice is hazardous: Voice is subject to special hazards as the organization attempts to silence it either by retaliation against those who voice or by extending special favors to them.
4. Voice is treacherous: Since voice is generally a process in which a few voice on behalf of a much larger dissatisfied or claimant group it is possible that the changes achieved through voice are primarily in the interest of the articulate few.

Viewed jointly in this way, certain relations between these four characteristics become evident. The peculiar strengths of voice in comparison to exit, that is its richness and exuberance, are balanced by its weaknesses, that is the hazards to which those who voice are exposed as well as the propensity to betrayal of the general interest that they may display. Moreover, the strengths and the weaknesses appear to be interrelated: It is precisely because voice can convey so large and varied an array of information (item 1) that those who actually do the voicing can pick and choose and emphasize those items that are most useful to their own interests (item 4); and it is because voice can become so joyful and exuberant an activity (item 2) that organizations faced with this sort of dangerous thrust become resourceful in deflecting and stunting it through efforts at retaliation and corruption (item 3).

The upshot would seem to be that the advantages of voice are counterbalanced by corresponding disadvantages, leaving the general argument on the comparative merits of exit and voice about where it was. But this is hardly the crux of the matter. Surely one should not look upon it merely as a contest in which points are scored by either voice or exit. My purpose, here, was rather to elaborate on the exit-voice polarity and, in the process, to discover some new uses to which it can be put.

11

Exit, voice, and the state

There are two main types of activist reactions to discontent with organizations to which one belongs or with which one does business: either to *voice* one's complaints, while continuing as a member or customer, in the hope of improving matters; or to *exit* from the organization, to take one's business elsewhere. *Exit, Voice, and Loyalty* was built on this dichotomy.

One of my main contentions was that economists, with their emphasis on the virtues of competition (i.e., exit), had disregarded the possible contributions of voice just as political scientists, with their interest in political participation and protest, had neglected the possible role of exit in the analysis of political behavior. The book, however, gave more attention to the former point and dealt only briefly with the political scientist's principal object of study: the state.[1] In the present essay, I shall attempt a more extensive survey. The importance of exit in relation to the state is the common theme of the diverse situations, ranging from the stateless societies of tropical Africa to the modern small welfare state, that I will explore.[2]

This paper was written for a symposium held in June 1977 at the University of Uppsala, Sweden, on the occasion of the 500-year jubilee of the foundation of the University, and was published in *World Politics* 31 (October 1978): 90–107. Reprinted by permission of Princeton University Press.
[1] Primarily in connection with the issue of resignation of officials who are in disagreement with public policies.
[2] In this volume, I am touching on emigration in relation to the state also in Chapters 9 and 10. Secessionist movements were brought into the exit-voice framework by Stein Rokkan, "Dimensions of State Formation and Nation-Building: A Possible Paradigm for Research on Variations within Europe," in Charles Tilly, ed., *The Formation of National States in Western Europe* (Princeton: Princeton University Press, 1975), pp. 562–600, and by Samuel E. Finer, "State-Building, State Boundaries and Border Control: An Essay on Certain Aspects of the First Phase of State-Building in Western Europe, Considered in the Light of the Rokkan-Hirschman Model," *Social Science Information* 13 (August-October 1974): 79–126.

I. Exit, Rousseau's savage, and stateless societies

Does the exit-voice model have something useful to contribute to the analysis of the state? It does, in the opinion of Jean-Jacques Rousseau. In the *Discourse on the Origin and the Foundations of Inequality among Men* he wrote:

> When the savage has had his dinner he is at peace with all of Nature and friends with everyone around him. What if a dispute arises about the meal? In that case, he will never become involved in a real fight without having first compared the difficulty of winning with *that of finding elsewhere the means of subsistence;* and since considerations of pride are of no consequence the fight is rapidly settled by the exchange of some fisticuffs: the winner eats, the loser *goes to look for better luck elsewhere (va chercher fortune)* and everything is at peace again; but with man in society things are altogether different. . . .[3]

Rousseau allowed here for a strictly limited amount of nonverbal voice – "some fisticuffs" in the unusual case in which there is a fight at all – and exit was for him the principal way in which the "savage" manifests nonconformity with other members of his group. This way of dealing with dissent has the virtue of minimizing conflict; it also is likely to keep any one group quite small. For exit to function in this beneficial manner, Rousseau's principal condition is the absence of "pride" – elsewhere he called it *amour propre* and contrasted it with the commendable *amour de soi* which is concerned with the satisfaction of basic physiological needs. The question whether the "savage" would be able to fill these needs after having exited from a group was taken up by Rousseau in his *Essay on the Origin of Languages* and, consistently enough, received a resoundingly affirmative answer.

> . . . the origin of languages is not due to the first needs of men; it would be absurd to hold that from the *cause that separates men* there should derive the instrument that unites them. Where, then, does language originate? In the moral needs, in the passions. Passions bring men closer together *while the need to stay alive obliges them to flee from each other.*[4]

Most readers of the *Essay* are of course interested in Rousseau's remarkable theory of language which is brought underway with these vigorous sentences. I choose to emphasize here

---

[3] Rousseau, *Oeuvres complètes* (Paris: NRF, Pléiade, 1966), Chapter III, p. 203; emphasis added.

[4] See Rousseau, *Essai sur l'origine des langues* . . . , edition, introduction, and notes by Charles Porset (Bordeaux: Ducros 1970), Chapter II, p. 43; emphasis added.

his view that breaking away from a group is not necessarily a bar to survival, so that exit becomes a feasible option in case of conflict. It is well to remember that the *Essay* was originally part of the *Discourse*;[5] the two quoted passages are different aspects of the same thought. Jointly they constitute a theory of a small, stateless society in which the availability of exit has the dual function of defusing conflict and of assuring a continuous process of fission—and thereby the continuation of the condition of statelessness.

Observation of certain so-called primitive societies in recent decades has turned up a number of situations that correspond to Rousseau's model. Writing in 1944, Claude Lévi-Strauss gives the following account of political life among the Nambikuara of Central Brazil:

> No social structure is weaker and more fragile than the Nambikuara band. If the chief's authority appears too exacting, if he keeps too many women for himself, or if he does not satisfactorily solve the food problem in times of scarcity, discontent will very likely appear. Then, individuals, or families, will separate from the group and join another band believed to be better managed. . . . Therefore, Nambikuara social structure appears continuously on the move. The bands take shape, they disorganize, they increase and they vanish. Within a few months, sometimes, their composition, number and distribution cannot be recognized.[6]

A similar pattern of social and political behavior, also from Central Brazil, is reported by Joan Bamberger about a tribe called Kayapó:

> Should traditional leadership fail to re-establish harmony after a dispute has broken out, the contestants and sometimes their supporters, which in the most dramatic instance includes the entire community, may engage in physical combat. Fighting of this kind is institutionalized among the Kayapó in the formal duel, known as *aben tak* ("hitting together"). . . . whoever loses an *aben tak*, whether it is a two-person fight or a community brawl, must leave the village. The Kayapó say that the vanquished depart because they have too much "shame" (*piaam*) to remain in the same village with those people with whom they have fought. . . .[7]

---

[5] *Ibid.*, II (introduction by Porset).

[6] Lévi-Strauss, "The Social and Psychological Aspects of Chieftainship in a Primitive Tribe: The Nambikuara of Northwestern Mato Grosso" (1944), reprinted in Ronald Cohen and John Middleton, eds., *Comparative Political Systems: Studies in the Politics of Pre-Industrial Societies* (Garden City, N.Y.: Natural History Press, 1967), pp. 53–4.

[7] Bamberger, "*Exit* and *Voice* in Central Brazil: On the Politics of Flight in Kayapó Society," in David Maybury-Lewis, ed., *Dialectical Societies: The Gê and Bororo of Central Brazil* (Cambridge, Mass.: Harvard University Press, 1979), p. 139.

The similarity to Rousseau's fisticuffs scenario is remarkable, even though the Kayapó seem to be afflicted with more than a trace of pride and *amour propre*. The disaffected Kayapó also resemble Rousseau's savage in that they simply exit without necessarily *entering* or joining some other group that seems to them to be better managed (as is the case for the group described by Lévi-Strauss); a breakaway group is here apparently willing and able to go it alone.

On turning from America to Africa, one meets with many more illustrations of the phenomenon of fissiparous politics – known to the anthropological literature under such titles as acephalous or stateless societies, segmentary lineage systems, fission and fusion, and the like. A large part of that literature deals with what in modern politics is known as "secession" rather than as "emigration." In other words, the tendency toward fission frequently takes the form of a group detaching itself from a larger one while staying (or moving about, in the case of nomadic tribes) in the same area as before. The exit concept could, of course, be extended to cover cases of this sort. I shall, however, limit myself here to situations in which physical moving away of individuals or groups is an essential characteristic of the splitting-up process.

Frequent recourse to exit in this sense appears to be an important ingredient of statelessness in a number of African societies. Evans-Pritchard says about the Nuer that "any Nuer may leave his tribe and settle in a new tribe of which he thereby becomes a member."[8] In their Introduction to *Tribes Without Rulers*, Middleton and Tait write, "In much of Central Africa, for example, there are politically uncentralized societies in which . . . the main political structure is provided by relations between chiefs and villagers of cognatic kin, related in various ways to a headman and free to choose their village residence where they please."[9] Reporting on Bushman bands in South Africa, Lorna Marshall points out that "the possibility of choice and change of

[8] Evans-Pritchard, "The Nuer of the Southern Sudan," in M. Fortes and E. E. Evans-Pritchard, eds., *African Political Systems* (London: Oxford University Press, 1940), p. 279.

[9] John Middleton and David Tait, eds., *Tribes Without Rulers: Studies in African Segmentary Systems* (London: Routledge and Kegan Paul, 1958), p. 3. It should be noted that the book does not deal with these societies; it concentrates on those having "segmentary lineage systems," where exit resembles secession rather than emigration.

members from one band to another . . . allows for adjustment in the size of the band to the relative scarcity of food and water" and that "a new band can be formed at any time that circumstances permit and people desire to form one." Friction in human relations is one reason for such new band formation.[10]

The most elaborate description of the fission process via geographical separation is in Turnbull's account of Mbuti pygmy bands in the tropical rain forest of Central Africa. Here fissions that have little to do with lineal relationships are frequent occurrences, specially on the occasion when a camp moves.

> Sites are even chosen because they afford greater privacy between the various sections, thus minimizing any serious disputes that are in progress. Some interpersonal hostilities will persist, however, and it is these and not lineal relationships that are reflected in the final fission, when the camp divides into a number of independent camps, or sub-bands, each going its own way. If the dispute is serious, one or another sub-band may go off to another territory, and seek to join up with that band. . . .
>
> So the monthly change of camp is an opportunity not only for a diplomatic rearrangement of the layout, minimizing latent hostilities, but it is also an opportunity for improving the economic strength of the band by either adding to it or subtracting from it.[11]

By bringing together these various situations – which Rousseau hit upon by pure deduction – I hope to have demonstrated that some forms of statelessness are closely associated with the possibility and regular practice of exit. But it is by no means easy to interpret the nature of this association. The fact that my most explicit examples in America and Africa come from bands living in thinly populated tropical rain forests or savannahs suggests that the availability of at least minimally fertile, unoccupied natural resources makes exit permanently attractive and prevents the emergence of any larger political grouping with statelike authority. Such availability, however, is not a sufficient condition for statelessness: within a lord-peasant or lord-laborer context, exactly the same situation has been quite plausibly invoked

[10] Marshall, "!Kung Bushman Bands" (1960), reprinted in Cohen and Middleton (n. 6), 17, 34–5.

[11] Colin M. Turnbull, *Wayward Servants: The Two Worlds of the African Pygmies* (London: Eyre and Spottiswoode, 1965), p. 106. Turnbull attempts to explain this constant "flux and instability" of the Mbuti bands by their antagonistic relationship with the settled villagers who, as a result of this confusion, are unable to assert the lineal and territorial rights they claim over the Mbuti.

by Nieboer and others as favoring the introduction of *slavery*.[12] The presence of "open resources" is no doubt important in shaping political forms; but, depending on other system determinants, it can lead either to a highly coercive system or to one that lacks any specialized and permanently constituted political authority. Moreover, these two polar opposites do not exhaust the universe of possibilities: after all, Nieboer's "open resources" are not so far from Turner's "open frontier."[13]

In any event, I do not wish to propound here an ecological theory of stateless societies. What interests me is not so much the fundamental reason for which exit takes place with such regularity as the political effects of institutionalized exit. One of these effects is the nonemergence of large, centralized societies with specialized state organs. Another is the apparent stability of the statelessness-cum-exit condition over wide areas and through time. Political arrangements that are unstable at the level of individual bands, with their constant fission and fusion, have been remarkably stable – as though frozen in this pattern of instability – when looked at from a slightly more macro point of view. One reason is that the exit pattern of conflict behavior, once set, is very difficult to change except through some outside event such as invasion or exhaustion of the "open resources." Once again, the practice of exit is self-reinforcing. Once this avoidance mechanism for dealing with disputes or venting dissatisfaction is readily available, the contribution of voice – that is of the political process – to such matters is likely to be and to remain limited.[14]

In accounting for stability, one would wish to know something about the feedback effect of exit on the organization that is being left: does the organization take notice of exits by its members and act in consequence in such a manner as to remedy its weaknesses and inefficiencies? Unfortunately, the anthropological studies I have cited do not supply much material in answer

---

[12] H. J. Nieboer, *Slavery as an Industrial System* (The Hague: Nijhoff, 1900); Evsey Domar, "The Causes of Slavery or Serfdom: A Hypothesis," *Journal of Economic History*, (March 1970): 18–32.

[13] Nieboer and Frederick Jackson Turner were contemporaries, but were probably unaware that one was speaking of "open resources" as a factor conducive to slavery and the other of the "open frontier" as conditioning American-style democracy.

[14] This is true even for so elaborate a function as that of the "leopard-skin chief" of the Nuer in mediating disputes. See Evans-Pritchard (n. 8), pp. 291–5.

to this question. When exit occurs as a result of disputes between the two parties, it probably just produces satisfaction for the one that remains, and a "good riddance" reaction. According to some of the descriptions, however, exit results not only from the push of internal dispute, but also from the pull of "superior management" of other bands. In such a case, the bands that are losing members are more likely to react to the loss by attempting to improve their own performance. In view of the stability of these societies through time, one may perhaps infer that such a stabilizing feedback process must be at work: if exit were always cumulative, with losing bands never being able to recoup their losses, a tendency toward consolidation of the many bands into one would have asserted itself. (Another explanation why this does not occur would be that there is some sort of optimal size for bands with diseconomies of scale setting in if this size is exceeded.)

The exit behavior characteristic of the societies just reviewed, particularly when exit from one band involves entry into another, "better managed" one, is remarkably similar to what has been called "voting with one's feet." Because it resembles the working of the market where a buyer is free to switch from one seller to another, some quarters have celebrated this mechanism as far more "efficient" than the "cumbersome" political process for the redress of people's grievances or the fulfillment of their demands.[15] Unfortunately, because of differences in income and wealth, the ability to vote with one's feet is unequally distributed in modern societies. In the United States, where the problem is compounded because of race discrimination, inequality in access to exit has had some appalling consequences, such as the "ghetto-ization" and partial ruin of our big cities. It is possible that a more satisfactory approximation to the neo-laissez-faire economist's political dream is found in the societies of the forest people in Central Brazil and Central Africa; in historical perspective, of course, theirs has not been a perfect solution either, since they have turned out to be no match for the perhaps less efficient, but more powerful societies – exitless and endowed with a centralized political organization – that arose elsewhere.

[15] Milton Friedman, *Capitalism and Freedom* (Chicago: Chicago University Press, 1962), Chapter 6; Charles M. Tiebout, "A Pure Theory of Local Expenditures," *Journal of Political Economy*, Vol. 64 (October 1956), pp. 416–24.

II. Movable property and its exit as a restraint on the state

The European state system of the seventeenth and eighteenth centuries is precisely that sort of society in one of its purest forms. To a considerable extent, the absolutist state arose as a result of a laborious and eventually successful fight for the formation and territorial unification of a geographical unit. Particularly on the European Continent, the state was, as Samuel Finer has remarked, "obsessed by the demon of exit," exit being taken here in the sense of territorial autonomy or secession.[16] It is ironic, then, and was so sensed by some eighteenth-century observers, that as soon as one form of exit had been brought under control, another raised its head because of the expansion of commerce and finance which was actively promoted by the absolutist state. With this expansion, a new form of wealth assumed increasing importance. It was named *movable* wealth, in contrast with the unmovable form – land and buildings – in which the bulk of assets had traditionally been held. Montesquieu defined it as "money, notes, bills of exchange, stocks of companies, ships, all commodities and merchandise"; he noted that this form of wealth could move about from one country to another.[17]

What was the reaction of the state and of enlightened opinion to the discovery of this new form of wealth and to the possibility of its exit? The fears and hopes aroused by the rise of movable capital in the seventeenth and eighteenth centuries offer many interesting parallels with similarly contradictory perceptions caused quite recently by the rise of the multinational corporation.[18] A comparative study cannot be undertaken here, but a brief survey of reactions to the earlier phenomenon will perhaps be suggestive.

Initially, there was a lag in the perception of the new form of wealth, and particularly of its possible importance for politics. The case of James Harrington is striking. He is justly famous for his theory relating political forms and stability to the concentration and distribution of property. Nevertheless, at a time when the major mercantilist tracts about trade and bullion were being

[16] See Finer (n. 1), 115.
[17] Montesquieu, *Esprit des lois*, XX, chap. 23.
[18] See Hirschman, *Passions and Interests*, p. 95, and Part Two, passim.

written, his principal work, *Oceana* (1656), focused exclusively on landed property and its distribution as a determinant of politics. Criticized on this score by some of his contemporaries, he later justified his position by pointing, with an elaborate metaphor drawn from falconry, to the superior ability of "Mony" to take to flight:

Tho Riches in general have Wings and be apt to bate; yet those in Land are the most hooded, and ty'd to the Perch, whereas those in Mony have the least hold, and are the swiftest of flight. . . . a Bank never paid an Army; or paying an Army soon became no Bank. But where a Prince or a Nobility has an Estate in Land, the Revenue whereof will defray this Charge, there their Men are planted, have Toes that are Roots, and Arms that bring forth what Fruits you please.[19]

Here was an eloquent defense of the model used by Harrington. But the very "flightiness" of money which he stressed for this purpose raised questions about favorable or unfavorable *political* consequences that were to be expected as movable property became a substantial proportion of a country's total wealth.

One century later a debate along such lines was in full swing. It was not ever fully joined: those who looked at the new phenomenon with hope or alarm, respectively, usually dealt with different varieties of movable property. For example, one of the strongest denunciations of the new form of wealth was issued by David Hume as he focused on the public debt. In one of his later "conservative" essays, he predicted that "a grievous despotism must infallibly prevail" were England to allow the public debt to expand indefinitely; he castigated the holders of the debt, the "stockholders . . . who have no connexions with the state, who can enjoy their revenue in any part of the globe in which they chuse to reside. . . ."[20]

Exit of the "stockholders," or "stockjobbers" as they were also called in a pejorative vein, is here judged as an act of disloyalty and near-betrayal, without any redeeming features. But this passage stands quite alone in Hume's writings; he had only praise

[19] See "The Prerogative of Popular Government," in James Harrington, *Oceana and Other Works*, ed. John Toland (3d ed.; London: A. Millar, 1747), p. 243.

[20] From essay, "Of Public Credit" in Hume, *Writings on Economics*, ed. E. Rotwein (Madison: University of Wisconsin Press, 1970), pp. 98–9. For a number of telling eighteenth-century quotes denouncing the new world of stockjobbers and finance, see Isaac Kramnick, *Bolingbroke and His Circle: The Politics of Nostalgia in the Age of Walpole* (Cambridge, Mass.: Harvard University Press, 1968), pp. 47–8, 71–6, 220, 246.

for the new forms of mobile wealth generated by trade and industry – as did some of his friends and contemporaries, such as Adam Smith and Montesquieu. Actually, the latter discovered grounds for hailing the newly emerging forms of property, not in spite but *because* of their capacity for self-expatriation. This is a rather unexpected argument that is worth reviewing in some detail.

Always on the lookout for ways in which the overweening power of the sovereign could be checked, Montesquieu saw much promise in the invention and expanding use of the bill of exchange.

. . . through this means commerce could elude violence, and maintain itself everywhere; for the richest trader had only invisible wealth which could be sent everywhere without leaving any trace. . . .

Since that time, the rulers have been compelled to govern with greater wisdom than they themselves might have intended; for, owing to these events, the great and sudden arbitrary actions of the sovereign (*les grands coups d'autorité*) have been proven to be ineffective and . . . only good government brings prosperity [to the prince].[21]

Thus, the fact that, with the bill of exchange, a large portion of wealth had become mobile and elusive and was capable of both hiding and expatriation is here celebrated as a restraint on the *grands coups d'autorité* of the prince and as a positive contribution to good government.[22]

The new inability of political authority to seize the citizens' wealth at will also struck others as making a fundamental difference to the way in which government was likely to be carried on; the argument was formulated in a general way (that is, not just with regard to the bill of exchange) by Sir James Steuart: As private wealth expands, it "avoids [the statesman's] grasp when he attempts to seize it. This makes his government more com-

---

[21] Montesquieu (n. 17), XXI, Chapter 20.

[22] Later in the century, Turgot based very similar hopes on the emigration of *persons*. Commenting on Richard Price's *Observations on the Importance of the American Revolution* he wrote: "The asylum which [the American people] opens to the oppressed of all nations must console the earth. The ease with which it will now be possible to take advantage of this situation, and thus to escape from the consequences of a bad government, will oblige the European Governments to be just and enlightened." (Letter to Price of March 22, 1778, in *Oeuvres*, Paris: Delance 1810, IX, 389.) Turgot here argues about the state losing citizens as though it were a firm impelled by the exit of customers to improve its performance. The actual political effects of emigration on the sending country and their considerable diversity are explored in the next section.

plex and more difficult to be carried on; *he must now avail himself of art and address* as well as of power and authority."[23]

Capital flight—the possible exit of capital (and of the capitalists)—was perceived as a salutary restraint on arbitrary government by both Montesquieu and Sir James Steuart, who put forward several far more sanguine speculations about the likely political effects of economic expansion. Although Adam Smith differed with them in these respects,[24] he went along to the extent of arguing that the mobility and elusiveness of "capital stock" make it impossible for taxation to be as "vexatious" as it might otherwise be:

There are . . . two different circumstances which render the interest of money a much less proper subject of direct taxation than the rent of land.

First, the quantity and value of the land which any man possesses can never be a secret, and can always be ascertained with great exactness. But the whole amount of the capital stock which he possesses is almost always a secret, and can scarce ever be ascertained with tolerable exactness. . . . An inquisition into every man's private circumstances . . . would be a source of such continual and endless vexation as no people could support.

Secondly, land is a subject which cannot be removed, whereas stock easily may. The proprietor of land is necessarily a citizen of the particular country in which his estate lies. The proprietor of stock is properly a citizen of the world, and is not necessarily attached to any particular country. *He would be apt to abandon the country in which he was exposed to a vexatious inquisition, in order to be assessed to a burdensome tax, and would remove his stock to some other country where he could either carry on his business, or enjoy his fortune more at his ease.* By removing his stock he would put an end to all the industry which it had maintained in the country which he left. Stock cultivates land; stock employs labour. A tax which tended to drive away stock from any particular country, would so far tend to dry up every source of revenue, both to the sovereign and to the society. . . .

The nations, accordingly, who have attempted to tax the revenue arising from stock, instead of any severe inquisition of this kind, have been obliged to content themselves with some very loose . . . estimation.[25]

It would almost seem, then, as though everything were for the best: on the one hand, the dangerous exit in the form of secession had been more or less successfully exorcised by the power of the seventeenth- and eighteenth-century state; on the

---

[23] Steuart, *Inquiry into the Principles of Political Oeconomy* (1767), I, ed. A. S. Skinner (Chicago: University of Chicago Presss, 1966), p. 181; emphasis added.

[24] *Passions and Interests*, pp. 100–13.

[25] Smith, *The Wealth of Nations*, Modern Library ed., p. 800; see also pp. 345 and 858 for related passages; emphasis added.

other, according to the converging testimony of Montesquieu, Sir James Steuart, and Adam Smith, that power was curbed by a new and beneficial variety of exit that surfaced as a result of economic expansion: the ability of capital and capitalists to "remove their stock" or, in modern terms, to "vote with their feet" for the best available "business climate."

It is useful to recall these early perceptions, if only to marvel at the distance by which they are separated from contemporary ones. Today the international mobility of capital is infinitely greater (within the capitalist world) than at the time of Montesquieu and Adam Smith. There are numerous varieties of such mobility: transnational corporations can move subsidiaries from one country, considered unsafe, to another; more threateningly, mobility can take the form of international banks refusing to "roll over" their loans to a country that is considered to be "out of line." Still, the principal weapon is wielded by the country's own citizens – particularly of course by the more opulent ones among them – as they engage in capital flight on a massive scale whenever they feel threatened by domestic developments.

Occasionally these various exits do occur, according to the eighteenth-century script, in response to the arbitrary and capricious actions of the sovereign. But a much less favorable interpretation may be in order: exit of capital often takes place in countries intending to introduce some taxation that would curb excessive privileges of the rich or some social reforms designed to distribute the fruits of economic growth more equitably. Under these conditions, capital flight and its threat are meant to parry, fight off, and perhaps veto such reforms; whatever the outcome, they are sure to make reform more costly and difficult. It looks, therefore, as though the availability of the kind of exit that was hailed by Montesquieu and Adam Smith were today a serious menace: it damages the capability of capitalism to reform itself.[26]

Actually, this situation does not affect all countries equally. Capital flight is obviously much less of a weapon in the largest and most powerful countries where the owners of capital feel that there is no place else to go. Here it can be expected that voice will be activated by the impossibility of exit. Capitalists will

[26] See also Chapter 12, Section III.

make elaborate attempts to influence public opinion and public policy. An ideology in defense of capitalism will arise. At the same time, concessions are likely to be forthcoming where reforms of the system are obviously needed and are essential to the demonstration that the capitalist system can itself evolve and ameliorate the problems it creates. Purely on the basis of the differential availability of exit for capital and capitalists, one might therefore expect that the largest and most central countries of the capitalist system would be, at one and the same time, the ideological bulwarks of the system and its most active problem-solvers; the more peripheral states, on the other hand, might be in the grip of an anticapitalist ideology, and would at the same time exhibit unconscionable extremes of wealth and poverty. This "prediction," based on a most parsimonious exit-voice model, is surprisingly correct in a number of respects. The combination of an attitude of "standing up for capitalism" with attempts to remedy the system's worst evils is exemplified by both Victorian England and the United States of the twentieth century; in many less developed countries, on the other hand, the absence of any strong ideological support for capitalism coexists rather oddly with extraordinary difficulties faced time and again by attempts at effective reform. Here is perhaps a key to the old puzzle why anticapitalist revolutions have consistently broken out at the periphery rather than at the center of the capitalist system.

Fortunately, the model does not explain everything. In particular, it does not deal satisfactorily with an important group of small countries. A few additional factors must therefore be introduced.

III. Exit as a threat to the small modern state and some defensive strategies

In the eighteenth century, as has just been noted, the potential exit of capital and of the capitalists was actively discussed in terms of its harmful or beneficial effects on the capital-losing state. This manner of looking at out-migration – so congenial to the exit-voice framework – almost disappeared in the nineteenth century, which witnessed human migration, mostly from Europe to America, on an unprecedented scale. Only recently have the economic and political effects of out-migration on sending (rather than receiving) states again attracted attention, primarily in conjunction with the so-called brain drain, a phenomenon that has more in common with capital flight than with mass migration.

The enormous out-migration from Europe during the nineteenth and early twentieth centuries did not occasion much reflection about the feedback effect on the sending states and their political system because the outflow did not provoke any visible political problems or dangers. On the contrary–and this also explains why emigration, long prohibited during the mercantilist and absolutist eras, was so freely permitted–it *alleviated* a number of problems, economic as well as political. From the social and economic points of view, the outflow dampened the rapid increase in population as well as the concomitant rural-urban migration, and in spite of its massive proportions, emigration never reached the point where it was perceived to interfere with the recruitment of labor for expanding domestic industry. From the point of view of the political managers, out-migration had similar and related beneficial effects. People who chose emigration were obviously dissatisfied in some way with the country and society they were leaving. With exit available as an outlet for the disaffected, they were less likely to resort to voice: the ships carrying the migrants contained many actual or potential anarchists and socialists, reformers and revolutionaries. The inverse relationship between emigration and the socialist vote has been statistically demonstrated for Italy, in a study for the decade preceding World War I.[27] Moreover, new immigrants tend to be, at least initially, relatively unvociferous members of society; mass migration thus reduced social protest in the European-American state system as a whole and not only in the sending countries.

But the containment of social protest was not the only political effect of out-migration. Throughout the nineteenth century and up to World War I, the right of suffrage and other civil rights were extended in many of the very European states from which large contingents of people were departing. In other words, exit and a certain kind of voice increased hand-in-hand, even though, at the same time, exit lowered the volume of another more militant kind

[27] John S. MacDonald, "Agricultural Organization, Migration and Labour Militancy in Rural Italy," *Economic History Review*, second series 16 (1963–64): 61–75.

of voice. These two developments may be causally connected: because a number of disaffected people had departed, it became comparatively safe to open up the system to a larger number of those who stayed on. In this manner, exit-emigration may have made it possible for democratization and liberalization to proceed in several European countries prior to World War I without political stability being seriously imperiled.[28]

Besides being intrinsically interesting, these connections could contribute to the understanding of contemporary attempts at democratization. Might it be said, for example, that the large-scale emigration of Greek, Portuguese, and Spanish workers to France and Germany during the prosperous sixties and early seventies has made it easier for these countries to negotiate the difficult passage to a more democratic order than would have been the case otherwise?

In part, this topic has not received attention because the connection is rather remote and counterintuitive. That emigration of dissenters will strengthen an authoritarian regime in the short run is obvious; not content with allowing emigration, many such regimes have taken it upon themselves to deport or ban their political enemies – that is, they dealt with them in this particular manner during their more humane moments. But the likelihood that opening the gates and permitting out-migration may allow a regime to liberalize itself seems farfetched – except to those who have taken an advanced course in exit and voice.

Probably the main reason for the lack of interest in the political effects of emigration is that, as explained earlier, these effects had long been so positive. We do not investigate whatever seems to be going well no matter how poorly we understand the underlying process.

In recent years, however, emigration has not been wholly benign in its effects on the migrant-losing countries. This applies first of all to the brain drain: the size of the literature that has grown up around this topic strongly suggests that it is widely

---

[28] I have looked in vain for any speculation along such lines in the notable monographic studies on European migrations to the United States published as *Dislocation and Emigration: The Social Background of American Immigration* in D. Fleming and B. Bailyn, eds., *Perspectives in American History*, VII (Harvard University, 1974). Professor Bailyn tells me that in his current work on seventeenth- and eighteenth-century emigration to North America considerable attention is being given to the social and political context of emigration in the sending country.

viewed as a problem. But even the nineteenth-century kind of emigration became a problem when it gave a repeat performance in the twentieth, such as, for instance, the large-scale Irish emigration to England during the postwar period. The long decline of the Irish population, due to low birthrates and emigration, had come to a stop during the twenty-five years following Independence (1922), which coincided with the Depression and the Second World War. But after the war and particularly in the fifties, emigration, mostly from rural districts into urban Britain, surged once again and reached the highest levels in a century, in relation to the resident population (15 per mille per year in 1956–61). This outflow aroused deep concern and became an important public and political issue that led to a decisive turn in economic policy. By the late fifties, the old description of emigration as a "safety valve" had been replaced by the image of a country suffering from hemophilia with "blood running out of its veins." The increasing concern that "Ireland was a dying country . . . led to calls for new economic policies, the adoption of various plans by the different political parties, the appearance of emigration as an issue in a parliamentary election for the first time, and finally the unopposed acceptance (in 1958) of a national economic plan designed to develop Ireland and prevent emigration."[29] The plan was successful in attracting foreign capital and spurring industrialization, but it is an open question to what extent the considerable drop in emigration in the sixties was due to the plan's success or to the diminished absorptive capacity of the British economy which itself became increasingly troubled during that period.

With the Irish immigrants encountering a similar environment and a familiar language in England, Irish emigration came to assume unusually large proportions and was eventually perceived as a threat to Ireland's national existence. A similar situation arose in East Germany, which in the 1950s experienced a flood of (illegal) emigration toward West Germany. Beset with concerns rather similar to those of the Irish, the government of the D.D.R. did not bother to look around for ways of making itself more attractive to its citizens: in 1961 it simply closed its frontiers more effectively than before by building the Berlin Wall.

[29] Nicholas R. Burnett, "Exit, Voice and Ireland, 1936–58," unpublished (1977), p. 15; also Burnett's doctoral dissertation, "Emigration and Modern Ireland" (School of Advanced International Studies, Johns Hopkins University, 1976).

The reactions of the two countries that felt threatened by mass emigration were thus very different, in parallel to similarly different reactions of various European countries to the sudden availability of cheap wheat from North America and Russia in the 1870s.[30] East Germany adopted a primarily defensive strategy – comparable to the imposition of higher tariffs on wheat by France and Germany in the late nineteenth century; Ireland, on the other hand, attempted to meet the challenge of mass exit by changing the underlying conditions that had resulted in the outflow – and this "creative response" is similar to Denmark's policies of agricultural transformation.

Both Ireland and East Germany, however, had something in common: a new perception of exit as a threat. They reacted with considerable determination, as though they were fully persuaded, in line with the thesis of the first section of this essay, that the existence of the state is incompatible with the virtually costless availability of exit and with resort of citizens to it as a routine response to dissatisfaction.

No doubt, these two countries and their experiences in the fifties were special pathological cases. But for that very reason they are of interest as they reveal potential trouble spots in the present state system. With closer communication, easy circulation of capital, and unprecedented international mobility of high-level manpower, states are today exposed to more exit pressures than ever before. Small states are particularly vulnerable to these pressures: a large country can often rather easily accommodate an inflow of capital or manpower from a small country, while as an outflow these resources may represent a critical loss for the small country.

Why is it that there have not been more Irelands and East Germanys in the last thirty years or so? In part, no doubt, because *entry* has by no means been totally unregulated.[31] But in view of the considerable freedom of movement that has prevailed for capital and people (especially for trained personnel), it

---

[30] See Charles P. Kindleberger, "Group Behavior and International Trade," *Journal of Political Economy* 59 (February 1951): 30–46; and Peter A. Gourevitch, "International Trade, Domestic Coalitions, and Liberty: The Crisis of 1873–96," *Journal of Interdisciplinary History* 8 (Autumn 1977): 281–313.

[31] See Aristide R. Zolberg, "International Migration Policies in a Changing World System" in William H. McNeill and Ruth S. Adams, eds., *Human Migration* (Bloomington: Indiana University Press, 1978), pp. 241–86.

is likely that many states, and particularly small ones, have hit on various devices and strategies through which they have parried excessive tendencies toward exit. I shall briefly investigate how such strategies might work.

In the case of Ireland, the remedy for exit consisted of improved economic policy and conditions; indeed, countries worrying about exit do well to satisfy the basic economic aspirations of their citizens, particularly of the more mobile among them. But fortunately, individual economic welfare is not the only criterion on the basis of which the difficult and often agonizing decision to exit from one's own country is made.

What is needed in order to avoid excessive emigration and crippling brain drain is for a society to provide its members with some "attractions" that will reinforce their normal reluctance to leave. Besides an adequate supply of goods available for individual consumption, such attractions can also consist of what is known to economists as "public goods"; that is, goods that any member of a society can enjoy (consume) without thereby depriving others of their enjoyment (consumption) of these goods. A country's power and prestige, for example, are a public good that may be enjoyed by all of its citizens, including the most lowly and powerless. Along these lines it has lately been pointed out that social justice may be a public good: individuals may find it enjoyable to live in a society where income distribution is comparatively egalitarian.[32] Other public goods that come to mind include a long record for not becoming involved in international conflict or for guaranteeing human rights and democratic liberties. The latter two would make a country attractive to its citizens, especially in a world where destructive warfare frequently erupts and where many governments habitually suppress criticism and mistreat their political opponents.

The availability in a country of any one of these public goods serves to hold exit at bay and to increase loyalty.[33] It is possible to visualize a state system in which, in spite of close contact and free movement of people and capital, exit would never assume

---

[32] Lester C. Thurow, "The Income Distribution as a Pure Public Good," *Quarterly Journal of Economics* 85 (May 1971): 327–36; David Morawetz and others, "Income Distribution and Self-Rated Happiness: Some Empirical Evidence," *Economic Journal* 87 (September 1977): 511–22.

[33] See *Exit*, Chapter 7, particularly p. 78.

threatening proportions because each country would supply its citizens with a different assortment of public goods, with emphasis on one area (or a cluster) as a special attraction for its own citizens. Different countries would then "specialize" in power, wealth, growth, equity, peacefulness, the observance of human rights, and so on. Such specialization would certainly result in a more stable situation than if performance of nations were rated only along one dimension, such as per capita GNP; in the latter case, it would become possible to establish an unambiguous rating among countries, and exits toward the best performers would mount dangerously. Achievements along the various dimensions just mentioned are not easily combined into a unique preference scale or welfare function; it is likely, however, that if a country's citizens were equipped with a modicum of loyalty to start with, they would value the particular area in which their country excels—whatever that may be—more highly than that of the others. An ethnocentric welfare function of this sort may therefore be a condition for a stable state system under modern circumstances of high potential mobility.

The foregoing "polyphonic" solution to the problem is perhaps too beautiful to be real. Among its difficulties is the obvious one that the pursuit of peace by one country may be incompatible with that of power by another. Then there is the fact that, frequently, "all good things go together": one or a very few countries may be doing best, or are perceived to do so, along several important dimensions such as power, wealth, education, and general opportunity. A related problem is that a hegemonic country may impose its own preferences and welfare function upon public opinion around the world. As a result, especially in a world with intensive communication networks, citizens of non-hegemonic countries would tend to give a higher rating to the achievements of the leading country than to those of their own.

In the face of such difficulties, do smaller countries have a second line of defense? Is there, in other words, some further highly valued public good that a smaller country can provide for its more mobile citizens so that they will still think twice before emigrating? A remark by the American sociologist Renée Fox, who has been studying Belgian society for many years, is illuminating in this regard. Explaining her long involvement with that country, she says that she originally found Belgium tempting because, among other things, she was led to believe that "a small country . . . would be simpler than a large country to comprehend in a sociological sense." But that premise turned out to be totally untrue; many years later she exclaims, "if I were now asked to formulate a sociological hypothesis about the relationship between the size of a country and the complexity of its social system, I would be tempted to suggest that there is an inverse relationship between the two; that is, the smaller the country, the more complex its social system!"[34]

In conjunction with the concern over excessive exit, this remark raises the question whether complexity could perhaps be part of a country's attraction for its citizens, as much as any positive achievement of the previously mentioned kind. For it is *understood* complexity insofar as the country's citizens are concerned; *they* know how to navigate expertly, not only in their country's language, but among its idiosyncratic ways, its conflicts and familiar frustrations.[35] When I first came to live in Colombia, explanations offered by Colombians of various to me puzzling situations would invariably start with the sentence "Es que ese es un país muy raro" ("you must realize that this is a very odd country"). Clearly, they took considerable pleasure in enlightening me about something *they* understood so well. *Understood complexity* may then be another public good a society can supply to its citizens, and that is perhaps a clue to Renée Fox's paradox about small countries being more complex than large ones. With the latter having so much going for them, the smaller countries defend themselves against excessive exit through a plentiful supply of understood complexity; and, with respect to this particular asset, there is full assurance that "you can't take it with you."

[34] Fox, "An American Sociologist in the Land of Belgian Medical Research," in Philip E. Hammond, ed., *Sociologists at Work* (New York: Basic Books, 1964), p. 349.
[35] On the difference between the "native's" views of his society and the outside observer's, see Clifford Geertz, "On the Nature of Anthropological Understanding," *American Scientist*, 63 (January–February 1975): 47–53.

12

Three uses of political economy in analyzing European integration

We have recently been taught by several works of large-scale historical interpretation that a group of competing states – such as France, Spain, and the other European powers that emerged after the Middle Ages – may acquire, augment, and maintain its collective influence over outlying areas precisely because of its divisions and interstate conflicts, because, that is, the group is *not* integrated into an imperial unit.[1]

If this conjecture has merit, some of our most hackneyed phrases and proverbs will have to be revised and inverted to read "be divided and rule!" or *"La désunion fait la force"* (Disunity makes for strength), etc. It is of course unlikely that these paradoxes can totally substitute for the older wisdom, but I can see at least one other field of application for the new insight: the influence and prestige of social science as a whole may owe much to the *lack* of integration and communication among the individual disciplines of economics, sociology, political science, and so on. It is this lack which may be responsible for the widespread conviction that *some* social science must hold the key to a full understanding of an ongoing and puzzling social process. When one discipline does not give too good an account of itself it is possible to appeal to another one, which, being totally isolated from

Originally prepared for a conference on economic approaches to the study of international integration, held at the European University Institute in Florence, Italy, in June 1979. Together with other conference papers this essay is to be published in a volume edited for the European University Institute by Pierre Salmon who organized the conference.

[1] See Perry Anderson, *Lineages of the Absolutist State* (London: N.L.B., 1974) and Immanuel Wallerstein, *The Modern World-System* (New York: Academic Press, 1974). The same point had been made in Jean Baechler, *Les origines du capitalisme* (Paris: Gallimard, 1971), translated into English as *The Origins of Capitalism* (Oxford: Blackwell, 1975).

the first, sets out, so to speak, with a clean sheet and honey-moonlike expectations.

Something of this sort may be happening with regard to the study of European integration. An attractive political science model of integration that was put forward in the fifties has been badly eroded, both by the evolving facts and by rival interpretations. The idea that political science is able to illuminate the dynamics of integration is owed in good measure to the 1958 book by Ernst Haas, *The Uniting of Europe*, and to its guiding concept of "spillover."[2] With this concept, which will be briefly discussed later in this essay, Haas essentially articulated what was the unspoken strategy – the "thinkful wishing" – of such architects of European integration as Jean Monnet. But already in the 1968 preface to the second edition of his book, Haas saw fit to qualify his earlier "neo-functionalist" analysis and enthusiasm. Another seven years later, he issued a paper whose very title, "The Obsolescence of Regional Integration Theory,"[3] appeared to deprecate the attempt to make sense of integration through the conceptual tools available to political scientists. In general, the literature on political integration, which was burgeoning in the fifties and sixties, has considerably abated in the seventies.

But this experience did not lead to a general stocktaking about the ability of social science to furnish explanations of certain processes and to formulate "laws of motion." The prestige of one social science discipline is not tarnished by the misadventures of another, so that it is possible for, say, economists to claim that they can "handle" a problem that has perplexed the political scientists. In recent years, this relay effect has in fact occurred in a number of areas long thought to be the exclusive province of political science as some economists, aided and abetted strangely enough by not a few political scientists, have as-

---

[2] First published in 1958 by Stevens and Sons Ltd., London. Reissued with a new preface by Stanford University Press, 1968. Another influential work on the dynamics of the integration process, written at approximately the same time, but more cautious in its conclusions and predictions, is Karl W. Deutsch et al., *Political Community and the North Atlantic Area* (Princeton, N.J.: Princeton University Press, 1957). Based on an intensive reading of the historical record over a wide area and a long historical period, this book also gave an important impulse to further studies of integration.

[3] Research Series No. 25, Institute of International Studies, University of California, Berkeley, 1975.

serted that their approach (based on the assumption of rational action in the service of individual self-interest) is applicable over a much wider field than it has traditionally occupied.

Now I must right away take my distance from this particular claim. As I wrote a few years ago:

> . . . there are serious pitfalls in any transfer of analytical tools and modes of reasoning developed within one discipline to another. As the economist, swollen with pride over the comparative rigor of his discipline, sets out to bring the light to his heathen colleagues in the other social sciences, he is likely to overlook some crucial distinguishing feature of the newly invaded terrain which makes his concepts and apparatus rather less applicable and illuminating than he is wont to think. [As in the case of] imported ideologies, the distance between reality and intellectual schema is here likely to be both wider and more difficult to detect than was the case as long as the scheme stayed safely "at home."[4]

Nevertheless, economists and economic reasoning can contribute a great deal to the understanding of the obviously interrelated processes of economic and political integration. The field for such explorations is in fact so rich that I propose to subdivide it into three distinct categories.

In the first place, we shall note a case – the economic theory of customs unions – in which the very distinctions made and concepts created for the purpose of analyzing the economics of integration have implications that throw light on the politics of the process. The economist who moves with ease among his own distinctions has of course a comparative advantage in getting hold of these unexpected dividends of his analysis. But often he fails to exploit his advantage, for lack of interdisciplinary motivation. Perhaps also, it is a sound, if partisan, instinct that makes him reluctant to venture onto the terrain of the political implications of his analysis: for once these implications have been spelled out, the policy conclusion of the economic analysis considered in isolation may have to be substantially modified, as will soon be shown.

The second category of useful interaction between economics and politics has to do with situations where economic and political phenomena are perceived to have analogical structures. In such cases – my example will here be economic development in comparison with economic-political integration – exploring the

---

[4] *Bias for Hope* (New Haven: Yale University Press, 1971), pp. 3–4.

analogy can be conducive to a better understanding of both phenomena involved. Some years ago an analogy of this sort was drawn between money and power and political scientists were quite excited about the possibility of learning something new about power–that perennial black box–by asking questions about the "earning," "accumulation" and "spending" of power. In such cases, one discipline serves essentially as a metaphoric language for the other and in the process matters are often seen in an entirely new light. In the end, however, every metaphor, illuminating though it may be, has its limitations. Coming up against them will actually be also useful, for it will lead to a better appreciation of the uniqueness of each of the two phenomena.

It is my belief that the major contributions economists can make to an understanding of the politics of integration fall within the two just noted categories which have the common characteristic of respecting the autonomy of the political. But I do not want to deny that occasionally there may be a third category: Here the economist would transfer concepts and modes of analysis originally elaborated for the purpose of understanding the economy to the political terrain. This is clearly a case of "imperialistic" expansion of one discipline and, as I have already stated, I have serious doubts about the practice (for reasons other than mere dislike of imperialism). In the third part of this paper, I shall nevertheless engage in this sort of enterprise which will, however, have the redeeming feature that the basic conceptual structure that will be transferred and applied–the exit-voice model–is itself a mixture of economic and political elements.

I. The politics of trade creation and trade diversion

Returning for a moment to the self-proclaimed demise of political science in relation to the analysis of integration, I feel that economists can offer some consolation to their distraught colleagues. Haas and his coworkers need not really have become so despondent over their inability to predict correctly the meandering movement and dynamics of integration: Economists make wrong forecasts all the time and have learned how to thrive on them! One of the principal excuses they have for their wrong predictions is the unfortunate fact that, just as in the case of private profit calculations, the most critical macroeconomic magnitudes, such as the prospective deficit or surplus in the balance of payments, or the rate of unemployment or inflation, are differences between gross values, such as foreign payments and receipts, total and employed labor force, etc. Hence, even if these values are estimated with an acceptable margin of error, the estimate of the critical difference may be off by a very large percentage and may even carry the wrong sign. Forecasting the progress of integration is similarly risky business: For that progress is the net outcome of opposing forces. Haas's "spillover" effect no doubt exists and has been felt continuously since the European Coal and Steel Community was first formed. But counterforces have also been at work and have in fact been aroused by the very successes of integration so that the net outcome or balance is continually in doubt.[5] Perhaps it is appropriate to recall here Paul Valéry's definition of peace as a "virtual, mute, continuous victory of the possible forces over the probable appetites."[6] Thus the outlook for peace, along with that for full employment, and the progress of integration, can all be viewed as depending on the *difference* between two gross magnitudes and all are subject to the same difficulty of prediction.

This does not mean that our whole enterprise is futile, but rather that prediction is not an appropriate test of the usefulness of social science analysis. The feeling that we have acquired a better *understanding* of a social process – even though, as is quite conceivable, it could become more *un*predictable as a result – is sufficient justification for the enterprise, particularly if, as is often the case, new ways of influencing the process become available through that enhanced understanding.

This more cautious but eventually more successful and useful way of proceeding has characterized economic analysis in the area of our concern. Take the already venerable debate about the positive or negative economic effects of customs unions. Jacob Viner, who initiated this debate thirty years ago, argued that the improvement in resource allocation due to the lowering of tariffs among the participating countries would lead to "trade creation," whereas the discrimination against nonparticipants im-

---

[5] See Stanley Hoffmann, "Obstinate or Obsolete? France, European Integration, and the Fate of the Nation-State," originally published in *Daedalus*, Summer 1966 and reprinted in his *Decline or Renewal? France since the 1930's* (New York: Viking, 1974), pp. 363–99.
[6] *Regards sur le monde actuel* (Paris, 1931), p. 51.

plicit in the arrangement would lead to "trade diversion."[7] In evaluating a customs union from the global welfare point of view, the benefits of trade creation therefore must be set against the harmful effects of trade diversion.

This sort of analysis refrains from making an outright prediction about the net economic effects (the prospective benefits) of a customs union; once again, it will be noted, this effect depends on the difference between two magnitudes (trade creation *minus* trade diversion) and prediction is thereby made hazardous. On the other hand, the analysis seems to lead to a straightforward policy advice: Trade creation should be fostered and trade diversion combated.

At this point in the argument, the political analyst may well seize upon the economist's categories for his own purposes. Suppose he wishes to gauge the likely political support for the customs union within the countries that are to enter it. To do so he can take over with profit the very categories of economic analysis—except that they work in a very different fashion. As a first approximation, the political chances for forming and maintaining a customs union will be bolstered by trade diversion and threatened by trade creation. The larger the trade-creating effects, that is, the greater the need to reallocate resources in the wake of tariff abolition, the greater will be the resistance to the union among various highly concentrated and vocal producer interests of the member countries. The gains from trade creation, on the other hand, lie in the future and are likely to be diffused among numerous firms and among the consumers at large. Thus trade creation is on balance a political liability. Trade diversion implies, on the contrary, that concentrated producer groups of the member countries will be able to capture business away from their present competitors in nonmember countries. These effects will therefore endear the customs union to the interest groups concerned and will provide some badly needed group-support for a union.[8]

It seems likely to me that this sort of analysis could be quite useful in understanding the dynamics of the European Commu-

---

[7] Jacob Viner, *The Customs Union Issue* (New York: Carnegie Endowment for International Peace, 1950).

[8] Even though Viner, in his book, devoted a chapter to the "Political Aspects of Customs Unions" he did not make use of the economic categories he had created for the analysis of that chapter.

nity. For example, the common agricultural policy had strong trade-diverting characteristics, but this was precisely the reason why it played a crucial role in gaining support for the Community within some very important but occasionally vacillating member countries whose farmers were–or were expected to be–the beneficiaries of that policy. It is, on the contrary, the prospect of trade creation in agriculture, that is, the prospects of a stepped-up degree of competition and consequent need to re-allocate resources which is the major obstacle in the way of enlarging the Community at the present time, through the accession of Spain, Portugal, and Greece.

Here, then, is a good example of economic analysis and its distinctions being useful to political analysis, but also of the way in which the introduction of political considerations modifies the prescriptions of the economist. The straightforward policy conclusion of Viner's theory was that in the formation of a union the principal task is to maximize trade creation and to minimize trade diversion. But bringing in political considerations leads to a very different advice: in view of its political benefits, it may well be desirable to arrange for some trade diversion so as to make use of interest group support for the union in its difficult formative years. The policy problem then becomes that of keeping trade creation to politically safe limits while providing for a vitally needed minimum of trade diversion–quite a difference from the original prescription!

II. Spillovers and linkages: a parallel between political integration and economic development

Economic and political objectives are not *always* antithetical, of course. As has often been pointed out, the two effects noted by Viner look at economic union from the point of view of the allocation of given, fixed resources, and one of the principal purposes of the union is to have a positive effect not on more effective utilization and allocation of existing resources but on their growth, through economies of scale, more intensive communication, more confident entrepreneurship and the like.[9] In-

[9] See Tibor Scitovsky, *Economic Theory and Western European Integration* (London: Allen and Unwin, 1958) and Paul Streeten, *Economic Integration* (Leyden: Sythoff, 1964).

sofar as such dynamic effects take hold and lead to sustained economic improvement, it seems not unreasonable to think that they will strengthen the political solidity of the union so that in this case, in contrast to the previous one, positive economic (growth-promoting) and positive political (union-strengthening) effects should go hand in hand. As a result of disappointing experience in many countries over the past twenty years or so, we have, however, become much more cautious in making such inferences from economic to political performance. Moreover, not only are the interrelations between economic growth and what was fleetingly called "political development" circa 1960 far more complex and ambivalent than had been thought: Even the concept of economic growth has lost its once uncontested solidity and unambiguous meaning.

But the very difficulties we have in comprehending both economic and political change, let alone their interaction, point to the possibility of a much more modest enterprise: that of opening up communications between those who attempt to analyze these processes so as to ascertain whether certain modes of thinking about economic development can be useful to the understanding of political change and vice versa. It is admittedly a case of the blind leading or trying to lead the blind, but this metaphor is not meant here in a dispiriting vein: in interpreting its use in the Bible, one must recall that most of the time the blind are in fact better off if they hold on to each other while moving about (as they still do today in many poor regions of the world), however desperate or laughable the enterprise may look to those who can see.

When the processes of economic development and of economic-political integration are examined in this spirit, there appears a certain formal similarity between them which makes it tempting to "borrow" or "translate" from one to the other. The essence of the similarity consists in some very elementary properties and characteristics: the pace and progress of both economic development and of integration depend on whether "one thing leads to another" in the face of strong resistance from existing institutions, social and political structures, attitudes, values and so on. The virtue and appeal of Haas's analysis was precisely that with his "spillover" he had identified forces that would make for progress toward European unification through incremental steps, in spite of the obvious resistance from the powerfully entrenched interests of the national state system. Thus he wrote:

> . . . it is inconceivable that the liberalisation not only of trade, but of the conditions governing trade can go on for long without "harmonisation of general economic policies" spilling over into the fields of currency and credit, investment planning and business cycle control. . . . The spill-over may make a political community of Europe in fact even before the end of the transitional period.[10]

The leading idea here is that, once freedom of trade is irrevocably established among a group of countries, compelling pressures will arise toward uniform tax, social security, and eventually also monetary and general economic policies, presumably because otherwise the disparities and uncertainties under which national producers would have to operate, would be intolerable. It sounds like *la force des choses* and a quite reasonable prediction, but something went wrong: either the pressures were not as compelling as was thought, or some unexpected counterforces arose. In general, the latter explanation has been appealed to in accounting for the stalling of the integration process in the sixties: but was it really all the fault of Gaullism? The more fundamental reason for which the spillover lacked in dynamism was that within the framework of a continuously and rapidly growing European economy the pressures for harmonization of economic policies were not nearly as compelling as seemed a priori likely. These pressures were thought to result from the much higher degree of competition and the consequently precarious positions of many firms and even sectors within national economies that the abolition of tariff barriers would bring. But this was essentially reasoning for a more or less stationary economy in which the trade-creating effects of a customs union make for painful reallocation of resources. In an environment of all-round growth, very few existing firms were or felt threatened and therefore were not particularly interested in further integration moves that would equalize the conditions of competition. *Perhaps it was then the vigorous growth of the Western European economies in the fifties and sixties that made the spillover dynamic so much less compelling than had been thought.* This conclusion is con-

---

[10] *Uniting of Europe*, p. 311.

firmed by events of the last twelve months: the new move toward a common European currency, known as the European Monetary System, is in large part a response to the continuing inflation, unemployment, and structural readjustment problems presently facing Western Europe.

So much for the interaction between theory and practice in the field of European integration. Now that I have told the story in broadest outline, it is easy for me to translate it into at least one view about economic development–my own. Merely at the linguistic level, Haas's "spillover" sounds rather like my "(forward and backward) linkage effects" and also has something in common with my characterization of development as a "chain of disequilibria."[11]

It may therefore be of some interest to pursue this surface similarity. Just as Haas, I was looking for a compelling dynamic that would unfold in spite of manifold and entrenched resistances. For that reason I emphasized the need for stronger spurs than the placid generation and investment of capital along the lines of the then popular Harrod-Domar growth model. The strategy of unbalanced growth in general and the backward and forward linkages in particular–primarily in connection with industrialization–were seen as supplying such a more compelling and directive push.

The parallelism goes further. For Haas's spillover to function, it was necessary that there first be some initial integration move (such as a customs union). Similarly, for the backward and forward linkage dynamic to get under way, some fairly important initial import-substituting industries must first be in place. The spillover arises in part because of the initiative of the "Eurocrats," but fundamentally because of interest-group pressures for further integration moves, in the name of assuring "fair play" and of equalizing the conditions of competition. The linkage dynamic, on the other hand, was based on the idea that investments in backward- and forward-linkage industries are privileged in relation to investments that are comparatively unrelated to already ongoing activities; a basic assumption was here that development would proceed under conditions of for-

---

[11] Haas's *Uniting of Europe* and my *Strategy of Economic Development* were both published in 1958; while we became later very much aware of one another's writings, our two books were written independently.

eign exchange shortage so that the imported inputs for the newly established industries would at some stage become highly eligible for being substituted in turn by domestic production.

As it turned out, both the spillover and the linkage dynamic were less reliable than had been thought originally. They worked nicely enough for a while; but just as the spillover dynamic failed the integration process in the mid-sixties, so there appeared at about the same time some evidence (and much talk) about a leveling off of the process of industrialization via import substitution.[12] While the label that was given this slowdown – the "exhaustion of import substitution" – was highly exaggerated, it became clear in retrospect that there was some justification for distinguishing between an "early and easy" stage of import-substituting industrialization and a more halting and difficult subsequent stage during which domestic production of basic industrial materials and of some capital goods would move into the center of the stage of the industrialization effort while the country would also become an industrial exporter of some consequence. This development became often possible only in the larger developing countries, such as Brazil and Mexico, and owed much to the new balance-of-payments pressures that arose in the seventies, largely as a result of the oil crisis and the concomitant recession in the advanced industrial countries. Once again, there is a parallel here to the current *relance* of European integration under the pressures of the special economic difficulties of the now-ending decade.

It is possible to draw some lessons from our parallel. One is that social scientists invariably seem to overestimate the strength and durability of whatever social forces and processes they uncover. Correlatively, as soon as these forces toward change meet with the first obstacles, their *total* demise is widely proclaimed when in fact there is still quite some life left in them. These first two lessons make interesting footnotes to the sociology of knowledge. Then there is a third, more basic lesson: forces that are expected to subvert quietly and a bit deviously the existing order through economic pressures rather than change it in the course of an open political confrontation tend to labor for that

[12] I have discussed these matters in "The Political Economy of Import-Substituting Industrialization in Latin America" (1968), reprinted in *Bias for Hope*, and in Chapter 5, this volume.

very reason under a specific handicap: the absence of a strong ideology under whose banners they can mobilize support when difficulties appear.

These are the kind of conjectures we might not have come upon, or might have less confidence in, if we had not–somewhat laboriously–translated the language of economic development into that of political integration.

III. Some uses of exit-voice reasoning

In the preceding section the autonomy of the political has been scrupulously respected. Concepts elaborated for the purpose of understanding economic development–the linkage effects– were not in any sense directly "applied" to the study of integration. They were merely shown to have a great deal in common with concepts such as the spillover that had arisen out of the study of the integration process, and, as a result, something was learned about both processes.

In this section I intend to be less respectful. I shall intrude the exit-voice model into the discussion and attempt to show that it permits a better understanding of the integration process, in connection with some specific problems.

A. Capital mobility, reform, and integration

As was pointed out in the preceding chapter, the possibility of exit of the wealthy and of their capital–a possibility that emerged with the rise of various forms of *movable* capital–was hailed in the eighteenth century as a restraint on the caprices and on vexatious or confiscatory policies of the sovereign. The power of capitalists to react through exit (capital flight) to actual or prospective policies they disliked was thus deemed a beneficial restraint on public policy. The eighteenth-century analysts did not perceive the possibility that exit or threat of exit could be used as a veto, not only of arbitrary exactions, but also of policies that might well be in the general interest. Once this is recognized, the veto weapon no longer looks so beneficent. Moreover, the possession of this veto reduces the need for the owners of movable capital to formulate proposals and policies of their own, that is, to develop their *voice*. This sort of situation can of course be quite damaging to the capacity of a state to achieve a meaningful consensus about needed reforms. Quite apart from competitive considerations, it becomes difficult for any individual state to undertake a reform opposed by its capitalists.

Suppose now this situation prevails in a group of states which serve mutually as safe havens for their national capitalists: how would it change as a result of full-fledged economic and political integration?[13] It is easy to perceive two consequences. In the first place, what was formerly the export of capital is now a mere interregional movement; as a result, the owners of capital may have to subject themselves to the indignity of actually having to argue their case in public. Exit will be transformed into voice. Secondly, the possibility of significant reform being adopted in one country *alone* is now formally ruled out. But this is not really a substantial change as in the previous situation such reforms were in effect subject to being vetoed or disrupted through capital flight.

The impossibility for a single country in the group to move ahead of the others with respect to, say, some social reform or some redistributive taxation was already a fact before integration, but it was hidden from the public and the policymakers and became apparent only after the futile expenditure of large-scale proreform energies. With integration this impossibility is visible to all and energies can now be productively directed to the adoption by the group as a whole of whatever reforms are believed to be called for. Through the exit-voice logic, we have here developed a perhaps important pro-integration argument: under modern conditions of mobility of capital, the ability of capitalist states to undertake reforms is enhanced by the formation of political-economic units that are large and inclusive enough to make the blocking of reforms through large-scale capital flight impractical.

B. Regional imbalances and integration

Whether integration alleviates or aggravates regional disequilibrium and conflict *within* states has become a major performance

---

[13] I should make it clear that I am writing in the hypothetical mood. The integration that is postulated in this section is much more far-reaching than the one presently achieved in Western Europe. The reasoning has nevertheless some relevance for possible European developments.

test for any project of closer economic and political union *among* states. The reason is that these persistent disequilibria and conflicts present many states with one of their major contemporary problems. An important argument *against* integration has therefore been the suspicion that it might aggravate these problems.

The reasoning that would lead to that suspicion is now well known: market forces as well as certain public policies favoring concentration would be given freer play as a result of integration and would lead to an even greater agglomeration of economic resources in the most advanced sectors and regions of the integrating countries, at the expense of the poorer and more backward portions of each cooperating country's economy and territory. These poorer regions would be left in a backwater at best; more likely they would be further depleted and exploited by the now even more weighty center or centers. I have no doubt about the existence of such "backwash" or "polarization" effects (as Myrdal and I, respectively, called them some twenty-odd years ago) nor about the likelihood that they would be strengthened as a result of economic union of two or more countries, *in the absence of countervailing policies.* But this last assumption is both crucial for the argument and anything but justified today. For the problem of polarization has by now become widely recognized as one that must be forcefully dealt with by public policy. In Europe the worry that economic union may widen the differentials between advanced and backward regions has inspired new institutions (in particular the European Social Fund) and policies specifically designed to pour resources into the poorer regions and to accelerate their development. These European-wide institutions and policies came of course on top of national policies attempting to deal with the problem.

Awareness of the problem and the existence of institutions and policies designed to deal with it provide of course no guarantee that the regional disparities will disappear or even narrow. Unintended effects of other community policies – the common agricultural policy, in particular – have in fact gotten in the way of the policies aiming at reducing interregional differences in income. Nevertheless, in comparison to what would be likely to happen under purely laissez-faire auspices, any actual polarization effects are going to be muffled and closely monitored in present circumstances.

But this is a somewhat weak conclusion, for it only says that regional underdevelopment and the ensuing region-center conflict will not get much worse as a result of integration. It seems intuitively plausible that integration can make a positive contribution by lessening the sharp conflicts and tensions that have arisen between certain regions and the national authorities. To understand why this should be so, attention must be focused on the more crucial noneconomic aspects of the center-region or region-region conflict. That economic underdevelopment is not a primary reason for the conflict is suggested by the fact that in a fair number of cases a region has developed considerable hostility toward the center (or another region) even though it is the economically *more* developed part of the country. In such cases – as with the Flemish part of Belgium and with Catalonia and the Basque provinces of Spain – the region feels aggrieved because it is made to pay for what it considers laziness, extravagant living, and parasitism of the people in the economically backward regions which in these cases often include the capital city. As both underdevelopment and superior economic performance are invoked as grounds for complaining about the center, one comes to suspect that the economic argument is subsidiary to the principal grievance of the region which is usually to be found in more basic matters, such as a protracted history of conflict and subjection as well as linguistic, religious and cultural differences.[14] Regional conflicts of this sort have multiplied and intensified in the post-World War II period because the European national states have lost their previous status as world powers, a position that implied special opportunities for *all* the citizens of these states; more important perhaps, that status was simply awe-inspiring and deterred any idea to challenge national unity. It is in fact surprising that there has not been more disintegration in the wake of the loss of status that European states have suffered.

Looking at the matter in this perspective makes it tempting to analyze it in terms of exit and voice. In the postwar period a number of regions have become disaffected from the national state as a result of old and new grievances or because of the

[14] Peter Gourevitch argues that economic grievances are the ingredient in the center-periphery relationship that will exacerbate the underlying tensions, in "The Reemergence of 'Peripheral Nationalisms': Some Comparative Speculations on the Spatial Distribution of Political Leadership and Economic Growth," *Comparative Studies in Society and History* 21 (July 1979): 303–22.

disappearance of certain benefits or disciplines. Normally dissatisfaction with an organization can lead to either voice or exit. As a result of centuries of domination, conflicts, and misunderstandings, the dissatisfied regions do not believe in the possibility of obtaining gains through the use of *voice*. Voice has become degraded. Hence the regions have been given more and more to uttering threats of exit. On its part, the center refuses to take such threats seriously or routinely represses them, as when they occasionally explode into terroristic acts. It looks as though we had here the worst of both worlds: voice is discounted as ineffective by one of the two parties while exit-like behavior and its threat are either ignored or suppressed by the other.

In this situation integration holds out hope for a break in the impasse. It creates a new interlocutor – the wider community in formation – which is not weighed down by the heritage of past conflicts and outrages. With integration the aggrieved region can put its case, or at least portions of its case, before a new forum. This regeneration of voice can be one of the major benefits of integration. Correspondingly, with the autonomy and prerogatives of the nation-state being deemphasized, the region will find that separation-exit from the nation-state is no longer essential; it also may strongly wish to be part of the new entity in formation. Even though the achievement of genuine supranational power by this entity may be a long way off, it can act as a concerned third party or even as an ombudsman in relation to the grievances of disaffected regions.[15]

We end up with a rather ironic conjecture: the European Community arrived a bit late in history for its widely proclaimed mission, which was to avert further wars *between* the major Western European nations; even without the Community the time for such wars was past after the two exhausting world wars of the first half of the twentieth century. Perhaps one of the Community's real missions will turn out to be the avoidance of civil wars or wars of secession *within* some of the Western European countries, as it provides the newly secession-prone regions with novel channels for voice.

[15] For some suggestions along these lines on the part or on behalf of presently embattled minorities in Corsica and Northern Ireland, see *Le Monde* of August 21 and September 1, 1979.

C. *Integrative and disintegrative crises*

In addition to the somewhat specialized contributions just attempted, the exit-voice framework might be called upon to help in the analysis of the European integration process in general, its progress, difficulties, and prospects.

Expectations ought to be fairly low in this regard, for two reasons. First of all, the process of voluntary integration among sovereign states is among the least frequent political phenomena – there simply is very little historical experience that could suggest, confirm, or refute hypotheses, no matter what the conceptual framework. Take, for purposes of comparison, processes such as the breakdown of democracies and their transformation into authoritarian regimes, or the opposite political change from authoritarianism to pluralism: even though these processes are highly complex and, in the latter case, quite rare, the empirical material at hand is still comparatively much richer and the invitation to generalize and theorize correspondingly stronger.

Secondly, there is some question as to the "fit" between the exit-voice framework and the integration process. The concepts of exit and voice have been developed and have been found most useful in analyzing *fully established* organizations and their capacity to react against decline in performance. But in the case of political integration, interest centers on a different topic: on the chances of the novel and insecure supranational organizations to grow, to *become* well established and to assume new functions. If the concepts of exit and voice are still to be of service in so different a context, the meanings they had on their native ground are likely to undergo substantial modification, as will now be shown.

Suppose an organization and its members live through events strongly affecting their interests and inviting some action; the organization is not specifically mandated to deal with the problem, but it stands ready to do so if invited by the members. The alternative facing the members in this situation is not exit or voice with respect to the organization and to some action conceivably proposed by it, but whether or not to invite the organization to act or to propose action in the first place. Exit simply means here that members decide to ignore the organization and to behave as though they were independent agents: in contrast to the ordinary exit situation there is not yet any door to go through or to throw shut behind one. Voice means precisely the building of such a door: it is the attempt to involve the organization in the new problem, with the expectation that some advantage will accrue to the members from a common approach.

Suitably and substantially redefined in this fashion the notions of exit and voice can perhaps be of some help in understanding the integration (or disintegration) process. We are led, not wholly unexpectedly, to distinguish between two types of crises: the *disintegrative crisis* that leads the individual members (i.e. nation states) to go it alone and the *integrative crisis* that, on the contrary, impels members to look for some concerted action recommended "from above," that is, from the common organization that is in the process of being built and that may well be strengthened as a result of the new task it is called upon to assume.

It is interesting to speculate about the respective characteristics of these two crisis types. Here we do have some recent historical experience to draw on: the sharp jolt of the oil crisis of 1973 led to a fairly universal go-it-alone, if not *sauve-qui-peut*, reaction on the part of the individual members of the European Community, whereas the subsequent common, protracted and poorly understood problems of unemployment, inflation, and slow growth experienced by the leading European countries in the course of the seventies made them rather more interested in exploring common courses of action. Is it possible to conclude that sudden crises with a clearly identifiable cause will be disintegrative whereas more slowly developing difficulties that are poorly understood will turn out to be integrative? For the time being we can do no more than ask this question while adding our suspicion that matters are in reality quite a bit more complex. For example, it is certainly not correct to look at each crisis by itself, without regard to what happened before. The disintegrative impact of one crisis will itself exert some force on the way in which the next crisis is tackled: if it is evident that the fledgling organization can hardly survive another similarly disintegrative crisis and if there is some desire to assure its survival, the next crisis may well be integrative regardless of its precise characteristics.

As I announced earlier, the various applications of exit-voice to integration problems that have been attempted here hardly qualify as expansionist expeditions of an economist intent on annexing territory hitherto controlled by political scientists. The reason is of course that the exit-voice dichotomy itself does not exclusively dwell in the economic sphere; at times, in fact, it rather seems to fall wholly within the political. Moreover, the injection of exit-voice reasoning has not pretended to produce fundamental new solutions to some major puzzles of integration. What then is the point of the exercise? Perhaps that it sensitizes us to certain situations which can be effectively *reformulated* in terms of exit and voice. Such reformulations will not leave things exactly as they were: occasionally they will make us see the forces at work as well as possible options and outcomes in a new light. And that is about as much, I have come to think, as we can expect from social theory.

Around
The Passions and the Interests

Introductory note

As was pointed out in the previous note, neo-conservative thought became more articulate in the sixties, a trend that has gone all but unnoticed because the then prevailing ideological winds were blowing in the opposite direction. Similarly, during the seventies when the welfare state and associated policies came under sustained and highly vocal attack on the part of conservatives, several intellectual enterprises unfolded that sounded a quite different note.

Foremost among these contrapuntal events was the publication of *A Theory of Justice* (1971) by John Rawls. The immense success of this book showed that interest in the idea of social justice was by no means dead – it just needed a work of intellectual power and originality to be rekindled. Around the same time and not unrelatedly, philosophers and economists rediscovered the "possibility of altruism" and the need to supplement the market mechanism by professional codes of ethics and other moral restraints. The strict limits any democratic order must impose on the market and the need for periodic redefining of these limits were eloquently pointed out by the late Arthur Okun.

The immediate impact of the new and seemingly intractable problems of the seventies, such as the coexistence of unemployment and inflation, was to incite criticism of Keynesian macroeconomic policies, which had become the conventional wisdom of the preceding period, and to raise correspondingly the prestige of the monetarist school of thought with its ready-made alternative approach. But another, more fundamental effect was to raise doubts about the scientific pretenses of *all* the contending models. Could it be that the behavioral assumptions built into them proceed from an excessively simplistic image of both human nature and the social system? Something of this sort was affirmed by Amartya Sen when he pointed out that any theory of human behavior must involve not only the concept of preference orderings, but that of metaorderings, that is, preferences about preferences. Though the possession of such desires about desires, or "second-order volitions," is even regarded as the distinguishing characteristic of the human person by some philosophers,[1] economists have yet to take cognizance of it. It is easy to see how the introduction of this richer concept of human nature makes the economic and social system less predictable than when its agents are assumed to have unique, stable and "well-behaved" desires and preferences.

I like to think of *The Passions and the Interests* (1977), as well as of the two following essays, as participants in the broad intellectual movement whose outlines I have just all too briefly sketched. In a sense, my book is the story of the progressive impoverishment of the prevailing concept of human nature over a period of some three centuries, from the end of the Middle Ages on. In the early modern age, man was widely viewed as the stage on which fierce and unpredictable battles were fought between reason and passion or, later, among the various passions. At mid-eighteenth century, some hope was held out that the interests, which were increasingly understood in the purely pecuniary sense of the term, would be able to tame the disastrous, if aristocratic, passions. But by the latter part of that century, the passions were collapsed into the interests by Adam Smith who pronounced "the great mob of mankind" to be safely programmed: From the cradle to the grave, its members were to be exclusively concerned with "bettering their condition."

The two essays that follow plead for a return to the earlier and richer views. Chapter 13, "An alternative explanation of contemporary harriedness," was published four years before my book, but was actually written alongside its first draft and is intimately related to it: The main point of the essay stems from the contrast between work and consumption, on the one hand, and what I call "obituary-improving activities," on the other, and that contrast is clearly a modernized version of the opposition between the interests and the passions.

---

[1] Harry G. Frankfurt, "Freedom of the Will and the Concept of a Person," *Journal of Philosophy* 68 (January 14, 1971): 5–20.

Chapter 14, "Morality and the social sciences: a durable tension," makes a similar plea, and shows how the concept of benevolence, once wholly exorcised from economic models, has slowly staged a comeback. At the same time this is an essay in understanding. If there is to be a fruitful reencounter of morality and social science, then the strength of the resistance against such an enterprise must be realistically appreciated. The essay thus explores the historical and epistemological reasons why the many well-meaning exhortations to build moral values into economic analysis have not been notably effective. A few suggestions on how to do better are also ventured, diffidently.

13

An alternative explanation of contemporary harriedness

Why would I make myself more harried than I already am by agreeing to participate in the present Symposium? Reflection on this question made me increasingly uneasy about Staffan Linder's explanation of contemporary harriedness and suggested an alternative way of looking at the matter.

Linder divides the time available to man into work and consumption. At a low level of development there may be such a thing as idleness, but this is squeezed out by expanding work and consumption time in wealthier societies. There also is "time devoted to cultivation of mind and spirit," but Linder thinks of it as just another variety of consumption time: theater going, book reading, and the like represent the consumption of culture. The exhaustive subdivision of time into work and consumption that underlies all the reasoning of the book (and is formalized in the mathematical appendix) leads directly to its principal thesis: as productivity of work increases, the individual will have command over more goods while consumption time hardly increases, if at all; hence there will be an increasing "goods intensity" of consumption time, and the individual is harried because he tries to engage in Linder's simultaneous or hectically successive consumption stunts.[1] The more entertaining parts of the book, the remarks on the changing time devoted to cocktail

Originally published in *The Quarterly Journal of Economics* 87 (November 1973): 634–7, as contribution to a symposium on Time in Economics with a focus on Staffan B. Linder's book, *The Harried Leisure Class* (New York: Columbia University Press, 1970). The symposium was organized and edited by Thomas C. Schelling. © 1973, by the President and Fellows of Harvard College. Reprinted by permission of John Wiley & Sons, Inc.
[1] *Leisure Class*, p. 79.

parties, sex, cultural activities, and religion are all extensions of this basic proposition.

Now I agree emphatically with Linder about the fact of harriedness. But I doubt that it can be explained, to more than a minor extent, by the attempt at stuffing an ever-increasing amount of real consumption into a limited amount of time.

The starting point of the alternative explanation I wish to propose is simple and none too new: man does not live by consumption alone. Linder has a fine time making fun of the notion that individuals might devote themselves increasingly to cultural pursuits as their income increases; but there are many other ways of spending time, outside of the consumption of ordinary goods and services. Here it is enlightening to recall Hobbes's view of men's favorite pastime: "men are continually in competition for honour and dignity." And it is particularly interesting that he declared this use of one's time to be highly *income-elastic:* "All men naturally strive for honour and preferment; but chiefly they, who are least troubled with caring for necessary things."[2]

What Hobbes views with some alarm here includes the activity also known as participation in public affairs that has been celebrated at other epochs as the noblest imaginable use of man's time, indeed as the justification for his existence. But no matter whether these sorts of time uses are viewed admiringly or apprehensively and disapprovingly, it begins to look as though Linder's subdivision of man's time into work and consumption is anything but exhaustive. There is a third set of activities that represents our truly final (or ultimate) demands: often mixed up in an inextricable jumble, they comprise the striving for power, prestige, and respect, the maintenance of old friendships and associations and the cultivation of new ones, participation in public affairs, and – why not? – the pursuit of achievement, truth, creativity, and salvation (this pursuit being something utterly different from the consumption of culture).

The high income elasticity of these pursuits does not, of itself, explain why the more affluent should be harried. Normally one would expect them simply to squeeze out some other equally time-consuming activities. But there is something about our

---

[2] Cited in Keith Thomas, "Social Origins of Hobbes's Political Thought" in K. C. Brown, ed., *Hobbes Studies* (Oxford: Blackwell, 1965), pp. 190–1.

mixed bag of "ultimate" activities (how is "obituary-improving" as a neutral term?) that makes people devoting lots of time to them peculiarly harried. What is it? First, these activities often become addictive beyond some threshold: in that case the time devoted to them expands autonomously and eventually encroaches on necessary work and essential consumption time. Second, and more important, the obituary-improving activities lend themselves, *more than other time uses,* to systematic and frequently wild *underestimates* of the time actually needed to accomplish what one sets out to do. Harriedness is typically the result of *time overruns* in relation to original estimates and intentions. It will surely be granted that such overruns are more likely to occur with respect to the intended "dashing off" of a letter to the *New York Times* than with respect to the eating of one's breakfast. The result is overcommitment, an essential ingredient of harriedness for which the view here presented is able to account.

One comment on income elasticity. It would of course be silly to say that low-income people do not worry about prestige, friendship, or creativity; often they do exceedingly well in all these respects. But at higher levels of material welfare, income earning and consumption are increasingly colored by these activities. The fee is the least important reason for which one accepts an invitation to lecture, and the need for drink and food is incidental to most cocktail parties.

Recognition of the obituary-improving activities as the principal source of harriedness alleviates, by the same token, the harriedness problem as described by Linder. A large part of these activities is incorporated into the national accounts on the product side. I am being paid for the conference I attend and for the bureaucratic fight I wage: they are part of my contribution to output solemnly registered in the national accounts as a portion of GNP. As a result, a considerable and probably increasing portion of the GNP in the "service economy" simply is not "there" to be consumed by anyone and, to that extent, the harrying problem of supply disposal does not exist.

By no means do I wish to dismiss altogether the phenomenon Linder has so amusingly depicted. It surely exists at some stage in the economic career of groups and individuals. At that stage people are intent on using their newly won affluence to the hilt, and they may well get into a bit of time trouble in the process. But this is likely to be a passing phase as they get used to their new purchasing power and possessions. The utility one gets out of his new gadget is apt to decay even faster than the gadget itself, for all of its built-in obsolescence. And just as there are few Don Juans in real life, so are there few people who continuously try to recharge their depleted utility batteries by trying out ever new gadgets, simultaneously or in rapid succession. Rather, they will at one point choose the much more vigorous and durable satisfactions to be gotten out of our bundle of obituary-enhancing activities, Hobbesian and the rest.

At the end of his book, Linder joins in the now familiar call against the "consumption society" and advocates a "change of heart of the individual." I have two comments:

1. The change Linder calls for is already vigorously under way. If my diagnosis of contemporary harriedness is correct, then a large portion of the leisure class—not only academics by any means—has already forsaken the consumption society for other far more fascinating pursuits.

2. When we invite others to step off the gadget treadmill, we should be aware that, as a result, they may become more rather than less harried as they expand their obituary-improving activities. Also, to the extent that they will then devote themselves, in Hobbesian fashion, to "honor and preferment," things are unlikely to resemble Huxley's *Island* [hopefully invoked by Linder] or any other utopia.

14

Morality and the social sciences:
a durable tension

What is the role of moral considerations and concerns in economics? More generally, what can be said about the "problem of morality in the social sciences"? In commenting on these questions – the second was the subject of a conference I attended not long ago – I shall first give some reasons why this sort of topic does not come easily to the social scientist; only later shall I show why there is today an increased concern with moral values, *even* in economics – that rock of positivist solidity. In conclusion, I shall suggest some ways of reconciling the traditional posture of the economist as a "detached scientist" with his or her role as a morally concerned person.

To deal usefully with the relationship between morality and the social sciences one must first realize that modern social science arose to a considerable extent in the process of *emancipating* itself from traditional moral teachings. Right at the onset of the modern age, Machiavelli proclaimed that he would deal with political institutions as they really exist and not with "imaginary republics and monarchies" governed in accordance with the religious precepts and moralistic pieties that have been handed down from one generation to the next by well-meaning persons. Modern political science owes a great deal to Machiavelli's shocking claim that ordinary notions of moral behavior for individuals may not be suitable as rules of conduct for states. More generally, it appeared, as a result of the wealth of insights discovered by Machiavelli, that the traditional concentration on the

Originally presented as a lecture on September 25, 1980 when the author received the Frank E. Seidman Distinguished Award in Political Economy in Memphis, Tennessee, and published as an occasional "Acceptance Paper" by the P. K. Seidman Foundation at Memphis in October 1980.

"ought," on the manner in which princes and statesmen ought to behave, interferes with the fuller understanding of the "is" that can be achieved when attention is closely and coldly riveted on the ways in which statecraft is in fact carried on. The need to separate political science from morality was later openly proclaimed by Montesquieu, another principal founding father of social science, when he wrote:

It is useless to attack politics directly by showing how much its practices are in conflict with morality, reason, and justice. This sort of discourse makes everybody nod in agreement, but changes nobody.[1]

A similar move from the "ought" to the "is" was soon to be made in economics. As the actual workings of trade and markets were examined in some detail from the seventeenth century on, a number of discoveries as shocking and instructive as those of Machiavelli were made by writers on economic topics. I am not referring just to Mandeville's famous paradox about private vices leading, via the stimulation of the luxury trades, to public benefits. Quite a bit earlier, in the middle of the seventeenth century, a number of deeply religious French thinkers, the most prominent of whom was Pascal, realized that an ordered society could exist and endure without being based on love or "charity." Another principle, so they found, could do the job of making the social world go round: the principle of self-interest. This ability of doing without love came to them as an uneasy surprise and as a worrisome puzzle: a society that is not held together by love is clearly sinful – how could it then be not only workable, but so intricately and admirably constructed that Divine Providence seems to have had a hand in it?

A century later, such worries had given way to outright celebration: Adam Smith evinced no religious qualms when he bestowed praise on the Invisible Hand for enlisting self-interested behavior on behalf of social order and economic progress. Yet, the idea of morality supplying an alternative way or ordering economy and society still lurks somewhere in the background as Smith mocks it in one of the most striking formulations of his doctrine: "It is not from the *benevolence* of the butcher, the brewer, or the baker, that we expect our dinner," so he writes, "but from their regard to their own *interest*."[2] Smith fairly

---

[1] *Oeuvres complètes*, ed. Roger Caillois (Paris: Pléiade, NRF, 1949), Vol. I, p. 112.

bubbles over here with excitement about the possibility of discarding moral discourse and exhortation, thanks to the discovery of a social mechanism that, if properly unshackled, is far less demanding of human nature and therefore infinitely more reliable. And, once again, the refusal to be satisfied with the traditional "ought" created a *space* within which scientific knowledge could unfold.

Marx remained strictly in the Machiavelli-Montesquieu-Smith tradition when, in his attempt to interpret and, above all, to change the prevailing social and political order, he consistently refused to appeal to moral argument. He scoffed at the "utopian socialists" precisely for doing so in their critique of capitalist society and for resorting to moral exhortation in putting forth their proposed remedies. In spite of the ever-present moralistic undertone of his work, Marx's proudest claim was to be the father of *"scientific* socialism." To be truly scientific, he obviously felt that he had to shun moral argument. True science does not preach, it proves and predicts: so he proves the existence of exploitation through the labor theory of value and predicts the eventual demise of capitalism through the law of the falling rate of profit. In effect Marx mixed, uncannily, these "cold" scientific propositions with "hot" moral outrage and it was perhaps this odd amalgam, with all of its inner tensions unresolved, that was (and is) responsible for the extraordinary appeal of his work in an age both addicted to science and starved of moral values.

The tension between the "warm" heart and the "cold" or, at best, "cool" head is a well-known theme in Western culture, especially since the Romantic Age. But I am speaking here not only of tension, but of an existential incompatibility between morality and moralizing, on the one hand, and analytical-scientific activity, on the other. This incompatibility is simply a fact of experience. Our analytical performance becomes automatically suspect if it is openly pressed into the service of moral conviction; and conversely, moral conviction is not dependent on analytical argument and can actually be weakened by it, just as religious belief has on balance been undermined rather than bolstered by the proofs of God and their intellectual prowess. The matter has been best expressed by the great German poet Hölderlin in a wonder-

---

[2] *Wealth of Nations*, Modern Library Edition (New York, 1937), p. 14.

fully pithy, if rather plaintive, epigram. Entitled *"Guter Rat"* (Good Advice), it dates from about 1800 and, in my free translation, reads:

If you have brains and a heart, show only one or the other,
You will not get credit for either should you show both at once.[3]

The mutual exclusiveness of moralizing and analytical understanding may be nothing but a happenstance, reflecting the particular historical conditions under which scientific progress in various domains was achieved in the West. These conditions have of course left strong marks on cultural attitudes, marks so well identified by Hölderlin.

But the hostility to morality is more than a birthmark of modern science. With regard to the social sciences in particular, there are some more specific reasons to think that antimoralist petulance will frequently recur, because of the very nature of the social scientific enterprise and discourse. Let me briefly explain.

In all sciences fundamental discovery often takes the form of paradox. This is true for some of the principal theorems of physics, such as the Copernican proposition about the earth moving around the sun rather than vice versa. But it can be argued that social science is peculiarly subject to the compulsion to produce paradox.

The reason is that we all know so much about society already without ever having taken a single social science course. We live in society; we often contribute to social, political, and economic processes as actors; and we think – often mistakenly, of course – that we know roughly what goes on not only in our own minds, but also in those of others. As a result, we have considerable intuitive, commonsense understanding of social science "problems" such as crime in the streets, corruption in high places, and even inflation, and everyone stands forever ready to come forward with his or her own "solution" or nostrum. Con-

---

[3] "Hast Du Verstand und ein Herz, so zeige nur eines von beiden,
Beides verdammen sie Dir, zeigest Du beides zugleich."
Hölderlin's distinction between *Verstand* (reason) and *Herz* (heart) reflects the rehabilitation of the passions in the eighteenth century that led to the "heart" standing for the many generous moral feelings, impulses, and beneficent passions man was now credited with while reason was becoming downgraded; at an earlier time, the contrast, not between the heart and the head, but between the passions and reason, or the passions and the interests, carried a very different value connotation. I have dealt with these matters in *The Passions and the Interests*, pp. 27–8, 43–4, and 63–6.

sequently, for social science to *enhance* our considerable, untutored knowledge of the social world it must come up with something that has not been apparent or transparent before or, better still, with something that shows how badly commonsense understanding has led us astray.[4] Important social science discoveries are therefore typically counterintuitive, shocking, and concerned with *unintended* and unexpected consequences of human action.

With the commonsense understanding of social science problems having usually a strong moral component (again much more so than in the natural sciences), the immoralist vocation of the social sciences can in good measure be attributed to this compulsion to produce shock and paradox. Just as one of social science's favorite pastimes is to affirm the hidden rationality of the seemingly irrational or the coherence of the seemingly incoherent, so does it often defend as moral, or useful, or at least innocent, social behavior that is widely considered to be reprehensible. In economics, examples of this sort of quest for the morally shocking come easily to mind. Following the early lead of Mandeville and his rehabilitation of luxury, many an economist has carved out a reputation by extolling the economic efficiency functions of such illegal or unsavory activities as smuggling, or black marketeering, or even corruption in government.

Lately this taste for the morally shocking has been particularly evident in the "imperialist" expeditions of economists into areas of social life outside the traditional domain of economics. Activities such as crime, marriage, procreation, bureaucracy, voting, and participation in public affairs in general have all been subjected to a so-called "economic approach" with the predictable result that, like the consumer or producer of the economics textbook, the actors involved, be they criminals, lovers, parents, bureaucrats, or voters, were all found to be busily "maximizing under constraints." Such people had of course long been thought to be moved and buffeted by complex passions, both noble and ignoble, such as revolt against society, love, craving for immortality, and devotion to the public interest or betrayal thereof, among many others. In comparison with this traditional image of man's noneconomic pursuits, their analysis at the

---

[4] See Gilles Gaston Granger, "L'explication dans les sciences sociales," *Social Science Information* 10 (1971), p. 38.

hands of the imperialist economist, with the emphasis on grubby cost/benefit calculus, was bound to produce moral shock; and, once again, the analysis drew strength from having this shock value.

In a book review, my colleague Clifford Geertz recently wrote a marvelous first paragraph that is eminently applicable to the writings to which I have just been referring:

This is a book about the "primary male-female differences in sexuality among humans," in which the following things are not discussed: guilt, wonder, loss, self-regard, death, metaphor, justice, purity, intentionality, cowardice, hope, judgment, ideology, humor, obligation, despair, trust, malice, ritual, madness, forgiveness, sublimation, pity, ecstasy, obsession, discourse, and sentimentality. It could be only one thing, and it is. Sociobiology.[5]

To most of us this sounds like a scathing indictment, but partisans of the book under review may well feel that its author deserves praise precisely for having cut through all those "surface phenomena" listed by Geertz to the *fundamental* mechanism which lays bare the very essence of whatever the book is about. In the same way, practitioners of the "economic approach" to human behavior probably take pride in their "parsimonious" theory, and whatever success they achieve is in fact largely grounded in the reductionist outrageousness of their enterprise.

One cannot help feeling, nevertheless, that this particular way of achieving notoriety and fame for the economist is running into decreasing returns. For one, the paradigm about self-interest leading to a workable and perhaps even optimal social order without any admixture of "benevolence" has now been around so long that it has become intellectually challenging to rediscover the need for morality. To affirm this need has today almost the same surprise value and air of paradox which the Smithian farewell to benevolence had in its own time. Second, and more important, it has become increasingly clear that, in a number of important areas, the economy is in fact liable to perform poorly without a minimum of "benevolence."

The resurgence and rehabilitation of benevolence got started in microeconomics. One of the conditions for the proper functioning of competitive markets is "perfect" information about the goods and services that are being bought and sold. We all know, of

---

[5] Review of Donald Symons, *The Evolution of Human Sexuality* (New York: Oxford University Press, 1979) in *The New York Review of Books*, January 24, 1980, p. 3.

course, that this condition is frequently far from being met, but imperfect information might not be too damaging to the market system if it were limited and widely shared among all citizens, be they sellers or buyers. What happens, however, if, as is often the case, the knowledge of the buyers about a certain commodity is far inferior to that of the suppliers and sellers? In that case the stage is set for exploitation of the buyers by the sellers unless the latter are somehow restrained from taking advantage of their superiority. Government could be and has been entrusted with that task, with varying success: we all know by now that government will not necessarily succeed where the market fails. An ingenious solution would be for the sellers to subject themselves voluntarily to a discipline that keeps them from exploiting their superior knowledge. For example, surgeons could take on the obligation, as a condition for the exercise of their profession, never to prescribe an operation when none is needed. This is the case, pointed out some time ago by Kenneth Arrow, where adherence to a code of professional ethics can remedy one specific form of market failure. So we are back to benevolence: in a somewhat institutionalized form, it is here invoked as an input essential for the functioning of a market economy in which sellers have more information than buyers.

The fact that there is a need for ethical behavior in certain situations in which the market system and self-interest, left to their own devices, will result in undesirable outcomes does not mean, of course, that such behavior will automatically materialize. Perhaps it tends to do so when the need is particularly imperious, as it is in the case of surgeons and surgery. In any event, we worry quite a bit more about "being had" when we buy a secondhand car than when we consult a doctor about the need for an operation. Economists have recently identified a number of areas, from the market for "lemons" to day-care services and psychotherapeutic advice, where the performance of the market could be much improved by an infusion of "benevolence," sometimes in the modest form of cooperation and exchange of information between suppliers and customers.

The need for ethical norms and behavior to supplement and, on occasion, to supplant self-interest appears with great clarity and urgency in the just-noted situations of "market failure." But this need is actually always there to some degree: if only because of the time element contained in most transactions, economic efficiency and enterprise are premised on the existence of trust between contracting parties, and this trust must be autonomous, that is, it must not be tied narrowly to self-interest. To quote a recent, sweeping statement of this point: "Elemental personal values of honesty, truthfulness, trust, restraint and obligation are all necessary inputs to an efficient (as well as pleasant) contractual society. . . ."[6] If all these needed personal values are added up, the amounts of benevolence and morality required for the functioning of the market turn out to be quite impressive!

So much for microeconomics. But the really giant, if unacknowledged, strides in the rehabilitation of morality as an essential "input" into a functioning economy have taken place in the macro area, as a result of the contemporary experience with, and concern over, inflation. In spite of all the noise caused by certain technical debates (demand-pull vs. cost-push, monetarist vs. Keynesian or post-Keynesian views), there is in fact wide agreement – because it is so self-evident – that the understanding *and* control of contemporary inflation require probing deeply into the social and political underlay of the economy. For example, suppose it is correct that increasing public expenditures must be blamed for the inflation, then the question surely is: Why is the modern state subject to ever increasing pressures for dispensing an ever more comprehensive set of public services to newly assertive interest groups? Similarly, if it is true that wage and price restraint could do much to hold back inflation, then why is it that such restraint is so difficult to come by? A British sociologist has written, in answer to such questions, that "conflict between social groups and strata has become more intense and also to some extent more equally matched, with these two tendencies interacting in a mutually reinforcing way."[7] Here is a well articulated expression of the widespread view that inflation reflects increasing combativeness or, in colorful British parlance, "bloody-mindedness" on the part of various social groups that have heretofore been viewed in our textbooks as "cooperating" in the generation

---

[6] Fred Hirsch, "The Ideological Underlay of Inflation," in Fred Hirsch and John H. Goldthorpe, eds., *The Political Economy of Inflation* (Cambridge, Mass.: Harvard University Press, 1978), p. 274.

[7] John H. Goldthorpe, "The Current Inflation: Toward a Sociological Account," in *The Political Economy of Inflation*, p. 196.

and distribution of the social product. The result of this sort of sociological analysis of inflation is then to plead for a "new social contract" which would hopefully result in inhibiting and reducing "bloody-mindedness" all around.[8]

The observation that is in order at this point will already have occurred to the reader: this nasty attribute, "bloody-mindedness," which it is so important to restrain, is nothing but the obverse of benevolence which it is therefore essential to foster. Hence, getting on top of our major current macroeconomic problem turns out to require the generation and diffusion of benevolence among various social groups! So it definitely would seem time for economists to renounce the amoral stance affected, at least in the *Wealth of Nations*, by the illustrious founder of our science: for the solution of both micro- and macroeconomic problems, the pursuit of pure self-interest on the part of each individual member of society is clearly inadequate.

So far so good. But have we gotten very far? We have learned that we should not scoff at benevolence and at moral values in general. We can also appreciate that Malthus had a point when, in endorsing the Smithian rule according to which everyone should be left free to pursue his self-interest, he systematically added the reservation "while he adheres to the rules of justice."[9]

But this sort of addition of a qualifying, moralizing afterthought is not really much of a contribution. Granted the important place of moral thought and values for economics, how should we map out the new terrain and become aware of all the insights we have missed because of our previous exclusive concentration on self-interest? One way to proceed is to attempt a

[8] An alternative solution is to fight fire with fire and to apply what might be called "countervailing bloody-mindedness." The recently much-discussed idea of making it expensive for management to increase wages through a special tax levied on payroll increases beyond a certain norm has the avowed purpose of "stiffening the back" of management as it faces militant labor. The monetarist injunctions can also be regarded as a proposal to counter the bloody-mindedness of various social groups by that of the Central Bank (something that in a number of countries turns out to require strong-arm regimes as well as *real* bloodletting). See also Chapter 8, this volume, for a more extended examination of the sociological aspects of inflation.

[9] *Principles of Political Economy* (London: John Murray, 1820), pp. 3 and 518. This qualifying clause was brought to my attention by Alexander Field; see his paper "Malthus, Method, and Macroeconomics," unpublished, May 1980. As Field points out, in the numerous expositions of the principle with which *The Wealth of Nations* is studded, Adam Smith added the similar phrase, "as long as he does not violate the laws of justice," only once. See Modern Library edition, p. 651.

head-on attack. The opposite of self-interest is interest in others, action on behalf of others. So the obvious way of making amends for their previous disregard of moral values and "generous impulses" is for economists to study altruism. A number of works on this topic have indeed appeared in recent years.[10] They are instructive and useful but suffer perhaps from the attempt to make up for lost time in too much of a hurry.

In my opinion, the damage wrought by the "economic approach," based on the traditional self-interest model, is not just the neglect of altruistic behavior. It extends to wide areas of traditional analysis and is due to far too simplistic a model of human behavior *in general*. What is needed is for economists to incorporate into their analysis, whenever that is pertinent, such basic traits and emotions as the desire for power and for sacrifice, the fear of boredom, pleasure in both commitment and unpredictability, the search for meaning and community, and so on. Clearly this is a task that cannot be accomplished once and for all by a research project on the injection of moral values into economics. Any attempt of this kind is likely to yield disappointing results and would thus invite an extension to economics of the French saying, "With beautiful sentiments one makes bad literature."

An effective integration of moral argument into economic analysis can be expected to proceed rather painstakingly, on a case-to-case basis, because the relevant moral consideration or neglected aspect of human nature will vary considerably from topic to topic. The task requires a conjunction of talents that is difficult to come by: first, familiarity with the technical apparatus of economics; and second, openness to the heretofore neglected moral dimensions whose introduction modifies traditional results.

A fine example of such a conjunction – and also of its difficulty – is Robert Solow's recent presidential address to the American Economic Association on the topic of labor markets and unemployment. In explaining why the labor market is not smoothly self-clearing, he stressed the fact that workers pay a great deal of attention to "principles of appropriate behavior

---

[10] For example, Kenneth E. Boulding, *The Economy of Love and Fear: A Preface to Grant Economics* (Belmont, Cal.: Wadsworth, 1973); Edmund S. Phelps, ed., *Altruism, Morality and Economic Theory* (New York: Russell Sage Foundation, 1975); David Collard, *Altruism and Economy: A Study in Non-Selfish Economics* (Oxford: Robertson, 1978).

whose source is not entirely individualistic," such as the reluctance of those who are out of work to undercut those who hold jobs. "Wouldn't you be surprised," so he asked, "if you learned that someone of roughly your status in the profession, but teaching in a less desirable department, had written to your department chairman offering to teach your courses for less money?"[11] Here is an important recognition of how certain moral-social norms profoundly affect the working of a most important market: they make it less perfect from the point of view of self-clearing, but certainly *more* perfect from almost any other conceivable point of view!

I now turn to the difficulty of coming up with such an observation. Note that its vehicle was Solow's presidential address. Is there perhaps a tendency in our profession to wait until one has reached the pinnacle before coming forward with such, after all, only mildly moralistic and heretical views? Now I am quite sure (at least in the case of Solow) that it is not pusillanimity and the desire for advancement that are responsible for such *late* blooming of moral emphasis; rather, the explanation lies in that mutual exclusiveness of heart and head, of moralizing and analytical understanding, on which I dwelt at the beginning of this essay. When one has been groomed as a "scientist" it just takes a great deal of wrestling with oneself before one will admit that moral considerations of human solidarity can effectively interfere with those hieratic, impersonal forces of supply and demand.

There is a notable instance here of what Veblen called a "trained incapacity." It is so strong, in fact, that we will often not avow to ourselves the moral source of our scientific thought processes and discoveries. As a result, quite a few of us are *unconscious* moralists in our professional work. I have a personal story to illustrate this point, and here is how I told it in the special preface I wrote – for reasons that will be apparent – for the *German* edition of *Exit, Voice, and Loyalty:*

> As is related in my book, its intellectual origin lies in an observation I made some years ago in Nigeria. But quite a while after the book had been published in the United States, it dawned on me that my absorption with its theme may have deeper roots. A large part of the book centers on the concern that exit of the potentially most powerful carriers of voice prevents the more forceful stand

[11] Robert M. Solow, "On Theories of Unemployment," *American Economic Review*, 70 (March 1980), pp. 3, 4.

against decline that might otherwise be possible. This situation is not altogether unrelated to the fate of the Jews who were still in Germany after 1939. Most of the young and vigorous ones, like myself, got out in the early years after Hitler took over, leaving a gravely weakened community behind. Of course, the possibilities of any effective voice were zero in the circumstances of those years no matter who left and who stayed. Nevertheless, the real fountainhead of the book may well lie in some carefully repressed guilt feelings that, even though absurd from the point of view of any rational calculus, are simply there.[12]

At this point, a further afterthought suggests itself: it was probably fortunate that I was *not* aware of those deeper moral stirrings when I wrote the book; otherwise the presentation of my argument might have been less general, less balanced as between the respective merits of exit and voice, and less scientifically persuasive. My excursion into autobiography thus points to an odd conclusion: One, perhaps peculiarly effective way for social scientists to bring moral concerns into their work is to do so unconsciously! This bit of advice is actually not quite as unhelpful as it sounds. For the reasons given, it seems to me impractical and possibly even counterproductive to issue guidelines to social scientists on how to incorporate morality into their scientific pursuits and how to be on guard against immoral "side effects" of their work. Morality is not something like pollution abatement that can be secured by slightly modifying the design of a policy proposal. Rather, it belongs into the center of our work; and it can get there only if the social scientists are morally alive and make themselves vulnerable to moral concerns – then they will produce morally significant works, consciously or otherwise.

I have a further, more ambitious, and probably utopian thought. Once one has gone through the historical account and associated reasoning of this essay, once we have become fully aware of our intellectual tradition with its deep split between head and heart and its not always beneficial consequences, the first step toward overcoming that tradition and toward healing that split has already been taken. Down the road, it is then possible to visualize a kind of social science that would be very different from the one most of us have been practicing: a moral-social science where moral considerations are not repressed or

---

[12] Original English text of preface to German edition in Albert O. Hirschman, *Abwanderung und Widerspruch* (Tübingen: J.C.B. Mohr, 1974), p. vii.

kept apart, but are systematically commingled with analytic argument, without guilt feelings over any lack of integration; where the transition from preaching to proving and back again is performed frequently and with ease; and where moral considerations need no longer be smuggled in surreptitiously, nor expressed unconsciously, but are displayed openly and disarmingly. Such would be, in part, my dream for a "social science for our grandchildren."

Index of authors cited

Afansas'ev, A., 110
Alejo, Francisco Javier, 164
Amin, Samir, 86
Anderson, Perry, 129, 266
Aronson, Elliot, 156
Arrighi, Giovanni, 16
Arrow, Kenneth J., 219–20, 300
Aufhauser, Keith, 94
Avineri, Shlomo, 168

Baechler, Jean, 266
Baer, Werner, 64, 191
Bailyn, Bernard, 260
Balassa, Bela, 113
Baldwin, Robert E., 62, 79
Bamberger, Joan, 248
Baran, Paul A., 61
Barion, J., 167
Barkin, David, 44
Bates, Thomas R., 129
Bazdresch, Carlos, 164
Beckerman, Paul, 191
Bell, R. R., 233
Bergsman, Joel, 113
Berry, Sara S., 79
Birch, A. H., 241
Birnberg, Thomas B., 71
Bonilla, Frank, 44
Boucher, Michel, 64
Boulding, Kenneth E., 303
Burnett, Nicholas R., 261

Calmon, Pedro, 78
Cancian, Frank, 42
Canitrot, Adolfo, 192
Cardoso, Fernando Henrique, 1, 27, 45,
  84, 86, 88, 91, 125
Cariola, Carmen, 69
Chenery, Hollis B., 1
Cobb, Richard, 47
Collard, David, 303

Collier, David, 98, 107, 191
Constant, Benjamin, 217
Corden, Max, 114
Crouch, Colin, 207

Davies, Hugh B., 235
Davies, James C., 48
Dean, Warren, 78
Deutsch, Karl W., 267
Diamand, Marcelo, 111
Diaz Alejandro, Carlos F., 167
Domar, Evsey D., 94
Downs, Anthony, 153–4
Duesenberry, James S., 41, 199

Eisenberg, M. A., 218
Elliott, J. H., 183
Evans-Pritchard, E. E., 249, 251
Evenson, R. E., 73

Faletto, Enzo, 84
Feldman, Arnold, 44
Ferguson, Adam, 101
Ferrer, Aldo, 107
Fetter, Frank Whitson, 68, 186, 204
Field, Alexander, 302
Finer, Samuel E., 246, 253
Fishlow, Albert, 22, 64, 81, 191
Forrester, Jay W., 161
Foster, George M., 42, 55, 56
Fox, Renée, 264–5
Franck, Thomas, 231
Frank, André Gunder, 18, 86, 88
Frankfurt, Harry G., 288
Freeman, Richard B., 236, 238, 241
Friedman, Milton, 177, 188, 211, 232, 252
Furtado, Celso, 92, 116, 189, 192

Galenson, Walter, 62
Geertz, Clifford, 77, 92, 154, 265, 299
Germani, Gino, 46

Gerschenkron, Alexander, 10, 11, 90, 126
Girvan, Norman, 84
Glazer, Nathan, 161
Goldthorpe, John H., 301
González Casanova, Pablo, 44
Gordon, Robert J., 180
Gourevitch, Peter A., 207, 262, 280
Gramsci, Antonio, 129
Granger, Gilles Gaston, 298
Grunwald, Joseph, 179
Guerra y Sánchez, Ramiro, 91, 94
Gurr, Ted Robert, 42

Haas, Ernst, 267, 273–5
Haberler, Gottfried, 185
Harberger, Arnold, 21
Harrington, James, 253–4
Hayek, Friedrich August von, 177, 185, 188
Hegel, Georg Wilhelm Friedrich, 135, 167–76
Hennessy, T. M., 230
Hilgerdt, Folke, 13
Hill, Polly, 79
Hirsch, Fred, 183, 301
Hobbes, Thomas, 52, 291
Hobson, John Atkinson, 171, 173
Hoffmann, Stanley, 270
Hölderlin, Friedrich, 297
Hoselitz, Bert F., 59, 63
Houck, J. P., Jr., 73
Hume, David, 254–5
Hunt, Shane J., 69
Huntington, Samuel P., 57
Hymer, Stephen H., 66

Innis, Harold, 65, 91

Johnson, Harry G., 113
Jones, Leroy P., 64

Kafka, Alexandre, 189
Kaufman, Robert, 107
Kaufmann, Walter A., 172
Kerstenetzky, Isaac, 64
Keynes, John Maynard, 6, 203–04
Kierkegaard, Sören, 32
Kindleberger, Charles P., 9, 262
Knox, T. M., 168
Kramnick, Isaac, 254
Krashinsky, Michael, 219–20, 235
Krasner, Stephen, 159
Kuhn, Thomas S., 59, 60
Kurth, James R., 91
Kuznets, Simon, 1, 162

Labrousse, Ernest, 47

Lafer, Celso, 106
Laidler, David, 186
Lamb, Geoff B., 241
Lancaster, Kelvin, 83
La Rochefoucauld, François de, 52
Laumas, Prem S., 64
Leal Buitrago, Francisco, 122
Leibenstein, Harvey, 7, 29, 41, 62, 194
Lenin, Nikolai, 175–6, 203–04
Levin, Jonathan V., 69
Lévi-Strauss, Claude, 248
Lewis, W. Arthur, 8, 9, 15, 16, 188
Lindblom, C. E., 148, 152
Linder, Staffan B., 66, 290–3
Linz, Juan, 66
Little, Ian, 113
Lorwin, Val, 229
Love, Joseph, 15
Lowi, Theodore J., 146
Luxemburg, Rosa, 171, 173

McConnell, Grant, 151
MacDonald, John S., 226, 259
McGreevey, William Paul, 92
Machiavelli, Niccolò, 129, 294
Magnet, Alejandro, 102
Mahbub ul Haq, 39
Maier, Charles S., 192
Malinowski, Bronislaw, 90
Malthus, Thomas Robert, 170, 302
Mamalakis, Markos, 189
Mandelbaum, Kurt, 7
Marer, Paul, 28
Martin, Andrew, 207
Marx, Karl, 3–5, 88–90, 94–6, 152, 167, 170–2
Meadows, Donella M., 161
Medoff, James L., 236
Michels, Roberto, 243
Middleton, John, 249
Miliband, Ralph, 147
Mill, John Stuart, 17
Miller, S. M., 161
Mintz, Sidney W., 91, 94,
Modigliani, Franco, 179
Montesquieu, Charles Louis, 101, 253, 255–7, 295
Morawetz, David, 2, 263
Morgenstern, Oskar, 55
Myint, Hla, 74
Myrdal, Gunnar, 16–17, 88, 279

Navarrete, Jorge Eduardo, 164
Nelson, Richard R., 153, 219, 220, 235
Nie, Norman H., 242
Nieboer, H. J., 94, 251
Nieto Arteta, Luis Eduardo, 92, 101, 103

Noyola Vásquez, Juan, 179
Nugent, Jeffrey B., 64
Nurkse, Ragnar, 7

O'Connor, James, 124
O'Donnell, Guillermo, 76, 104–9, 112,
  118, 192
Okun, Arthur M., 287
Olson, Mancur, 211
O'Malley, Joseph, 167
Orbell, John M., 232–4
Ortiz Fernández, Fernando, 90, 94
Ospina Vásquez, Luis, 100
Owen, E. R. J., 81

Packenham, Robert, 20, 142
Parkin, Michael, 186
Pascal, Blaise, 96, 216
Paz, Pedro, 84
Pearson, Scott R., 64, 66
Peattie, Lisa, 45
Pettigrew, Thomas F., 42
Phelps, Edmund S., 188, 303
Pike, Frederick B., 102
Pinto, Aníbal, 18, 69, 128
Piore, Michael, 180
Prebisch, Raúl, 15, 60, 120, 122
Price, Richard, 255

Rawls, John, 22, 287
Rein, Martin, 161
Resnick, Stephen A., 66, 71
Reyna, Jorge Luis, 45
Riedel, James, 64
Roemer, Michael, 64
Rokkan, Stein, 57, 213, 224–5, 246
Rosenberg, Nathan, 63
Rosenstein-Rodan, Paul, 7, 10
Rostow, Walt W., 10, 11, 63
Rothschild, Michael, 39
Rousseau, Jean-Jacques, 128, 217, 247–8
Rubel, Maximilien, 170
Runciman, W. G., 42
Rustow, Dankwart A., 57
Ruttan, Vernon W., 73

Samuelson, Paul A., 60
Schaffer, Bernard B., 241
Schelling, Thomas C., 290
Schultz, Theodore W., 8
Schultze, Charles, 180
Schydlowsky, David, 111
Scitovsky, Tibor, 113, 199, 272
Scott, Anthony, 83
Scott, Maurice, 113
Seers, Dudley, 6, 179
Seldon, Arthur, 177

Sen, Amartya, 181, 288
Serra, José, 107, 112, 191, 196
Shaw, Jerry I., 53
Sheahan, John, 99
Shefter, Martin, 193–4
Simon, Herbert, 9, 147–8
Simon, John G., 219
Simonsen, Mario Henrique, 199
Singer, Hans, 15, 60
Singer, Paul, 5
Sismondi, Jean Charles de, 169–70
Skidmore, Thomas E., 204
Skolnick, Paul, 53
Smith, Adam, 256–7, 288, 295–6, 302
Solow, Robert M., 303–4
Spechler, Martin C., 223
Spraos, John, 15
Steuart, Sir James, 101–4, 255–6
Stevens, Carl M., 237
Stouffer, S. A., 42, 48
Streeten, Paul, 1, 272
Sunkel, Osvaldo, 27, 69, 84, 179
Sutcliffe, B., 5
Symons, Donald, 299

Tait, David, 249
Tavares, Maria da Conceição, 106
Tendler, Judith, 64, 80, 92
Thomas, Clive Y., 20
Thomas, Keith, 291
Thurow, Lester C., 263
Tiebout, Charles M., 211, 231, 252
Tobin, James, 180
Tocqueville, Alexis de, 46, 94, 99–100, 101
Tolstoy, Leo, 29
Tucker, Robert C., 157
Tumin, Melvin M., 44
Turgot, Anne Robert Jacques, 255
Turnbull, Colin M., 250
Turner, Frederick Jackson, 251

Uno, T., 232–4

Valéry, Paul, 270
Verba, Sidney, 242
Viner, Jacob, 8, 271, 272

Wallerstein, Immanuel, 266
Warren, Bill, 19, 86
Watkins, Melville H., 65
Weil, Eric, 168
Weisband, Edward, 231
Weisskoff, Richard, 64
Wellhofer, E. S., 230
Williams, Oliver P., 231–2
Williamson, Oliver E., 222, 236, 238

Winslow, E. N., 170   Yotopoulos, Pan A., 64
Wionczek, Miguel S., 164   Young, Dennis R., 234, 236–9
Wittfogel, Karl, 81
Wolff, Edward, 64   Zolberg, Aristide R., 262